Illustration 1

Published by

MELROSE BOOKS

An Imprint of Melrose Press Limited
St Thomas Place, Ely
Cambridgeshire
CB7 4GG, UK
www.melrosebooks.co.uk

FIRST EDITION

Cover designed by Melrose Books

ISBN   978-1-909757-90-5

Printed and bound in Great Britain by:
Latimer Trend & Company Limited,
Estover Road, Plymouth PL6 7PY

FSC
www.fsc.org
MIX
Paper from
responsible sources
FSC® C013436

Shipyards of the Upper Mersey

Being a Study of the Ship and Boat Yards of Runcorn, Frodsham,
Widnes, Ellesmere Port, Sankey,
and Warrington

An in-depth look at these facilities with focus also on the other
maritime industries of the area

Robert Ratcliffe

LIST OF CONTENTS

LIST OF ILLUSTRATIONS

Front Cover and Frontispiece

1   Photograph of Stubbs's Yard with two vessels on the slip. By permission of "Mr. Salty Dog" (contributor to the Flickr online photo album website).

After Section on Castle Rock (see pages 9–10)

2   *Despatch* being launched from Mersey Street Yard in roughly the same location as the above picture (care of Ken Stubbs).

3   Runcorn waterfront in 1887 with details by Ross Bullock of Runcorn and District Historical Society. By permission of Ross Bullock.

4   View of the Belvedere Yard of Blundell and Mason (postcard used in *Schooner Port* by Starkey). By permission of Avid Publications.

5   Anderton and LeCouteur of Castle Rock (care of the author's cousin once removed, Frank LeCouteur).

6   Photograph from the early 1890s as the Ship Canal was under construction, showing a fore-and-aft building berth at Castle Rock that was previously unknown to the author (from the late Geoff Wheat's article Manchester Ship Canal, in *Narrowboat* magazine, winter 2011/2). From the Geoff Wheat Collection.

7   Abel's Castle Rock Yard , slightly to the west of the above picture (from Runcorn Photos page on Facebook). By permission of "Mr. Salty Dog" (contributor to Flickr).

8   RUTH BATE under construction at Castle Rock Yard. Source investigated by the Runcorn and District Historical Society but unknown.

9   A sailing vessel aground at low tide beside Castle Rock Wharf apparently under survey or repair, perhaps by shipwrights from Castle Rock Yard, or maybe another concern. Source investigated by the Runcorn and District Historical Society but unknown.

10   Just to the west of the last picture, a group of fishing vessels being painted or repaired on the beach at the end of Castle Rock Wharf. Source investigated by the Runcorn and District Historical Society but unknown.

After Section on Weston Point

11   Weston Point ("The Point"), 1911–19. A drawing by G. Alfred Holloway, from his book *Weston Point Remembered, 1911–1920*. I tried to find out from Cheshire Libraries if I had permission to use this image but I had no answer. The book was a privately produced one from 1988 with an introduction written by a staff member from Cheshire Libraries but no other clue as to publisher. The map shows Wright's Dock and the southern end of Weston Point Docks.

11a The key to Mr. Holloway's map. Note the map shows the Bridgewater Canal flowing into the Weaver Navigation. This is actually the Runcorn and Weston Canal, which linked the Weston Point and Runcorn Docks systems, and thus, ultimately, linked into the Bridgewater. Also, the part marked as the "Weaver Navigation Canal" is actually the Old Basin in Weston Point Docks, which used to have a further dock, the New Basin, between her and the Manchester Ship Canal. This has now been filled in but was still there in the period covered by Mr. Holloway's book). The Weaver Navigation is the waterway running alongside the "Stoney Wall", and "Stoney Beach" where local children used to play, marked on the right of the map.

12   Scan of the 1958 chart showing Weston Point Docks. With thanks to the Hydrographic Office.

After Section on M.S.C. Co. at Old Quay and Beyond

13   Sprinch Yard (centre); Simpson, Davies Yard above and left of her; Samuel Taylor's Yard above that; Victoria Yard (a separate entity to the Sprinch, which had this as her official title initially) to the bottom left; and triangular-shaped "The Baulks" opposite the Sprinch Yard to the low right of centre. Source investigated by the Runcorn and District Historical Society but unknown.

14   Author's photograph of the Bridgewater Motor Boat Club graving dock (the former double graving dock at the Sprinch, seen in the above to the bottom left of the yard).

15   Packet dry dock in centre of postcard view, with MSC STRETFORD in dock (unknown source).

16   JENNY LIND on the graving grid at Bridgewater Docks (care of Percy Dunbavand).

17   EVA on Dry Dock at Runcorn Docks in 1954 (from Flickr). By permission of Frank Brown.

two tugs with white superstructures, above which is the entrance to the former No. 1 Slipway Basin, now filled in. In the background of both images is the large gate repair shed, at the eastern edge of the yard. By permission of Peel Ports.

31 Photo of DANIEL ADAMSON on the end of Top Wall at Old Quay, and showing part of the mobile crane tracks (care of Roy Gough).

32 Photo of Old Quay taken by author's father, Ian Ratcliffe, from TENACITY (cabin cruiser built in Ellesmere Port).

33 Main gate at Old Quay, taken by the author in the early 2000s.

34 Author's shot of the last slipway at Old Quay (left of the above) taken in the early 2000s.

After Conclusion of Chapter on Runcorn

35 DENNIS BRUNDRIT (care of Mr. Pitaluga, the owner of the land and foreshore where the wreck of the ship now resides).

36 Wreck of DENNIS BRUNDRIT shortly before the storm of 1942 (care of Mr. Pitaluga, as above).

37 Part of the face of the figurehead of DENNIS BRUNDRIT, on display at the Falkland Islands Museum and National Trust, held by Colin Patterson-Smith, a friend of the author and former employee of the museum (author's photo).

38 Remains of the figurehead of DENNIS BRUNDRIT, held in storage at the Falkland Islands Museum, allowed to be viewed by the author by kind permission (and seen here in the author's photo with the face temporarily restored).

39 Author's shot of the wreck of the DENNIS BRUNDRIT with the plaque he had made to commemorate her planted in place on Centre Island, Falklands.

After Section on the DENNIS BRUNDRIT

40 VOLANT under repair at Stubbs's Yard, with shipwright Harold Whitby stood in foreground (care of Ken Stubbs).

After Section on the Stubbs Family

41 Map of Runcorn waterfront in the late 1800s, scanned from archives at Halton Lea Library.

42 Map of Runcorn (formerly Bridgewater) Docks in the 1960s, scanned from old Manchester Ship Canal brochures at Halton Lea Library. By

permission of Peel Ports. Note that today the majority of docks and basins have been filled in, as have the locks. The remaining three are Alfred, Fenton and Francis Docks (the latter being the new name for the old Tidal Dock).

upper portion of the chart and the continuation inland is shown in the lower section. Close-ups of each set of docks along the Ship Canal are inset within the chart. I am obliged to point out that this is NOT to be used for navigation purposes as it has not been updated with the appropriate changes from Notices to Mariners, etc.

DEDICATION

This book is dedicated to all those men and women of Cheshire, Lancashire and the Mersey region who worked in the nautical, marine, river and canal environments. To all those sailors, bargemen, boatmen, lightermen, longshoremen, dockers, shipwrights, shipbuilders, ostlers, fishermen, beatsters, engineers and all others who made and make our area the rich bed of maritime history it is.

Nautical, marine, maritime... all great words that encompass a lot of trades and lifestyles. But none of them really connects all those people who had a way of life connected to the water. There are those who sailed the oceans and seas; those who navigated the rivers and canals; those who pulled barges and narrowboats by hand or by horse; those who built or repaired ships, boats, craft of whatever kind, and their engines or sails, masts, and spars; those who worked building the anchors and cables, ropes and rigging; those who supported the aforementioned as dockers, lighthouse keepers, chandlers, etc. The list goes on. I wanted to try to invent a word that would capture all these great occupations and I have, I hope, done so satisfactorily. To discover what it is, please see the appendices.

I would especially like to dedicate this work to all my family and friends that fit the above description. I discuss my family at some length in this work and I do so because I wish to make it clear just how intricately their lives have been woven into the maritime history of our town, as have the lives of many other Runcornians. I hope this inspires some research into family history in others in our part of the world, and that others find this work as fascinating and rewarding as I have.

Finally, I dedicate this work to my naval mentor and good friend, Chris Rickard. Chris served in the Navy for twenty-four years and then many more as a civilian instructor. As a Communications Yeoman, he had no equal, and his expertise was always sought and shared in equal measure. He conducted much research for institutions such as the Flag Institute on the subjects of national Colours, visual signalling and tactics in battle. His love of naval lore and history was as infectious as his obvious dedication and consummate professionalism. He was an inspiration to so many and always there to assist, encourage and contribute. RIP Chris and thanks for everything.

ACKNOWLEDGEMENTS

Thank you to the following (in no particular order):

Microsoft for the Word programme this book is written in, for the PowerPoint system used for the graphs in this work and the Paint programme used on some of the illustrations.

The late H.F. "Bert" Starkey, for his research and writings, which form the basis of this work and which led me to expand upon his initial findings to begin my own work in this field. His contribution to the preservation of our history is evidenced by a colossal library of works and I am only one of many to have learned from his long years of study and research. Thanks also to Avid Publications for permission to use a photo from Bert Starkey's work.

The many authors, researchers and photographers whose work I have studied and analysed from books, booklets, websites and maps over the last twenty or so years of looking into this subject.

To the many contributors to the internet chat site Tug Talk for their memories and pictures. Many of them are former Manchester Ship Canal tug and dredger crewmembers or staff from Old Quay Yard. I cannot name all contributors but among their number are David Asprey (especially for information on Weston Point Steam Towing), Stephen Carter, Daniel Cross, Carl Lechey, George Robinson, Arthur Taylor, Dave Waller, and Michael Williams.

To the many contributors to the Facebook pages Runcorn Photos, Runcorn past an present (sic), You know your from Runcorn when… (sic), and COBWEB (Canal Old Boys Web) for their memories and pictures. In particular, I would thank ex-Ship Canal workers Frank Brown, Tony Dowling, John Lunt, John Taylor and the late Kenneth Morgan. Thanks also for the photographs to Frank Brown and also Kenneth Morgan, who sadly passed away in October 2014 at the time I was submitting my work to the publisher.

Ross Bullock of the Runcorn and District Historical Society for his time and for his labelled photograph of Runcorn's waterfront.

Percy Dunbavand for his research, memories and time. Also for his photographs.

Evelyn Hayes of Scribes and Scribblers in Runcorn for her time, for putting me in contact with the two gentlemen asterisked below, and also (on a separate note) for help with tracing my family tree.

Liz Howard of the Curiosity Bookshop, Runcorn, for her local history books and for her time and advice.

Ray Miller, for his advice and time, and also for printing so much of my ramblings over the years!

Ron Turner*, for his memories and time.

Roy Gough* for his book, his photographs and for his memories and time.

Ken Stubbs, for his time and his memories and pictures.

David Keenan, for his memories and time.

Charles F. Foster, for his advice and time and for his picture of Frodsham Dockyard.

Hugh Potter, editor of *Narrow Boat* magazine, for his help and advice regarding the picture from the Geoff Wheat Collection.

Peel Ports Group marketing director Julia Bradley and commercial controller Joe Blythe for their time and help with details of work carried out by the Manchester Ship Canal Company at Old Quay Yard. Also for permission to use some old M.S.C. Co. plans and images from its corporate magazine *Port of Manchester Review*.

Cheshire Libraries and their staff in Halton Lea and Egerton Street, Runcorn, Warrington and Chester.

Paul Wright (a friend of my father), the editor of the railway enthusiast *8D Society* magazine for his advice.

Roy Fenton of *Ships in Focus Record* (and a contributor to so many nautical magazines) for his advice.

David Roberts of Avid Publications for his permission to use material from books by the late Bert Starkey.

Reverend David Long and the Sankey Canal Restoration Society for permission to use several photographs and for the research conducted for publications and for its website.

The staff of the UK Hydrographic Office for their help and for Copyright Licence #17517 that has allowed me to use the Manchester Ship Canal and Upper Mersey chart in this work.

Commander Paddy Allen, R.N., my boss as Commander, Sea Training at Devonport, for his reading of my proof copy and for his enthusiasm, support, and advice. My report has been finalised, so this is NOT sycophantic!

Thanks also go to:

My late great uncle Frank for his memories.

To his son, Frank for his research.

Dad, for his memories and help piecing things together; for the long walks along the canal and riversides locating and photographing the locations discussed in this booklet. Thanks to him for his enthusiasm and support for me in this project.

Also, thanks to him for the photos of Old Quay Yard taken from TENACITY. This was the cabin cruiser built by our friend the late Reg Lindop of Ellesmere Port.

Mum, for her support and guidance as ever.

And to my wife, Julie, for encouraging me to put this book forward for publishing.

FOREWORD

Cheshire[1] is a county of contrasts. It is thought of as a flat county, the vast Cheshire Plain being famous. Yet Cheshire has a number of well-known and once strategically-important hills, from Frodsham and Helsby to Beeston.

On the one hand, it is renowned as a rural area of farms and beautiful vistas, yet Cheshire also has a vast array of industrial heritage to call upon. There were the iron and copper industries at such places as Runcorn and Wallasey. There are the chemical refineries at Stanlow and the chemical plants at such places as Runcorn, Widnes (within the county since 1974), Chester and Northwich.

There were the salt mines of Northwich and Winsford and coal mines and sandstone quarries at various locations. There are also the railway engineering plants at such places as Crewe.

Within the county there are motor car manufacturers, such as Rolls-Royce and/Bentley at Crewe and Vauxhall Motors at Ellesmere Port.

Then there are the aircraft building plants, such as the Avro facility at Woodford, which merged into Hawker Siddeley, then British Aerospace. This was renamed BAE Systems before the factory's eventual closure in 2011. Avro also built aircraft at Ringway, now Manchester International Airport.

More aviation facilities also reside within our county boundaries, such as the former Vickers-Armstrong plant at Hawarden/Broughton near Chester. This too went through various changes, from de Havilland to Hawker Siddeley, then British Aerospace to its current owner, Airbus. Finally, in the Seventies there was also Crosby Aviation of Knutsford, which built light aircraft.

There were leather and textile/clothing industries throughout the county, paint manufacturers, breweries, and lead works, etc.

---

1   When I speak of Cheshire, I refer to both the historic "teapot-shaped" county that existed from antiquity until 1974, and also the modern version that includes Warrington and Widnes. The Mersey formed a natural border at the north of the county for hundreds of years until the political boundary changes brought in these two towns from the opposite bank that had previously been in Lancashire. The changes also took the Wirral Peninsular away from Cheshire and gave it to the newly-formed Merseyside, and took Stockport and other areas to the north-east for the new Greater Manchester, as well as some land for Derbyshire.

Our green and pleasant land was also very much at the heart of the "workshop of the world" that was England.

However, one particular facet of industrial might particularly fascinates me, and it is one that Cheshire also had more than her fair share of: ship and boat building. Birkenhead and Northwich are probably the first towns one thinks of when considering Cheshire and shipbuilding. But there were others at Bromborough, Chester, Winsford and elsewhere[2]. The county was very much a maritime one, with ports across its extensive coastline, nautical schools at Heswall (Training Ship AKBAR, replaced by the Akbar Nautical School, later Heswall Nautical School) and Birkenhead (such as TS INDEFATIGABLE at New Ferry and TS CONWAY between Rock Ferry and New Ferry[3])

There was an observatory at Bidston that used to calculate the exact time (firing the One O'Clock Gun near Morpeth Dock, Birkenhead) and provide the tide tables to the world (as used in the D-Day landings) before being replaced by computers in the 1960s. Cheshire was very much part of the great seafaring tradition of the British Isles.

Within these pages we shall look at those shipyards that existed on the Upper Mersey. That is to say, that part of the river furthest inland, beyond Bootle, Liverpool and Garston; Birkenhead, Wallasey and Bromborough.

Therefore, we shall look at Runcorn, Frodsham, Widnes (including Fiddler's Ferry[4]), Ellesmere Port, Sankey and Warrington. The reason for this order is simply the volume of work conducted in each of these towns (including Sankey, which is today a suburb of Warrington but worthy of separate note due to its earlier pedigree in this trade compared with the rest of the borough to which it now belongs) and the tradition for shipbuilding therein, listed in descending order.

I have more information about Runcorn than I do the other towns, largely because there was so much more maritime industry there than in the other places. It is for this reason that I have made graphs for the figures for Runcorn

---

2   These locations were home to both merchant and Naval shipbuilders, there being yards that built ships for the Royal Navy and the wider use of the Admiralty at Birkenhead, Bromborough, Chester, and Northwich.

3   Not to forget that we also had a brief spell as home to Royal Navy officers' training when BRITANNIA Royal Naval College was moved to Eaton Hall in Chester during World War II.

4   Fiddler's Ferry is just inside the border of Warrington Borough but I group it with Widnes because, during most of this period, Warrington did not stretch as far west as it does today.

and Frodsham shipbuilding but not for anywhere else. There are simply not as many ships from the other towns to list in this format.

It is my desire to preserve this information for future generations so that we can all remember and honour our forebears for their tireless industriousness and for all the benefits they brought to the area. The work is an amateur one, as I am not a professional writer, and it is a labour of love; I have involved myself in this study because it fascinates me. I hope it provokes similar emotions in others.

It is no exaggeration, however, to say there is much more work to do. As you can see from the pages herein, there are many gaps in the archives, missing and garbled information, and researchers at odds with each other over facts. All of this is because record keeping was perhaps not as efficient as it is today.

Also, for many of the craft built in this locale, there was no official registry; certainly there was no requirement for such when the vessels were only meant for the inland navigations and not for the river and sea crossings of their sister-ships.

Either way, this work is not complete but it is as far as I have got in twenty years of research and is ready to be shared. If anyone can provide more information, or perhaps correct any of the statements I make in this book, I would be very grateful to hear from them.

For example, I have tried very hard to come up with evidence of war work undertaken locally and I am sure there must have been work conducted on Royal Navy ships or, those of the Army, RAF and various auxiliary organisations. I have failed to find any such documentation but I feel it must have taken place, especially with the Western Approaches Command being based at nearby Liverpool during World War II.

In any case, any information, photographs, diagrams or maps can be sent to me for inclusion in an updated version of this study, should the demand be there for it. And if not, then will be just for my own interest, so I look forward to hearing from you.

Bob Ratcliffe
bobratcliffeuppermersey@gmail.com

Postscript: I don't normally "do" modern over traditional but in this book I have chosen to accept the advice given in *Fowler's Modern English Usage* and add the extra "s" in the possessive tense for that belonging to a person whose name ends in "s". Thus, there will be reference to Stubbs's Yard, rather than the way I was taught at school, which is Stubbs' Yard.

An Account of Runcorn's Shipbuilding and Boat Building Industry, Focusing Primarily on the Old Quay Area

Introduction

To write down in a short work the entire nautical history of a town such as Runcorn (as for many towns in our great seafaring nation), would be impossible. But I hope to give some sort of feel for the true diversity and range of maritime industries that existed in that town and even those which remain today, probably out of mind of most inhabitants of the area.

Largely, I'd like to reflect on the commercial ship and boat building and repair work of Runcorn, rather than spend any great amount of time focusing on the large number of pleasure craft currently manufactured within the town. Yet a reference to these businesses should be made, if only to show some of the skills developed over the centuries have not disappeared entirely.

The nautical history of Runcorn and its various outlying villages and settlements undoubtedly stretches back into antiquity. The fact people settled there along the River Mersey implies some sort of ties with the water, be it for fishing or trade. Later would come defence, with Mersey meaning "boundary river", and this evident natural border marked the northern end of the Mercian kingdom (and later the county of Cheshire) for many centuries.

A castle built at the order of Aethelflaed, Lady of the Mercians, in AD 914 (Runcorn Burgh) at the later site of the Castle Rock Shipyard[5] shows the defence of this settlement and kingdom from attack by the sea was given serious support, so some sort of shipping was in use locally, even if it was only by enemy forces! Earlier settlement at the waterfront of Runcorn is likely but not proven, despite the circumstantial evidence of Roman settlement and trade in the immediate area (and archaeological evidence of a Roman settlement at Halton Brow), including a supposed ferry or ford across the Mersey from Ditton to Runcorn.

---

5   The place-name of Castle Rock, or Castle Rock, comes from this ancient fort, whose last vestiges were swept away with the building of the Runcorn Railway Bridge. The ramparts of that bridge were designed in memory of the castle.

H.F. (Bert) Starkey's *Old Runcorn* states that shipbuilding and repair began in Runcorn in 1790, although the author of that book shows records in his earlier work *Schooner Port* of vessels built there from 1778 and a comment that Runcorn shipbuilding began in the late 18th Century. The presence of a ferry at Runcorn since medieval times suggests also that some boat building and repairing experience, however simple, was to be found locally since that period. The ferry was originally at Boat House Pool (which was at the site of the later Old Quay Docks) but was moved by the Bridgewater Trustees a quarter of a mile upstream to a place that then became known as Ferry Hut (due to the shelter built there for waiting passengers). Its service lasted until 1905, when it was replaced by the world's largest transporter bridge.

Nickson, writing of the year 1821, states in his *History of Runcorn* that 'there must have been some boat building or repairing at this time but the trade does not seem to have been of sufficient importance to merit a notice or to be added to the annual value of the town'.

Nickson goes on to say (whilst discussing the shipyard of J. Sothern) that by 1836 'shipbuilding had now become a staple industry of the town, and two other shipyards were under the management of the late Messrs. Samuel Mason and John Anderton respectively'.

Later in that tome, Nickson says of Runcorn in the 1880s that 'its industries comprise the manufacture of the various alkalies [sic] and acids, the making of soap, ship and boat building, the smelting of lead, silver refining, copper extraction, the making of steam engines, gas plant and well sinking apparatus, tanning, the extraction and distilling of glycerine…'.

Shipbuilding grew out of an earlier repair industry and became permanent, going on to gain what Starkey calls 'something of a national prestige for the building of small coastal craft'. Runcorn shipwrights became 'widely esteemed for their expertise', according to Starkey's *Schooner Port*. The centres of this industry were at Old Quay and along Mersey Road (roughly following the line of what was once Mersey Street) to Castle Rock, Runcorn Docks and also the Big Pool and Top Locks along the Bridgewater Canal. There were others at various locations near to these areas, suggesting they used the same accesses to the water for the launching of their vessels, but there were many others that are difficult to tie down to a location or to accurately state the exact nature of their business. This work shall focus on the larger, more famous concerns.

Shipbuilding at Runcorn ended with the building of the Manchester Ship Canal from 1888, although ship repair and boat building and repair continued until the very end of the Twentieth century, with modern pleasure craft still being built and repaired in the town to this day.

Today, as you look along the Runcorn waterfront to the east of the Jubilee Bridge (the steel arch road bridge), a new development is taking shape at what was once the last remaining, and also largest, of all the numerous ship and boat yards of the town. It is called The Deck and it promises to bring residential, retail and leisure facilities to a town that has desperately needed all three for some time. Its location is at the heart of the Old Town, from where Runcorn as we know it today gradually grew[6].

This area, once a creek known as the Boat House Pool or Old Gut, developed into a dock system known as Old Quay, and this is the name that most Runcornians would know the locale by today. The area saw much investment and at least three times (the building of the Mersey and Irwell, Bridgewater and Manchester Ship canals and their associated facilities), such development signalled a new lease of life for Runcorn. We can only hope that the latest changes do the same and that it was worth the price of what was a fine and self-sufficient shipyard.

Beginnings

Old Quay

The ancient ferry at Runcorn seems to have begun in 1178, although there may have been a boat earlier than this run solely for the benefits of the barons of Halton and Widnes. By at least the 1500s, this enterprise was run from the public landing place at the Pool of Runcorn, Old Gut, the creek where Sprinch Brook flowed into the Mersey. This area (which had become known as the Boat House Pool), where Bridge and Mersey Streets (and their predecessor lanes) once met, was eventually surrounded by the works of the Mersey and Irwell and Bridgewater Companies, as well as others, as they formed their shipyards and other works.[7] Whether or not any form of building or repair of

---

6   The most important ancient settlement of the area appears to have been Halton, seat of the Baron (later Duke of Lancaster) and home to the baron's castle. Around Halton came the Anglo-Saxon settlements of Norton, Aston, Sutton, and Weston, the settlements/farms of the north, east, south and west respectively. Runcorn, 'the wide or spacious cove/bay' in old English, came later, split between Lower Runcorn and Higher Runcorn. These have been known, respectively, over the centuries as Runkhorne Abatis; and Alterior Runcover, Runcoure Superior or Over Runcorne.

vessels occurred here in antiquity is a matter of debate but it seems logical to assume the long history of ferry operations here also summoned a boat building and repair industry. As a footnote, the eventual spread of Mersey and Irwell facilities and the building of the Bridgewater Navigation Yard at Old Gut meant the removal of the Runcorn Ferry to its latter home at Ferry Hut (with Ferry Hut Slip) near the parish church.

The earliest shipbuilding firm on record at Runcorn was a partnership of William Wright and Charles Hickson, whose Mersey Street Shipyard was in business by 1802 at the latest (earlier ship and boat launches are recorded but the details of who built them are lost), when they launched the 57 ton Flat, SARAH. By 1815 however, William Wright was building ships as the sole proprietor of the yard. The following year, a druggist and stone merchant named Dennis Brundrit married Wright's daughter Elizabeth. On the death of William Wright, the Mersey Street Yard passed to his son-in-law. The Brundrit Company, after various re-inventions, became the largest of the yards at Runcorn by 1848 and the Brundrit family controlled quarries (some inherited from William Wright) and owned ships and boats, becoming a sizeable business empire.

Shortly after the first records for the Wright and Hickson company, another significant builder made an appearance, in this case, around 1804. This was the Mersey and Irwell Navigation Company, the firm that built canals and canalised river stretches to create an inland navigation system linking Runcorn to Manchester. The last stretch of waterway, the Runcorn to Latchford Canal, terminated in a new set of docks at Runcorn, just east of Mersey Street. These Mersey and Irwell Docks became known as the Old Quay Docks (Old Quay being the name usually given to the company and canal as a whole) and the name stuck for the area from then onwards.

The Mersey and Irwell built a shipyard for the manufacture and repair of its own vessels. This consisted of a graving dock, which was a wet dock leading to a sideways entry patent slip of two ways (capable of lifting vessels of 200 tons). In 1837, all boat building and repair facilities of the company at

---

7   Old Gut is not to be confused with Duke's Cut, which was later corrupted to Duke's Gut. This was the name given to the channel dug by the Duke of Bridgewater to improve navigation at Runcorn by funnelling water around what is now known as Runcorn Bend to the entrance of his docks, preventing the build-up of silt and creating Runcorn Island as a separate entity from the mainland. Runcorn Island (later also known as Duke's Island) was more or less destroyed by the building of the Ship Canal and its remains can be seen on maps and charts as No Man's Land. Castle Bridge, which linked the island to the mainland near the ancient castle at Castle Rock, also had to be destroyed for the canal building.

Manchester were transferred to the yard at Runcorn. This yard later came into the possession of the Bridgewater Trustees in 1844. The trustees had taken control of the late Duke of Bridgewater's canal and shipping interests upon his death and they became the Bridgewater Navigation Co. Ltd. when they took-over the Mersey and Irwell company.

By this time, the area of the Boat House Pool had been partially enclosed by the developments by the Mersey and Irwell and the remaining area of the creek had been taken-over by the Bridgewater concern as a shipyard (later to be known as the Bridgewater Navigation Co. Yard), which was its principal yard out of all its facilities across the North-west. From this time, public access to the area was denied and the ferry to Widnes was moved to Ferry Hut, further to the east.

The Bridgewater Navigation Co. continued to use the Old Quay Yard alongside its own facilities already at the site as well as elsewhere in the town. These facilities were a graving grid on the outer wall of Bridgewater Docks (today's Runcorn Docks) at the end of the Old Line of Locks down to the River Mersey (and later to access the Manchester Ship Canal, before the locks were closed in 1949, with the new line being closed in 1960 and both subsequently in-filled). Also at this location was a graving dock and a boat yard at the Sevastopol Arm, part way down the Locks. These facilities may have been in operation as early as 1785 for the building and repair of company vessels. At Top Locks, where the Bridgewater Canal now terminates since the infilling of the locks themselves, the Bridgewater company also had the packet dry dock (a graving dock) between the Old and New Lines of locks for the repair of its Little Packets, or canal tugs).

By 1823, Dennis Brundrit was in partnership with Philip Whiteway, who became another local man of great importance (he actually laid the first stone of the Runcorn Railway Bridge on 12th April 1864 as a member of the Runcorn Improvement Commissioners). An 1839 survey of the Port of Liverpool (of which Runcorn was then part) recorded the land immediately east of the railway bridge was owned by Dennis Brundrit, who had "shipbuilding and other yards" there. Below the present Belvedere Buildings there were coal and timber yards belonging to Messrs. Brundrit, Whiteway and Forster, although later the Brundrit shipyard facilities seemed to be solely at the Old Quay site.

Further shipbuilders at Old Quay were Okell and the later Okell and Webster, who had a timber yard and smithy adjacent to the Brundrit works. Okell begun his business around 1821 and by 1840 his partnership with Webster had started.

J. Southern and Co. carried on "the timber and ship yard of Mr. Okell" according to Nickson's *History of Runcorn*. This firm was in business at least as early as 1836, so either the Okell firm continued its business elsewhere, or the yard at Old Quay was shared between the two firms. Either way, by the 1840s, the yard had been subsumed into that of the Brundrit concern.

At some point around the 1850s or '60s, business directories list John and William Brundrit and also Robert C. Whiteway as shipbuilders in their own right. Whether a continued partnership or some sort or a shared occupancy of the yard was the reason, the firm had morphed into Brundrit and Co. by around 1874. It was around this time that the yard had expanded, to include a patent slipway for sideways launching as well as two smaller slipways for fore and aft launching of ships. The company built the two largest ships ever to be launched from Runcorn, namely the 451 ton ANNE CHESSHYRE and the 462 ton DENNIS BRUNDRIT (which was claimed to be the smallest full-rigged ship in the world).

A later incarnation of the business appears to be as Brundrit and Hayes, Mr. Hayes being mentioned in *Smith's Directory of 1888* as "Hayes, Wm., Esq. (BRUNDRIT and CO.)", so presumably he was a senior man at the company who later became a partner in the firm. Evidence suggests he was a full partner in the quarrying business alongside Messrs. Brundrit of Runcorn and Higson of Liverpool in this venture. It appears, however, that the firm reverted to the Brundrit and Co. name in later years, before finally winding-up in 1891.

James Boot was known as a foreman shipbuilder and his address was listed as Cooper Street. This road was adjacent to Mersey Street and there was a James Boot who was manager of the Brundrit yard. He may have operated independently but more than likely he was part of the Brundrit empire.

Mill Street

Thomas and John (Junior) Johnson were brothers who took-over their father's soap works and very rapidly formed a massive business empire, all centred on Mill Street in Old Runcorn (around the Old Quay area). The brothers were soap, salt and rosin works owners; colliery, mine and quarry owners; and farmers. They were also deeply involved in the maritime scene.

They were ship owners and rope makers and they also built and maintained their own vessels. In fact, they built an important merchant fleet that became one of largest on Merseyside and the brothers became important local dignitaries.

Then, it all went horribly wrong: the brothers' fleet was caught blockade running to the Confederate states and destroyed or captured by the US Navy.

The brothers were bankrupted. Little evidence remains of the Johnsons' former wealth but among the visible remnants is the current town hall in Runcorn, which was once the private residence of Thomas Johnson.

Also near the Mills adjacent to Old Quay was the home of Fred Abbott, another local boat builder. He was once in partnership with a man called Walton and owned his own boats that traded to Liverpool.

Mill Street was the location of the later Belvedere Yard (see next section) and so this may well have been the same location where one or both of the firms above operated from. Belvedere and Mill Street Yards were separate entities but were likely to have been adjacent to each other.

Belvedere Yard

Immediately to the west of Old Quay was the shipyard of the Mason family. This began in around the 1830s under Samuel Mason. He started at Belvedere Building but his address was listed as Belvedere Yard shortly after 1840 and was in business as a 'ship and anchor smith'. The premises were below the former waterfront property of Belvedere Building, which was a boarding house in the times when the town was a health resort famed for its salt water baths and river bathing before industrialisation replaced the famed clean airs. Mr. Mason's address was Mill Street from about 1850 and he may have taken on the Johnson yard; he certainly seems to have retained his original yard as well.

Later incarnations of the firm included John Mason and Co., Mason and Craggs (John Mason being in partnership with George Craggs from 1857) and Blundell and Mason from around 1868 until 1879.

The yard seems then to have fallen into disuse except that a photograph from the book, *Cheshire Railways* by Mike Hitches shows several vessels on the stocks/slipway at the yard, with the transporter bridge to Widnes in the background. This dates the picture to sometime in or after 1905 and it is possible that someone was in the business of ship repair there at this date. It may even be possible the M.S.C. Co. used the yard for its vessels as it owned the land by this time. In later year,s the remains of the Belvedere slipway was used for the storage of the Ship Canal lock gates.

Other shipbuilders were addressed as on or near Mersey Street, where the Belvedere Yard lay, and these included such people as the "ship and anchor smith" John Ravenscroft of Church Street. They too, perhaps, used the Belvedere Yard under some sort of lease system, which may have been prevalent in the town given the large number of people engaged in these businesses.

Castle Rock

The small promontory next to the railway bridge where once stood the Mercian castle was for many years home to a shipyard/boatyard that existed until the 1960s.

The Anderton family worked the yard from around 1810 but Philip Speakman was also building ships and boats there from this period, perhaps in some sort of sharing scheme. The Speakman firm later acquired the Belvedere and Mill Street Yards as well as the Albion Yard on Big Pool.

Anderton later went into a new partnership and Anderton and LeCouteur ran Castle Rock Yard for some years. The LeCouteurs were a seagoing family from Jersey who moved to Runcorn under Captain John LeCouteur, the grandfather of my late Great Uncle Frank (who married my Great Aunt Alice Ratcliffe in 1942).

Eventually the well-known Runcorn family Abel took-over the Castle Rock Yard from around 1900 and they continued to build and maintain their own vessels there until the mid-1960s. They were carriers of gravel and sand for the glass industry and were one of the largest carriers in north-west England, according to researcher Terry Kavanagh.

The yard had a patent slip for the sideways launch of vessels and, at one point, there was a fore-and-aft slipway for building larger vessels, as evidenced by a photograph shown in *Narrowboat* magazine.

The last ever Mersey Flat to be built, RUTH BATE, was constructed at Castle Rock and launched in the 1950s. The second last built (also by Abel's), OAKDALE, is now a houseboat at Millom in Cumbria.

The firm had other yards in Runcorn but none as long-lived and famous as that at Castle Rock.

Ferry Hut

Wedged between Castle Rock and the Belvedere Yard was Ferry Hut, where the small waiting room and slip for the Mersey Ferry once stood. It was the site of a salt water baths dating from when Runcorn was a health resort and was still something of a holiday spot into the latter half of the last century, when summer-time crowds flocked to the small beach there beside what was by then the Manchester Ship Canal.

This small but well-known local area was also the site of some repair work because, as well as work that was likely to have been carried out on the ferry boat, there were a number of local fishing vessels that used to be beached there for repair as and when needed.

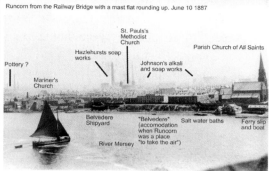

Runcorn from the Railway Bridge with a mast flat rounding up. June 10 1887

St. Pauls's
Methodist
Church

Hazlehursts soap
works

Johnson's alkali
and soap works

Parish Church of All Saints

Pottery ?

Mariner's
Church

Belvedere
Shipyard

"Belvedere"
(accomodation
when Runcorn
was a place
"to take the air")

Salt water baths

Ferry slip
and boat

River Mersey

Illustration 2

Illustration 3

BLUNDELL & MASON,
Iron and Wood Ship and Boat Builders and Repairers
BELVEDERE YARD, RUNCORN.
PATENT SLIP ON THE PREMISES.

ANDERTON & LE COUTEUR,
SHIP AND BOAT BUILDERS,
Castle Rock Yard
Runcorn.
All kinds of Smiths & Joiners Work Executed on the most reasonable terms
PATENT SLIP ON THE PREMISES.

Illustration 4

Illustration 5

Illustration 6

Illustration 7

Illustration 8

Left: *Illustration 9*
Above: *Illustration 10*

Big Pool

The once large expanse of water above the Old Town in Runcorn was home to several yards and these include the renowned Simpson, Davies and Co., builders of its own and others' narrow boats (it was probably the largest producer of the Runcorn Six-Planker type of narrowboat, made deeper for the large Bridgewater Canal).

It was a commercial builder that later carried out repairs for pleasure boat owners, going out of business in the 1960s.

It was not alone because there was also the aforementioned Albion Yard and various boat builders, such as Samuel Taylor, Thomas Binns, John Crippin and John Clucas. The already listed Speakman family also operated a yard here at one time.

Today, the Big Pool is largely gone as it was filled-in for road works.

Top Locks

The current terminus of the Bridgewater Canal once led to two flights of locks down to Runcorn Docks and also had a graving dock. That is fairly well-known but what is not so widely acknowledged is the large number of boat builders that once operated here.

These included Withington and LeCouteur (the latter being my late Great Uncle Frank's father, James), William Bate and the Stubbs family, who were also involved with boat and ship repair at Old Quay and before that at Runcorn Docks.

Runcorn Docks

Finally, Runcorn Docks housed a number of builders of ships and boats and there was a boat yard along one of the lines of locks.

The businesses included the Stubbs family under Samuel and later Jack Stubbs, before their move to Old Quay, and the Knowles Brothers, as well as the Potter firm, which operated a dockyard midway down the Locks.

Weston Point

Weston Point ("The Point") is famous for its "church on the island". The church, Christ Church, was built by the River Weaver Navigation Company Trustees for the watermen, boatmen and their families. It is a famous landmark that has survived the decades even as all its neighbouring buildings did not during the many changes at the docks. New docks have been built, and subsequently expanded or filled in, with the adjacent warehousing suffering a similar cycle of alteration. Yet the church remains, now deconsecrated but thankfully still listed and thus protected, on its island created from the lock system separating the docks from the Manchester Ship Canal (and originally the River Mersey). Current plans to fill in the remaining dock area to the south (leaving only the expanded Delamere Dock at the northern end of the complex, along with a new layby and expanded wharfage) will finally connect the church to the mainland, removing its island status. However, should the plans come to fruition, it will remain a landmark, testament to an age when the great entrepreneurs spent money on the well-being of employees and not just on speculation for greater profit[8].

I have heard that canal craft were occasionally launched here but I have only discovered a couple of vessels listed as such so far. However, as well as having its main yard at Castle Rock, Abel's was at Weston Point, where I believe it had a repair yard. This was perhaps at the basin on the Runcorn and Weston Canal parallel to Delamere Dock.

Charles Hickson also moved his business to Weston Point when his partnership with William Wright dissolved. The exact location of this concern is still unknown to me. He later went into business at Ellesmere Port and seems most likely to have been the man of that name mentioned in Starkey's *Old Runcorn* as being an Ensign in one of the two companies of volunteers raised in Runcorn as a precaution against invasion during the Napoleonic Wars[9]. Mr Hickson was, indeed, an interesting man whose history deserves greater research.

The Upper Mersey Navigation Commission based its vessels here and conducted maintenance on its buoys and markers at its yard beside Weston Point Docks.

Lastly, the engineers Henry Branch and Sons was also based at Weston Point, beside Wright's Dock, which was originally built for the loading of stone from the local quarries via a private railway. The entrance to the dock was blocked by a footbridge, which would be rolled on its wheels to move it out of the way of vessels.

---

8   Many local businessmen and landowners devoted time and effort to improving Runcorn and helping its people. Amongst the shipbuilders who did so were the Johnson brothers, who built a ragged school on Mill Brow for the benefit of the poor, and the Bridgewater Trustees, who opened a school along the locks to Bridgewater Docks for the children of boatmen.

9   The Loyal Runcorn and Weston Volunteer Infantry, raised in 1804 and disbanded in 1818.

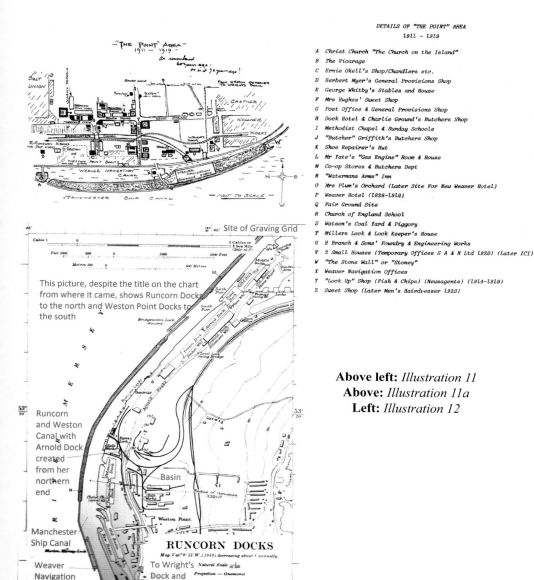

DETAILS OF "THE POINT" AREA
1911 - 1919

A   Christ Church "The Church on the Island"
B   The Vicarage
C   Ernie Okell's Shop/Chandlers etc.
D   Herbert Myer's General Provisions Shop
E   George Whitby's Stables and House
F   Mrs Hughes' Sweet Shop
G   Post Office & General Provisions Shop
H   Dock Hotel & Charlie Ground's Butchers Shop
I   Methodist Chapel & Sunday Schools
J   "Butcher" Griffith's Butchers Shop
K   Shoe Repairer's Hut
L   Mr Yate's "Gas Engine" Room & House
M   Co-op Stores & Butchers Dept
N   "Watermans Arms" Inn
O   Mrs Plum's Orchard (Later Site For New Weaver Hotel)
P   Weaver Hotel (1828-1919)
Q   Fair Ground Site
R   Church of England School
S   Watson's Coal Yard & Piggory
T   Millers Lock & Lock Keeper's House
U   H Branch & Sons' Foundry & Engineering Works
V   2 Small Houses (Temporary Offices S A & N Ltd 1920) (Later ICI)
W   "The Stone Wall" or "Stoney"
X   Weaver Navigation Offices
Y   "Lock Up" Shop (Fish & Chips) (Newsagents) (1914-1919)
Z   Sweet Shop (Later Men's Hairdresser 1920)

This picture, despite the title on the chart from where it came, shows Runcorn Docks to the north and Weston Point Docks to the south

Above left: *Illustration 11*
Above: *Illustration 11a*
Left: *Illustration 12*

The Coming of the Ship Canal

Although we have come up to the near past in our look at some of the Runcorn yards, it is an appropriate juncture here to look in more detail at how the maritime industry at Old Quay and Mersey Road changed when the "pride of Northern Britain", and the greatest engineering feat of the Victorian age, the Manchester Ship Canal, was completed.

The Ship Canal was cut through the foreshore directly beside the Bridgewater Yard at Old Quay and so, in 1890, the Sprinch Yard opened at Big Pool to take on the job of maintaining the Bridgewater Canal Department vessels, as they now had become. We shall discuss this new yard later.

The Brundrit yard, like all other shipbuilding businesses along the Runcorn waterfront, suffered from the building of the Manchester Ship Canal and its "gantry wall", as it is known locally, which prevented any further launches of larger vessels from that area. Brundrit went out of business around the time of the building of the canal and its remaining larger slipway was retained as the public slipway for the town. The rest of the yard was leased to the Stubbs family as a repair yard, with them also using the public slipway. The Manchester Ship Canal Co. had promised the town of Runcorn a graving dock in payment for the loss of its shipbuilding industry so that at least some sort of repair business could be continued there. In the end, a settlement was agreed whereby the town was granted a strip of land along the waterfront at what is today Mersey Road and the idea of a graving dock was swept aside for a public slipway. It seems the company acquired with the rest of the former shipyards and docks at Old Quay when it took possession of, and later granted to the town, the larger of Brundrit slipways. The company re-built the Brundrit slipway and it became known as Runcorn Town Slip. It also had a second slipway at the site, known as Old Quay Slip (the former Bridgewater Navigation Yard's slipway) and these two slipways appear to have been the agreed payment to the town in place of the graving dock.

The geography of the Old Quay area was changed massively. As well as having a much larger canal cutting through the vicinity, there was also the loss of many buildings and businesses and of the three docks that once marked the terminus of the Mersey and Irwell. The last of these docks was the Lower Dock, which was eventually to join the others, being filled in sometime in the early Twentieth century.

From early in the Twentieth century until the mid-1950s, the Stubbs family continued to maintain the remaining sailing craft (and others), under the leadership first of Jack Stubbs, and then his eldest son, Fred. Fred Stubbs's son Ken wrote an excellent article for the *Runcorn Weekly News* in 2013 that detailed his reminiscences of the yard when he was a boy. He also kindly gave me some help putting together a fuller understanding of his family's business, which began with his great grandfather Samuel Stubbs. However, even this dynasty of shipbuilding artisans have left the business now and Runcorn is a poorer place for it.

By this time, the entire Old Quay site had been subsumed into the Old Quay Yard of the Manchester Ship Canal Company. Stubbs's Slip (or Runcorn Town Slip as it was more properly known) was then one of two slipways remaining at the site, becoming known as Slipway No. 2 (by which name the M.S.C. Co. had long since referred to it). It was alongside Slipway No.1 (as built by the M.S.C. Co. in its earliest days on the site of the Bridgewater Navigation Yard) before the latter was filled in in the 1970s to make way for new workshops. When this happened, it was the end of a link back to the ancient Runcorn Ferry and the boathouse adjacent to the Old Gut, as this spot was the same location: Boathouse Pool, on whose right bank the boathouse had been and on whose left bank the patent slipway stood. At the isthmus of the left bank had once been the Boathouse Pier and later Boathouse Slip (from before the ferry to Widnes had been moved to Ferry Hut further to the east). Now all were gone along with the link back to the old crossing, which had finally been retired in 1905.

With the building of the new Deck project, it would seem that the commitment to keep such a facility at the site has now unfortunately lapsed. A report to the Halton Borough Development Control Committee dated 9th August 2004 admitted that "the importance of this proposed residential development [the Deck] in encouraging further regeneration of the older parts of Runcorn is considered to outweigh the possible prejudice to the need to facilitate direct use of the Ship Canal at this point [Old Quay]". This is despite the acknowledgement that the M.S.C. Co.'s original commitment to the town had been to provide two slipways (the refurbished Brundrit Slipway and the former Bridgewater Slipway, which was filled in in the 1970s). The ignorance of the committee to affairs of the canal and its history is evident when it quotes the Old Quay site as having been engaged in "shipbuilding and boat building since 1880", despite massive evidence to prove that the date is actually at least as far back as 1802. Furthermore, with regard to boat building, that date could go back to the existence of the Runcorn Ferry at Boat House Pool (on the Old Quay site) in the Middle Ages, as the ferry would in all probability have also been maintained at the site.

The only pleasing thing about the report is the statement that, with regard to the former slipway, "if it is possible to incorporate some facility as part of the successful development of the site [Old Quay/the Deck] then this should be welcomed". Perhaps a new but smaller yard may yet be opened there.

The Manchester Ship Canal Company at Old Quay and Beyond

The Old Quay Yard (or Old Quay Workshops) was now the largest shipyard that Runcorn had ever seen and it was a fine establishment, with facilities for the upkeep of the M.S.C. Co.'s myriad vessels as well as many others. At its height the yard, which in later years became known as the Runcorn Yard of the M.S.C. Co., employed 280 people. It had its own Millwrights, Sail Loft (where any tug crews not employed at sea would be turned to for repair work under the sailmaker) and various workshops. It latterly only had one slipway, which was still a public slipway, but one which the M.S.C. Co. continued to keep in constant use for the survey, refit and repair of its vessels. It was said by those who worked for the Manchester Ship Canal Company there was nothing that could not be made, fixed or augmented at Old Quay, and I can well believe it.

Among the many diverse jobs carried out there was the preparing of several large wooden timbers for use as a helicopter landing pad for the Piper Alfa oil platform. This was due to the large woodworking machines at the Lock Gate Repair Shed within the yard. By 1989, perhaps due to work on company vessels being so reduced from the heyday of the Ship Canal (when there was such a large number of craft belonging to the enterprise) and with the outsourcing of dredging and tug operations to independent operators, commercial work returned to this area with Old Quay Yard conducting repair work for vessels from other firms. Thus, in its latter days, Old Quay Yard returned to the same work that its predecessors had been engaged in from at least 200 years earlier.

However, this was not the only facility the M.S.C. Co. owned in Runcorn. It also operated, under its Bridgewater Department, the Victoria Dockyard (later to be known as the Runcorn Dock Yard). This was opened in 1883 and was reputed to be the best and best-equipped boatyard in the country. Sited on Big Pool and formerly connected to the waterfront at Old Quay via a small brook known as "The Sprinch", this yard was a masterpiece of canalboat maintenance and building. It had four graving docks (two of them double-sized), so it could accommodate six barges at once for repair work. It also had a building berth/slipway for sideways launching. Various workshops existed, including a boiler shop, fitting shop, blacksmith's shop and a sawmill. There were also several cranes. Although only three boats were built there, the maintenance of 300 flats and twenty narrowboats, floats and maintenance craft was centred on this facility. The workforce of 120 knew the yard as either the Sprinch Yard or Top Yard as it was at the top of the Sprinch Brook and up from Old Quay, which they called Bottom Yard.

On the opposite bank of the Bridgewater Canal, between Ellesmere and Caithness Streets, was an area known as The Baulks. This was where the timbers for use in the Sprinch Yard were kept.

By 1977, road works in the town as well as the inevitable run down of maintenance facilities for the canals due to the shift to rail and then road transport, meant the Sprinch Yard had closed. It was soon to become home to the first cruising club on the Bridgewater Canal, the Bridgewater Motor Boat Club. It still runs a slipway and double graving dock for members' use.

Furthermore, the old Bridgewater packet dry dock at Waterloo Bridge was used by the M.S.C. Bridgewater Department for the repair of more than twenty narrowboat tugs (as well as other vessels). This facility has been filled in since the lines of locks down to Runcorn Docks were abandoned in the 1960s.

At Runcorn Docks, the M.S.C. Co. Resident Engineer had taken an office adjacent to the former Bridgewater graving grid. The grid seems to have been enclosed on three sides by this time and used as a draw dock for the repair of vessels.

The Ship Canal Company also had divers at each of the locks into the Mersey, who would inspect and repair the lock gates as well as being employed on ship repair. The larger facilities of the company at Ellesmere Port and Manchester have been covered by other works and are outside the scope of this book but, save to say, the firm had a large infrastructure for the repair and building of its own and others' vessels. The last remaining of these complexes was the Runcorn Yard at Old Quay, which tenaciously clung on to a link with the town's past for many years, providing much-needed and traditional employment for many families who (like my own) had worked there at that sort of craft for generations.

Today, the entire Old Quay complex has gone. The eastern part of the old Mersey and Irwell terminus has long since lain empty, surrounded by the developments on the Astmoor Industrial Estate and the more recent housing project on the site of Runcorn Amateur Football Club's former Canal Street ground. The area to the west of the Old Quay Swing Bridge (which leads to what is today a nature reserve on Wigg Island) has been transformed into the Deck housing project and, although the slipway remains at the far west of the estate, its infrastructure has been removed. The lands further west were once also part of the yard but many years ago they were given over to the sea cadets of TS ASHANTI (who used an old shipyard workshop for their Drill Hall) but they too have now gone.

The M.S.C. Co. now has repair facilities at Runcorn Docks but it does not have a graving dock or slipway and very little can be achieved compared to what it was once capable.

In fact, Runcorn seems a lot less the hive of maritime activity it once was, and partly this may have to do with the M.S.C. Co. now coming under Peel Ports (a branch of Peel Holdings). Peel is a massive group that also own the Mersey Docks and Harbour Company and hence, Liverpool and Birkenhead Docks. Its maritime HQ is now in Liverpool, and so the days of the Ship Canal leading from Runcorn (where Port Division head office, the tug depot and repair facilities, and the gate repair centre were all once located) have gone.

Illustration 13

Illustration 14

Illustration 15

Illustration 16

Illustration 17

Illustration 18

Illustration 19

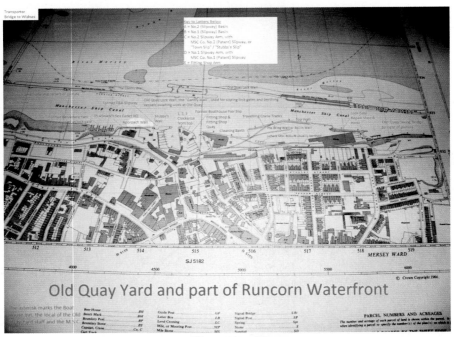

Old Quay Yard and part of Runcorn Waterfront

Illustration 20

Illustration 21

Illustration 22

Illustration 23

Illustration 24

Illustration 26

Illustration 25

Illustration 27

Illustration 28   *Illustration 29*

Now and then
Over recent years there have been marked changes to the appearance of Old
Quay. These are vividly illustrated in these two photographs by K. M. Holt,
taken in 1960 and 1973 respectively.

Illustration 30

Illustration 31

Illustration 32

Illustration 33

Illustration 34

Elsewhere in Runcorn

Although the bulk of the maritime scene of Runcorn can be placed in the various areas of the town headlined above, there were other facilities for ship and boat repair. These included the Marine Engineering and Naval Architecture firm of Drammen Maritime (U.K.), once run by my father, Ian Ratcliffe, with my mother, Rita, running administration. There was also the firm of William Dunbavand, an ancestor of the well-known Runcorn tug skipper Percy, without whom no book on maritime Runcorn would be complete (he is a friend of the family, having worked with my grandfather, George Ratcliffe, on the tugs out of Old Quay for many years).

The late Bill Leathwood, another great Runcornian who has given so much to us from his repository of knowledge, gave a speech to the Runcorn and District Historical Society in April 2005. In it he painted a picture of Runcorn in 1929-30 and spoke of "seven boat repairing yards" in the town at that time. This for a town with a population of just 17,000. The outline of this talk, Mr. Leathwood's last public speech, can be found on the Historical Society website and is well worth a read.

Today

Runcorn now appears to the casual observer as just another inland town but this is incorrect. Commercial shipbuilding and repair have disappeared; the local ship owners, brokers and chandlers have all gone; many of the docks and linking canals have been infilled; and the Ship Canal and Mersey seem very quiet. Yet two of the town's three dock complexes remain. Runcorn Docks (and the adjacent, private, facilities such as the Salt Union Berth) as well as Weston Point Docks are both still going. In fact, Weston Port or Port Weston, as the latter has become known, is now being regenerated by the Stobart group as part of a massive investment in the Borough of Halton (Runcorn and Widnes) and forms part of a multi-nodal transport hub. On top of this, the Marine Engine builders and repairers James Troop and Company have for the last few years been based at Astmoor Industrial Estate, thus providing an extra facet of nautical flavour to Runcorn.

But what of the ship and boat yards? Well, believe it or not, secreted in little nooks and crannies of the town, there are still several firms employed in this trade, although today we are dealing with pleasure craft and, in some cases, yards that are basically owned by small clubs having taken over the former facilities of the old-time commercial builders. But either way, the yards are there and you can still see many boats built or repaired in Runcorn by various companies in locations such as Weston Port, Preston Brook and along the Bridgewater Canal. And perhaps one day a small commercial enterprise will again grace the slipway at the Deck and continue a tradition older than memories and records remember.

Conclusion

This book will hopefully be an interesting eye-opener for the reader, showing a glimpse of the wide range of ship and boat building and repair that one town (and originally a small one at that) had. The might of the industrial United Kingdom was such that many towns had a great deal of manufacturing muscle and it is impressive to see what the country achieved so many years ago as well as what it still achieves, despite the best efforts of many in Whitehall and beyond to outsource such tasks to other countries. I hope this article and the lists in the annexes help to expand the readers' knowledge of what there once was in my home town and local area and open the imaginations of all to what there once was across the length and breadth of this great nation.

To put in context what you are about to read in the following lists and text, imagine how the ever-shifting channels of the Mersey precluded lengthy periods of deep water access to Runcorn and the surrounding towns that at one time were within its customs port boundaries. Picture how the coming of the Manchester Ship Canal was a double-edged sword, for just as it brought the benefits of access to a deep water port, it took away any chance of significant ship launching, as well as taking away the independence Runcorn had gained as a customs port. Yet, despite these setbacks, there was a wealth of such industry locally.

Among these industrial people were some ambitious and pioneering men. Builders of some of the early steam vessels of the Mersey, builders who took risks in investing in iron vessels and builders who eventually made steel ones. There were many vessels built in the area, and a reputation soon grew nationally for the expertise of the shipwrights who constructed many long-lived, sturdy and highly-regarded ships that gained coveted A1 status from the insurers Lloyd's of London.

Many of the businesses worked in collaboration, with ship-owning shipbuilders buying from their fellow shipwrights. There was certainly some sharing of facilities, such as the three main yards at Runcorn likely to have been used for most of this period by different builders at the same time. There was also migration, with the Frodsham shipwrights likely to have moved to Runcorn when their businesses closed, and artisans moving from Runcorn to Widnes and vice-versa over the years either permanently or in line with the shifting Mersey channels and the associated loss and gain of launching sites on the river. Beyond that, two Runcorn men were pioneers in the shipbuilding industry at what became Ellesmere Port. Ralph Manley, who had started a carrying firm out of Chester, and Charles Hickson (who was a shipbuilder at Runcorn and Weston Point), enjoyed some success as ship owners who built vessels for themselves and others.

The DENNIS BRUNDRIT and the Mersey Street Shipyard of Runcorn

The largest ship ever built in Runcorn, DENNIS BRUNDRIT, was a wooden, fully rigged ship built in 1856. She was built by Brundrit and Whiteway at its Mersey Street Shipyard; the largest of Runcorn's ship and boat yards, before it was subsumed into the Manchester Ship Canal's Old Quay Yard.

Illustration 35

Illustration 36

Illustration 37

Illustration 38

Illustration 39

Facts and Figures

Tonnage: 462 tons
Length: 141ft
Beam: 27ft
Depth of Hold: 18½ft
Cargo Capacity: 800 tons

Birth of the Ship

Designed by James Boot, then manager of Brundrit and Whiteway's Mersey Street Yard, DENNIS BRUNDRIT was a ship that caused much interest locally. She was felted and yellow metalled for voyages in tropical waters and was recognised by assessors from Lloyd's of London as a ship of superior build. She was said to be the smallest full rigged ship of her day.

Mrs. Robert Cheshire Whiteway launched the ship at around 1pm on a Tuesday of an unknown date in September 1856 to the sound of cannon fire and the yells of onlookers. At the launch, spectators crowded in the streets of Runcorn, which were hung with banners. Crowds also formed along the banks of the Mersey, at both Runcorn and Widnes, and aboard many boats in the river itself.

Career Details

May 1879: On passage from Cardiff, the DENNIS BRUNDRIT survived a storm to reach Stanley, Falkland Islands. She suffered the loss of her mainmast, foretop gallant mast, yards and sails, and her mizzen mast was sprung.

2nd October 1879: Sold by public auction to George Dean/J.M. Dean and Co. of Stanley for £355. J.M. Dean and Sons (or J.M. Dean and Co.) was a trading firm with a ship repair business. It was the main rivals of the F.I.C. (Falkland Islands Company), with whom it merged in 1889. Today's West Store (a collection of shops in a small complex) was the home of the company's sail loft, carpenter's workshop and boat repair workshop. Presumably, then, repairs to the DENNIS BRUNDRIT were carried out there, and probably across the road on the foreshore, as the ship was re-rigged as a barque by her new owner(s).

After Refit: Re-rigged as a Barque, the now 563 ton,

DENNIS BRUNDRIT continued her career, trading locally and sometimes between London and Stanley (nine such voyages) for seven years:

Morning of 20th November, 1892: Wrecked on Centre Island, near Salvador Settlement (then known as Port Salvador), Falkland Islands, while loading wool, hides and tallow for London. All 14 crew were saved and part of her cargo salvaged.

1940: Picture taken of the remains of DENNIS BRUNDRIT, which now resides in the Museum in Stanley, Falkland Islands.

1942: A storm blew the remains of DENNIS BRUNDRIT off the rocks she had been wedged on and into the waters surrounding Centre Island. Some of her ribs are still visible at low water. Charts clearly mark her position (funnily enough, as that's what charts do).

Remnants of the DENNIS BRUNDRIT Today

Apart from the wreck herself, some remnants remain in the museum in Stanley. These are:

> The figurehead, in an old barn serving as a storage facility near the museum.
> Left side of the face of the figurehead, on display in the museum.

The figurehead (or the bulk of it; from the knees up) was originally kept in a chicken pen at Salvador Settlement. The pen was also used as a private bar and on one occasion a particularly drunk man, for reasons of his own, swung at the figurehead with a shovel or spade. Hence the damage to its face.

Other remnants still surviving are the jetty at Salvador settlement, which was built around the remains of one the ship's masts. The sheep run and cow shed at Foam Creek House, which were built from wood from the ship.

A memorial to the ship exists at Centre Island after I had a brass plaque and wooden post made to tell visitors about this great vessel. I sought permission from Mr. Pitaluga, the owner of the land there, and planted the sign with help from the ship's company of HMS *Leeds Castle*, who got me there and then helped me search for remains. A record of this was made by Ray Miller of the *Runcorn Weekly News* when he published a full-page article after I contacted and met him on my return from my six-month stint in the Falklands in 2002.

When I was in the Falklands (so far, the middle of three periods spent in and around those islands with the Royal Navy), I bought a poster that displayed a drawing of the DENNIS BRUNDRIT.

It is titled "A Plan of the Falkland Islands Drawn by John Smith: With Details of Historical and Maritime Interest". It is available from the Falkland Islands Company.

A History of the Mersey Street Yard and the Wright-Brundrit Business Empire

1802: First record known of a vessel being launched from the yard. The vessel was SARAH, a flat of 57 tons. The shipyard was under the ownership of William Wright and Charles Hickson.

1815: By this time, William Wright was building ships under his name alone. The first known record of a vessel produced by William Wright's firm is of JANE, a flat of 65 tons.

The yard passed to Dennis Brundrit, druggist and stone merchant, after his marriage to Elizabeth Wright (daughter of William) and the later death of William Wright.

1823: By this time, Brundrit was in partnership with Philip Whiteway in the business of stone merchant and shipbuilder, under the name of Brundrit and Whiteway.

1839: According to a survey by the Port of Liverpool (of which Runcorn was then a part), the land immediately to the left of the Ethelfleda Railway Bridge belonged to Dennis Brundrit, who had "shipbuilding and other yards". Further along, below the present Belvedere Buildings, were coal and timber yards belonging to Messrs. Brundrit, Whiteway and Forster.

1848: By this time, the Mersey Street yard of Brundrit and Whiteway was the largest shipyard in Runcorn.

1856: Launch of the DENNIS BRUNDRIT.

1878: First record known of a vessel built under the new company name of Brundrit and Co. The vessel was MARTYN, a ketch of 67 tons.

1880: By this time, the yard was the last one in Runcorn engaged in building seagoing ships.

1887: Last known record of a vessel built under the Brundrit and Co. name. The vessel was PERCY, a flat of 85 tons.

The building of the Manchester Ship Canal brought about the end of shipbuilding at Runcorn, due to the restrictions imposed on large vessel launchings by the Gantry Wall. The M.S.C. bought the Mersey Street Yard and modernised one of the slipways; it became the public slipway for ship repairs. In this way, the M.S.C. tried to compensate Runcorn for the loss of its once proud industry.

The larger slipway and another small one, with the surrounding yard, were leased to Messrs. Stubbs (firstly, John Stubbs and Sons/John James Stubbs, and later F. Stubbs), who repaired schooners and barges until the last days of sail (at least the 1950s?).

Eventually, the two smaller slipways disappeared, and only the patent slipway used by the Stubbs family remained. Later, the two smaller yards merged again, forming the Old Quay Yard.

The slipway could be seen up to the time of Peel Holdings' (owners of the M.S.C. Co.) instigation of plans to develop the yard into retail and commercial land, off what is now Mersey Road. It is the site of the M.S.C. Co.'s Small Craft Repair Yard, the Runcorn Yard of the M.S.C. Co.

The Stubbs Family

Samuel Stubbs operated a yard at Percival Lane near Bridgewater Docks (the former terminal of the Bridgewater Canal and today known as Runcorn Docks) in the 1800s. The business later passed to his son, John (better known as Jack), and hence John Stubbs and Sons began life as "Shipwrights, Blockmakers and Makers of Masts and Spars", originally operating from Percival Lane around 1878.

Several members of the family ran their own businesses in senior partnership with each other. So, for example, there was Robert Stubbs and Company at Runcorn Docks, which also had Samuel and John James Stubbs on the books as partners.

Samuel Stubbs eventually moved to the Belvedere Yard and, by 1887 or so, John Stubbs was operating from the former Brundrit yard. The firm also built flats and later became a ship repair concern.

By the 1930s, the outfit was known as John James Stubbs, Ship Repairer. It built wooden boats as well as repairing and upkeeping various sailing and other wooden vessels. Jack Stubbs ran the yard all through World War II, working into his seventies.

A sad part of this tale was the loss in 1943 of Jack's younger son, Harry, who was only 41. Ken Stubbs said it is clear his grandfather, Jack, never got over the loss of his son, whose death would probably have been prevented if not for the shortage of antibiotics brought on by the war.

Illustration 40

Harry Stubbs was a skilled shipwright in the employ of his father and he was also responsible for the firm continuing as long as it did. This is due to his heroic action in 1917 when aged just 15. His father, Jack, had been taking a flat out of the dock at the foot of the slipway when the boathook he was using came loose from the pole and he fell backwards into the Manchester Ship Canal. Although he reached the wall, it was 17ft above the waterline and there was nothing to grip. Harry Stubbs leapt in to save his grandfather and pulled him from under the water, holding him there until a sailor from a passing ship also jumped in to join the rescue. Another boy then launched himself from the flat he was sailing past on and tried to bring the original flat (that Jack Stubbs had been trying to pull out of the dock) to the rescue of the other three. However, he was exhausted and could not climb in. By this time, workers from the yard had thrown a line to the party in the water, so Jack and Harry Stubbs and the sailor clung to that, while the other boy clung to the flat. Finally, a W. Booth of Church Street came along in his tug and rescued all four. So, if it had not been for the timely and brave intervention of Harry Stubbs, the firm that he helped to build the reputation of over many years would surely have perished along with its manager, his father, Jack Stubbs.

The firm later passed to the eldest son and thus became known as Fred Stubbs, I believe at some stage in the 1940s, before finally closing in the 1950s.

Probably related were two other Runcorn concerns. They were at Top Locks and were operated by Charles and Peter Stubbs respectively.

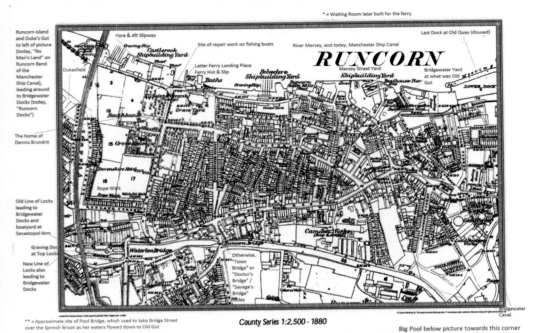

Illustration 41

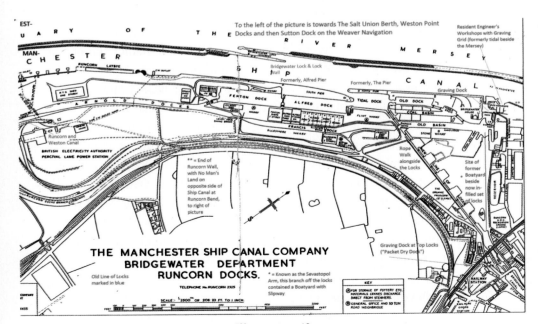

Illustration 42

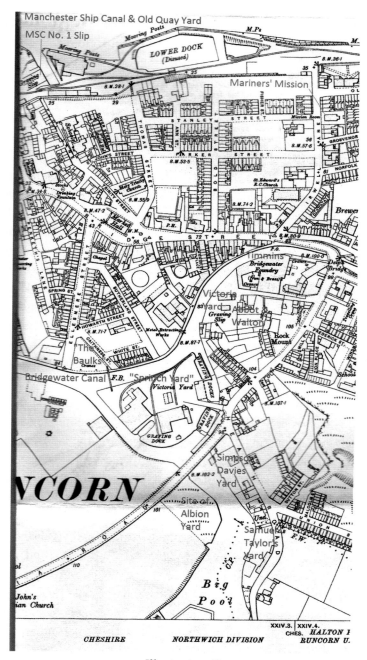

Illustration 43

A Brief Stroll Along the Waterfront from Old Quay

This is an updated version of details I sent to Peel Holdings, the owners of the Manchester Ship Canal and thus the surrounding foreshore, and to Taylor Woodrow, the developers of the complex now known as the Deck. It was sent in the hope of sparking an interest in erecting a plaque to honour the legacy of Runcorn's shipbuilders but, probably due to financial constraints (and perhaps the wishes of the developers of the Deck housing project), fell on deaf ears.

The revamp of Runcorn's waterfront along Mersey Road and the Deck has brought new life to the very heart of the town. The creation of a park and promenade along the canalside with the statue dedicated to Ethelreda (the Saxon Princess who founded a castle and settlement at Castle Rock in 959 A.D. at the western end of the park) and Runcorn's maritime heritage came some years ago and is now complemented by the new residential development to the east.

The redevelopment has taken place at the heart of the township of Runcorn, which grew separately from the castle, out of the former Boat House Pool (known as Old Gut, from where the ferry to the north shore (today's Widnes) plied the River Mersey at Runcorn Gap for hundreds of years. The ferry later moved to a new slip further west, towards Castle Rock (to a place known as Ferry Hut), but further passenger services came to the site in the form of various packets to Liverpool, Warrington and Manchester.

As the town grew, so too did its transport links. First came the Mersey and Irwell Navigation, a collection of river improvements linking Runcorn to Manchester and terminating at what was known as Old Quay Docks (today's Deck). The company was later bought by the Duke of Bridgewater and the Bridgewater Canal was soon completed, linking Runcorn and Manchester in a more efficient waterway. The two waterways helped bring wealth and prosperity to Runcorn under the guidance of the influential duke and his successors in running the businesses he founded. The duke helped improve local navigation conditions and safety. His home, Bridgewater House at Runcorn Docks (formerly Bridgewater Docks), can still be seen today by walking to the end of the Runcorn Promenade leading from the Deck, past Castle Rock.

The third and final maritime transport development came when the Manchester Ship Canal Company (now owned by Peel Holdings, the firm behind the creation of the Deck) bought the Bridgewater company and built its own canal to Manchester; this time creating the county's fourth largest port and a seaway for ocean-going ships stretching more than thirty-five miles inland. Again, as with the last two canal enterprises, there came a series of developments at Old Quay, in shipbuilding and other trades as well as in passenger services.

Old Quay stretched for the length of today's Deck and beyond. It actually went beyond the Old Quay swing bridge into Astmoor. Eventually, the whole area came under the ownership of the Manchester Ship Canal Company and it turned the entire plot to the west of the swing bridge into Old Quay Yard: its tug and tender depot and repair yard, and Lock Gate repair store and workshops. Later, the facility became known as Runcorn Yard and it was one of the big employers of the town, beside the tanneries, and I.C.I. and other chemical firms.

Further links with all things water include the town's former reputation as a health spa, with people once travelling from far and wide to bathe at the salt water baths near Ferry Hut. There was also the former Sprinch Brook that flowed from the Boat House Pool to Big Pool, a quarter of a mile to the south. Later, the Ship Canal Company and other firms had boatyards at the Big Pool after the Bridgewater Canal was built through the top of it. The brook that fed that body of water also fed the town's drinking needs as well as the needs of various industries, such as the brewery just to the south of Old Quay at the top of Big Pool.

These industries were also well represented at the site of the Deck, as there would once have been tanneries; alkali, acid and soap works; blacksmiths; and other industries, such as a mortar works, sailmaker and ropeworks, to support the maritime scene.

All in all, the Old Quay site represents the very beginnings of the town as well as the impetus behind its growth into the union and market town it became. It saw the passenger and tourist trade as well as the busy facilities of a port that at one time rivalled Chester and Liverpool (a city younger than Runcorn). The area was home to the primary industries that shaped the town over the years: Ship and boat building, tanning, the chemical industry and a home to watermen and longshoremen, stevedores and officials involved in port operations and passenger services. The further two major industries of its heritage were also touched by Old Quay: Firstly brewing, which took place near to the site using the stream that flowed from there; and secondly quarrying, which saw much input from individuals such as Dennis Brundrit and Robert Whiteway, whose main works stemmed from the area.

Now hopefully, the regeneration of the site will bring new residents and visitors to Runcorn and breathe some fresh life into the centre of this historic, ever-changing town.

The following firms operated ship or boat yards in the area of Runcorn that became today's Deck residential complex:

William Wright and Charles Hickson
William Wright
Dennis Brundrit
Brundrit and Whiteway
John and William Brundrit
Robert C. Whiteway
Brundrit and Co.
Brundrit and Hayes
Okell
Okell and Webster
Thomas Sothern
J. Sothern/Sothern and Co.
John Stubbs and Sons/John James Stubbs
Fred Stubbs
Mersey and Irwell Navigation Co.
Duke of Bridgewater/Bridgewater Trustees/Bridgewater Navigation
   Co. Ltd.
Carmet
Frederick John Abbott
T. and J. Johnson
Philip Speakman/Philip Speakman and Sons
Manchester Ship Canal Co. (M.S.C. Co.)
Bryant's
(public slipway)

Yard names included Mersey Street Yard; Mersey Road Yard; Mill Street Yard; Mersey and Irwell Yard; Bridgewater Navigation Yard; Stubbs's Yard/ Slip; Town Slip; Old Quay Yard; and Runcorn Yard (of the M.S.C. Co.).

The last two were the names of the large yard operated by the M.S.C. Co. and which occupied all the land once incorporated into the other individual yards at the site. It was known as Bottom Yard by the men that worked there, to distinguish it from Top Yard, the M.S.C. Co.'s Bridgewater Department Yard at the top of the old Sprinch Brook, at Big Pool.

The many vessels of the Manchester Ship Canal Company were maintained at Old Quay, along with other vessels and other work was carried out there (including the repair of the canal's lock gates).

The following businesses may have operated at the site or nearby, along today's Mersey Road:

James Boot

The following firms operated at what was the Belvedere Yard, immediately to the west of the Deck, where the Ship Canal Company stored the lock gates of the canal until a few years ago as part of an extended Old Quay Yard:

Samuel Mason
John Mason and Co.
Mason and Craggs
Mason
Blundell and Mason
Philip Speakman/Philip Speakman and Sons
Samuel Stubbs

Furthermore, a shipbuilder called John Ravenscroft operated from nearby Church Street and probably had a yard along Mersey Road on today's Runcorn Promenade.

The following firms operated at what was the Castle Rock (sometimes written as Castlerock) Yard, along the Runcorn Promenade to the west from the Deck and the former Belvedere Yard:

John Anderton and Co.
Anderton and LeCouteur
James B. Anderton
Philip Speakman/Philip Speakman and Sons
Richard Abel and Sons

Furthermore, Widnes shipbuilder Samuel Stock had an office at Castle Rock and perhaps conducted some building or repair from there.

These firms represented some of the finest ship and boat builders in the town, perhaps rivalled only by some of the yards at Big Pool and Runcorn Docks and producing several Lloyd's A1 registered vessels of impressive longevity.

For a further look into the past of central Runcorn Old Town, a short walk from Runcorn Promenade along the Manchester Ship Canal will take you to the new residential area of the Maritime Quarter beside the historic (grade II listed) Bridgewater House and the Runcorn campus of Riverside College. This was at one time earmarked to be the new home of Runcorn Linnets Football Club at a public sports facility but that fell through and now Runcorn plays home matches in Murdishaw.

One can only hope a reprieve for this once promising site of development can come soon and make this area once again a busy and vibrant scene, as it was for many decades.

A further walk along the footpath leading from Bridgewater House, following the line of old locks that used to link the Manchester Ship and Bridgewater Canals, will take you to a good vantage point over the docks of Runcorn. The locks are the subject of a campaign by the Runcorn Locks Preservation Society to have them reopened for leisure use.

Around the area of Runcorn Docks and Percival Lane, the following firms operated ship or boat yards:

> Duke of Bridgewater/Bridgewater Trustees/Bridgewater Navigation
>   Co. Ltd.
> M.S.C. Co.
> Knowles Brothers
> Samuel Stubbs
> John Stubbs
> Robert Stubbs and Co.
> Ira Withington
> Mick Mills

Yard names included Duke's Yard or Bottom Locks Yard. The following may have operated at the site:

> John Caine

Walking on from the line of locks, a short detour will take you to Waterloo Bridge (where the locks originally terminated), where the Bridgewater Canal currently ends due to road building schemes developed a few decades ago, cutting off the last stage of locks from the Bridgewater Canal.

This area is known as Top Locks and here the following firms operated boat yards:

Richard Abel and Sons
William Bate
John Hitchmough
John Rawlinson
Charles Stubbs
Peter Stubbs/Peter Stubbs and Co.
Withington and LeCouteur
Bridgewater Department of the M.S.C. Co.

Walking along the Bridgewater Canal heading east you will soon come to what remains of Big Pool (the remainder having been filled during further road building schemes at around the same time as those which affected the old lines of locks).

Here the following firms operated boat yards:

Abbott and Walton
A. Barton
Thomas Binns
John Clucas
John Crippin
Simpson, Davies and Co./Simpson, Davies and Sons Ltd.
Philip Speakman/Philip Speakman and Sons
Samuel Taylor
Bridgewater Department of the M.S.C. Co.

Yard names included Albion Yard; Runcorn Yard; and two yards known as Victoria Yard.

Victoria Yard and later Runcorn Yard were the names of the large facility operated by the Bridgewater Department of the M.S.C. Co.. It was considered to be the finest boat building yard in the country when it opened in the very late 1890s.

Furthermore, the following engineering firms built marine engines beside the Big Pool at the former Bridgewater Foundry:

A. Barton
E. Timmins and Co.

Now, a quick hop over on to the main road from the footpath and a cross over to Irwell Lane (the site of sailmakers Greigs) and Old Quay Street will lead you back down to the Deck.

This is the briefest of introductions to Runcorn's maritime heritage and it has hopefully whetted the appetites of readers to learn more about the town's extensive nautical past. Try to conjure up an image of old Runcorn replete with ship, boat, mast, spar and block makers; sailmakers, rope and twine makers; ship and boat repairers and painters; chain and anchor smiths; ship chandlers and marine store dealers (including those who sold and hired nautical instruments and butchers who advertised that they were "shipping butchers"); ship and boat owners and brokers/chartering agents; carriers by water and ferrymen; sailors/seamen (including a large number of Master Mariners); watermen/lightermen; bargemen/boatmen; fishermen; pilots; sailors' outfitters; stevedores/dockers; porters; and all associated officials.

Runcorn had a Mission to Seafarers and a Life Saving and Grappling Corps, as well as many businesses that depended upon shipping to survive (quarries, chemical producers, tanneries, etc.). It had a staggering amount of pubs and alehouses , many of which had nautical names, reflecting the vast amount of visiting sailors the town attracted. Finally, there was Dutton's tinsmiths, makers of the Dutton Jazz Horn famed throughout the north of England carnival band circuit. It made its famous musical instruments and also did other work, including making decorated kettles and pots for narrowboat families.

My main fascination is in the ranks of shipwrights and smiths, the caulkers and other artisans who brought my, for many years tiny, town such a great reputation far and wide for their build and repair quality. Runcorn was a true "Venice of the North", or "Little Venice"[10] as some knew it, and its canals and rivers gave employment to many who formerly or latterly served deep sea or coastal concerns. However, many port towns of the UK could claim to have many veterans of sea or river service, so perhaps that is not as remarkable a fact as that of our shipyard heritage.

The fact is Runcorn was, at different but some overlapping times, the terminus of two great canals to Manchester (the Mersey and Irwell and the

---

10 With intricate sets of inter-connecting docks, locks, and canal and river communications, and with local port facilities at other towns in the area, it was very much like Venice and its canals. Even down the Weaver Navigation could you find complexes such as Sutton Locks and the Frodsham Cut linking into the River Weaver just above Frodsham Bridge. A true set of maritime engineering masterpieces.

Bridgewater), the site of the Weaver Navigation to help make a more navigable pass to the River Weaver and the ports of inland Cheshire at Northwich, Middlewich, and Winsford, and a port on both the River Mersey and Manchester Ship Canal. It was the hub that linked into the Trent and Mersey Canal at Preston Brook. Runcorn was the base for the Ship Canal operations headquarters, and for its tugs (at Old Quay) and dredging department (with an office on No Man's Land and berths both there and at Runcorn Wall by Runcorn Bend)[11]. It had three sets of docks, the most extensive being what was originally the Bridgewater Docks, and the latter were linked into the Weston Point Docks via another canal, the Runcorn and Weston. Thus there was an inter-connected set of navigable waters all centralised on Runcorn, where many businesses and operators based themselves.

To consider that my town had such a number of yards building so many vessels despite the competition from larger firms at nearby Northwich, Birkenhead and Liverpool, among other places, is to realise something quite remarkable. Furthermore, the constantly shifting navigable channels of the Mersey, favouring the above locales on her banks and giving preferential circumstances to places such as Northwich, meant it was something extraordinary that Runcorn had the shipbuilding industry it did.

The coming of the Manchester Ship Canal and the consequential degrading in ship launching ability (certainly for any sizeable ships), should maybe have meant an earlier death for this industry but the shipbuilders carried on. The last Mersey flat, the local style of vessel developed since the Middle Ages and launched along the Weaver, Mersey, Lancashire and north Welsh coasts, as well as all the canals thereabouts, was actually built at Castle Rock. This Runcorn yard, owned and operated by Abel's, built RUTH BATE in the early 1950s, just before the final closure of the business. Ship repair continued locally though until the closure of Runcorn Yard in 2003 and pleasure boats are still built in Runcorn to this day.

---

11   The tug and dredging work have both been contracted-out to other firms so there is no longer a dredging fleet but various firms doing the work when required. The tugs are run by Carmet, based at Eastham.

Illustration 44

Illustration 45

Illustration 46

Illustration 47

Illustration 48

An Account of the Shipbuilding and Boat Building Industry of Frodsham

Introduction

Frodsham is an ancient town that records such as the Domesday Book make clear was of more importance than her neighbour, Runcorn. Whereas Runcorn may have been a small and sparsely populated area in the Middle and Tudor Ages (as Starkey records in *Schooner Port*, the antiquarian John Leland stated Runcorn is "now a poore hamlet by a salt creke"), Frodsham was a small port of some importance. It was the place where salt and Cheshire cheese was taken for transfer to larger vessels that could not reach further inland beyond Frodsham Bridge. There was also supposedly a ferry in the area now known as Frodsham Bridge. As a result, some sort of boat and ship building and repair industry may have existed from an early date. For the record, and as reported in *A Towpath Walkers Guide to the History of the River Weaver Navigation Volume 2* by Colin Edmondson, the original bridge was some 30 yards downstream of the current one in a line following the lane past the former Aston Arms public house (now a nursery). This road was the first main road into Frodsham from the east and was carried over the river in a route that led past the former Bridge Inn (now an access road to a car repair garage and some flats).

Frodsham once had a Mersey shoreline and, before the silting of the Mersey created the marshes, the river came up along a line approximating the route of Ship Street. Until a few years ago, there were still some bollards visible along this route and maybe there are still a few in existence? The Mersey therefore flowed into the Weaver, creating a much wider mouth than today's confluence with the Manchester Ship Canal. Thus, there was ample opportunity for a range of vessels to be built and launched in this part of the world. Frodsham produced a fair number of ships but seems to have focused on repair work as the yards continued for years while new builds are not so extensively reported from that period.

The Builders

Bert Starkey's research shows a number of vessels built at Frodsham since 1728, starting with the sloop ARMITAGE, of 40 tons. No builder's name has been traced yet for this vessel or the next seventeen recorded Frodsham-built ships, and then a William Hayes appears in 1795 as the builder of the 48 ton flat BETSEY.

Various other shipbuilders came and went from Frodsham, and it seems there were at least two separate local shipyards. A look at the list of vessels built at Frodsham will show the various firms in existence, and it may well be these companies shared facilities just like their counterparts in Runcorn appear to have done. This is an assumption based on the fact three or four shipbuilders appear to have been in business at Frodsham at the same time.

Among the builders, there were some who also owned ships. These were William Hayes, John Urmson and William Hazlehurst. They built and probably repaired their own vessels, as well as those of others. They were among a number of ship owners from the town (or village as it was until only a few years ago) that traded not only along the coast but as far afield as the West Indies, in ships built locally. This is an impressive fact for such a small settlement.

The End of Shipbuilding at Frodsham

William Hazlehurst would appear to have finished shipbuilding at Frodsham when, in 1856, there was a sale of shipbuilding tools and timber at Frodsham Bridge. This must have been taken up by Edward Jones, who was supposedly the last of the Frodsham builders, and continued until 1860 according to *Schooner Port*.

However, the last vessel launched at Frodsham in this period was the 40-ton Flat, FANNY, in 1862. It is not clear whether this craft was built by Jones or another shipbuilder. Either way, the end of the industry had come and perhaps a number of the men involved moved to Runcorn to continue their livelihoods.

In modern times, a brief resurgence of the skills of these former masters came to Frodsham with Ron Turner building several narrowboats in the village and with Frodsham Watersports conducting repair work on boats and jet skis to this day.

Otherwise, all that is left is the small minor port at Frodsham Bridge on the east bank of the Weaver, opposite the site of the medieval port. It is usually visited by small coasters operating between Frodsham and Liverpool and long

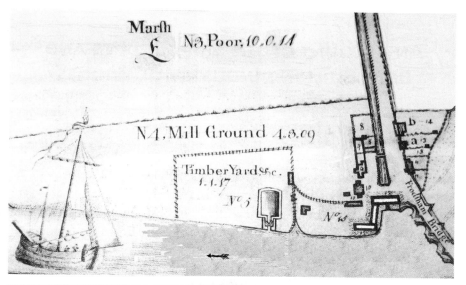

Above: *Illustration 49*
Left: *Illustration 50*
Below: *Illustration 51*

An Account of the Shipbuilding and Boat Building Industry of Widnes

Introduction

Although today there is no commercial river or canal traffic to Widnes, the town was once a thriving and busy minor port that saw much innovation. For example, the world's first purpose-built railway dock was built at Woodend by the St Helens to Runcorn Gap Railway Company[12]. It was the terminus of the extended St Helens, or Sankey, Canal. On the opposite side of town was West Bank Dock, now remembered in the name of an industrial estate built over the top of the now infilled basins (it was formed in two long arms that formed separate bodies of water). The author's great uncle, Frank LeCouteur, was Chief Engineer of Abel's ROSSENDALE when she was the last vessel to use West Bank Dock on 28th October 1970.

With the port of Widnes came much shipping, all linked to the local industries and industrialists. Chemical works had their raw materials and finished products shipped via the many craft plying the Mersey to Widnes. Coal was also transported from Widnes, brought via canal and railway from the mines of Lancashire.

The Shipyards

Various yards for the building and repair of vessels were established in Widnes over the years, and some were tied into considerable business empires.

Samuel Stock was the owner of a colliery near St Helens and he had his own private railway to bring the coal to Widnes, where it was loaded into his own fleet of ships. These ships were maintained, and some cases built, in

---

12 Woodend was a small settlement at the east end of the area of land known as Runcorn Gap (the same name given still to the stretch of water separating it from Runcorn). The stretch of the Mersey further east is Runcorn Sands. This is just north of Old Quay and also Wigg Island, the latter being accessible from Runcorn via Old Quay Swing Bridge and today a nature reserve (as well as home to a working wharf on the Manchester Ship Canal). Beyond Runcorn Sands on the northern shore of the meandering Mersey as it narrows further inland towards Warrington is Fiddler's Ferry.

Samuel Stock's own shipyard in Widnes. He ran this array of businesses from his offices in Castle Rock in Runcorn.

William Cooper and his successors also ran a fleet of vessels. The firm was a sand, gravel, and concrete aggregate dealer, quarry owner, It also owned two shipyards, one at St Mary's Road and the other the former Edward Gandy yard at Spike Island. My grandfather, George Ratcliffe, worked as a barge skipper for Cooper's after World War II but, after an accident in which he broke his leg, he ended up losing this job as the company could no longer hold the position for him. He then re-trained as a stoker with the M.S.C. Co. tugs, rising to Chief Engineer. Cooper's was the main rival of Runcorn-based Abel's and was a huge firm with interests across the Mersey region just like its competitors, having berths in Liverpool and Manchester.

Other yards were owned by the Wilkinson family and Hill and Grundy, both at Fiddler's Ferry. A further builder was Concrete Seacraft, which was one of a large number of manufacturers across the country that constructed ships from concrete due to shortages of steel during World War I. It used the "Ritchie Unit System" of manufacture, whereby the vessels were built in sections and were thus able to be built of thinner hulls due to the stronger interlinked parts of the ship being less susceptible to weakness during build than their all-in-one constructed counterparts. The yard was also at Fiddler's Ferry and was a sizeable concern, having a large area of Mersey foreshore, five building slips and a more than 200 workers. These included some Royal Engineers personnel as the whole scheme was initially part of one backed by the then First Lord of the Admiralty, (later Sir) Winston Churchill, designed to provide barges to ship arms and other material for the war effort to France.

A wide variety of shipbuilding, in fact, seemed to have existed in Widnes but it all spawned from seemingly nowhere. In *Schooner Port,* Starkey tells us the largest ship built in Widnes was the 172-ton schooner JANIE, launched from Samuel Stock's yard in 1875. As the first ship recorded as built in the town was in 1861, he is right in saying Widnes was a "young town with no tradition for shipbuilding". He goes on to say it "is reasonable to assume that Runcorn craftsmen were engaged for her [JANIE's] construction", and this seems a very fair assessment. The concrete vessels that briefly renewed the shipbuilding industry of Widnes surpassed their predecessors in terms of size of ships but the business was short-lived, perhaps due to the end of the war and a return to traditional methods of shipbuilding with steel.

The Future

Several boat builders and repairers exist today in Widnes, making the most of the town's marina facilities and tourist attractions to carve an existence. Widnes is no longer a port, however, so there could not be a return to shipbuilding.

On the other hand, the future of the shipping and transport industries would seem to be assured. The Stobart group has centred a lot of its business in Widnes, linking its facilities there with the port at Weston Point as part of its intermodal concept to interlink road, rail, and river/canal. This seems very much like everything coming full circle for Widnes, with the Sankey Canal and St Helens to Runcorn Railway being the forerunner of the intermodal ideas of today's business leaders.

Left: *Illustration 52*
Below: *Illustration 53*

Illustration 54

Illustration 55

Illustration 56

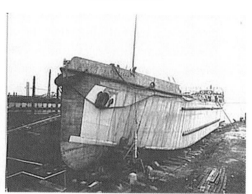

Illustration 57

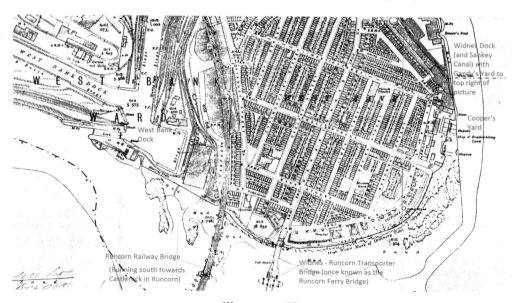

Illustration 58

An Account of the Shipbuilding and Boat Building Industry of Ellesmere Port

Introduction

Ellesmere Port is the epitome of the canal port town, born out of the canal age when the Ellesmere Canal was dug to the Mersey. A small shipbuilding and repair industry grew from modest roots and with some investment by Runcorn men, it seems, but altogether the new town would appear to have suffered from the same curse that Runcorn did: The ever-shifting channels of the River Mersey meandering from the south shore and away from that burgeoning industry. Nevertheless, as the dock system developed and grew at Ellesmere Port, so too did her ship and boat building and repair trade.

The Shipyards

There appear to have been at least four different shipyards in existence in the town, all within the dock complex that now constitutes the Boat Museum. The first was the timber yard built by Chester ship owner Ralph Manley and later taken-over by the Ellesmere Canal Company. They created a proper shipyard at the site (that I am classing as the second there), with a slipway, probably at the southern end of the Tidal Basin. This was between the aforementioned basin and the High Level Canal Basin which was later extended to form the large dock at the highest point of the complex, where the museum today has a row of period cottages. The lock connecting these two bodies of water would have been driven straight through the original building yard.

To the right of the docks was later built the Morton's Patent Slipway and another slip, both in use after the building of the Manchester Ship Canal. Nothing much remains, but today the site is between the car park and the museum's various open buildings. This facility was a yard in its own right, operated by the Ellesmere Canal Company and then the Manchester Ship Canal Company until the early 1920s.

By the time that the latter yard was closed, the M.S.C. had much more work on at Ellesmere Port's largest shipyard, centred on the pontoon dock or floating dry dock further to the east of the docks. This was a large and modern yard used for vessels on the company's books as well as for commercial repairs for other ship owners. It had a large workforce, who also conducted voyage repairs to ships at Stanlow, and worked at the Eastham wharves to remove and re-attach high masts and funnels from vessels voyaging beyond Runcorn and her bridges. This yard was complemented by one at Manchester Mode Wheel, but did not last as long, winding-up in 1969 with the loss of a hundred and fifty jobs.

There were other sections of the port engaged in boat or ship building too, and at one time or another the Tidal Basin, the North Pier, the South Pier, and the Victoria Arm were all used for this purpose.

The Future

There are a handful of small firms across Cheshire and Merseyside engaged in the manufacture of canal pleasure craft, and so too they are at Ellesmere Port. However, the commercial builders are all gone and all that remains apart from these small concerns is the boat museum.

The good news is the museum continues to restore and maintain a large number of historically important craft and with the opening of the heritage boatyard at the site recently, the future for this sort of work looks promising.

For a full and detailed account of the shipyards of Ellesmere Port, see *Waterways Journal Volume 15*.

This is not a means of cutting short my work: I have read this article thoroughly and absorbed the information into my book as I have from so many other sources. My work was all about providing information not available in full elsewhere, not at hand in one tome, and not obtainable without some considerable legwork as well as study. The history of these towns in the shipbuilding trade has never before been captured in this way, with the exception of that for Ellesmere Port in the *Waterways Journal* article by Terry Kavanagh. An attempt at prose on this topic by myself would be pointless when such a work already exists.

It is available to buy from the boat museum and is a good excuse to go and visit this local gem. Even if you have been before, do yourself a favour and visit again as a reminder of all that local history, all those local trades our ancestors were involved in, and all the new displays that had maybe not been built when you last visited.

Illustration 59

Illustration 60

An Account of the Shipbuilding and Boat Building Industry of Sankey and Warrington

Introduction

Although not generally famed as a shipbuilding town, Warrington seems to have been at the forefront of iron boat building from the outset of the industry. On top of this, it was also the centre of a huge industry in steel wire, complementing its other metal-working industries (copper, brass, steel, and aluminium). This industry is associated with the topic of this book due to the manufacturing of steel wire rope for a number of maritime uses (ships' hawsers, derricks' and cranes' falls, etc.). Warrington's dominance of the market for wire manufacture earned its local rugby league team Warrington Wolves its nickname of The Wire, and gave its local independent radio station its name, Wire FM.

The Shipyards

From Victorian times until fifty years or so ago, various primitive single-log carved boats have been unearthed near Warrington, suggesting a local seafaring community there since antiquity. The late Mike Stammers presented this evidence in his *Liverpool Sailing Ships*.

The earliest yard I know about is the Sankey Dockyard, founded in the very early 1800s below Sankey Bridges on the St Helens Canal. This yard produced many fine vessels and was, under the ownership of various firms through the years, the longest-lived of any Warrington shipwright firm thus far unearthed. By the 1920s, however, it had closed. Sankey was the last place, according to the research of the late Mike Stammers, that built sailing flats. The very last was the SANTA ROSA of 1906.

Winwick, further up the St Helens Canal, was the site of a maintenance yard for the vessels of the canal company, which was in use, I believe, until the 1960s.

There may have been yards in existence on the River Mersey's Warrington shores for many years, if not centuries, and certainly this is what Janice Hayes and Alan Crosby argue in their book *Warrington at Work*. I have not found any evidence of this as yet but there were two larger yards that produced some iron vessels there from the 1840s onwards. These were the Bridge Foundry and Bank Quay yards, and they were responsible for some very impressive vessels.

Bank Quay Yard went through various changes in management in its short existence but it produced some of the largest ships built on the Mersey up to then. Some were larger than any ship yet built at Birkenhead at that point, despite the latter town's fame for being the giant of Mersey shipbuilding and one of the major international centres of the trade.

Diversification

The end was almost inevitable for shipbuilding in Warrington, the shifting and treacherous tides of the Mersey forever making navigation along its upper course precarious at least, and perilous at worst. Thus, as the ships of the world grew ever bigger, this industry was to fade from the town, with only the Bank Quay Yard struggling on into the latter years of the late 1850s.

Once the realisation that further orders were not forthcoming had been accepted, the Bank Quay concern sold off its shipbuilding equipment and focused itsr energies on the other trades in which it had long been involved. Thus, the foundry concentrated on other ironwork, such as fabrications for bridge building.

And so the enterprise had come full circle, diversifying into shipbuilding before returning to its core business and eventually becoming part of a great business empire when it was bought by the Vulcan Foundry of Newton-le-Willows. The latter firm bought Bank Quay Foundry in 1847 and adapted it for manufacturing heavy castings for shipbuilding as well as gun, shot and shell making. The shipbuilding business died off and eventually so too did the whole foundry, which closed in about 1860[13].

---

13 See the website Anson Engine Museum at www.enginemuseum.org/evp.html.

Above: *Illustration 61*
Left: *Illustration 62*
Below: *Illustration 63*

A List of Ship and Boat Builders and Repairers of the Upper Mersey

This list will include builders/repairers within the boundaries of the old customs port of Runcorn (5th April 1847–16th April 1850 and 1st January, 1862–31st December, 1893, when Runcorn was a sea/river port in its own right and also the country's foremost canal port), although not all of these firms operated at times when Runcorn was an independent port.

Note that there were many ship and boat builders in the local area, on the rivers Dee, Mersey and Weaver as well as on the many canals/navigations of the region. In Cheshire (including those areas later subsumed into Merseyside and Greater Manchester) there were ship and boat yards at Chester, Connah's Quay and Saltney, Neston and Parkgate, Birkenhead and Bromborough, and also at Northwich (including Witton) and Winsford. In Lancashire (including those areas later subsumed into Merseyside and Greater Manchester) there were yards at Liverpool and Garston, St Helens, Manchester and Worsley, further afield at Lytham, Preston, Wigan, Barrow-in-Furness and even Rhyl and Conway in Wales. They all made flats and other local vessels associated with the Mersey and Weaver and their tributaries. Further boat yards were to be found at smaller ports and inland/trans-shipment ports throughout the region. Many related industries also existed in the area, from engine builders to sailmakers.

According to *Schooner Port*, with the coming of more maritime activity with the Bridgewater Canal came the establishment of the shipbuilding industry at Runcorn. Originally, mainly occupied with repair and rebuilding of river craft, the local yards began to build some reputation for the construction of river craft and sea-going vessels.

By 1850, Runcorn had gained a considerable reputation for building ships of quality (according to *Schooner Port*, Runcorn was to gain "something of a national prestige for the building of small coastal craft"). The town continued for many years as a busy shipbuilding and repair town and, even after the majority of the firms had closed, Runcorn continued to be home to one yard for the repair of vessels (Old Quay) after the building and repair industries of most of the above towns (as well as all the other towns once part of the customs port of Runcorn (see below) had disappeared. In fact, in the English north-west, only Birkenhead, Bromborough and Barrow-in-Furness outlived Runcorn as centres of that once booming British industry, being the homes of, respectively, Cammell Laird, McTay and BAE Systems Maritime – Submarines.

On a brighter note, the building and repair of pleasure craft (as distinct from the work of commercial yards) continues in most of the above towns today, including most of the towns in the old customs port; notably Runcorn itself.

Key to Survey, Clean and Repair Facilities

Note: This is a list of the central facilities of a ship or boat (repair) yard or dockyard; it does not include all the various ancillary concerns such as cranes; blacksmith's smithies/workshops (with bellows); other workshops; timber/ mast pits, ponds, houses and yards; saw pits; steam tanks/boilers/chests; rope walks/roperies; sail lofts and foundries, lathes, drilling machines, etc.

Shipyard and boat yard:
An area for the building and/or repair of ships or boats (respectively). Also known as a dockyard or dock yard, if actually having a dock or several docks (see below). Often, dockyard is the name given to a facility used for the main-tenance of a company's own vessels.

Repair yard:
A yard solely for repair work.

Basin/dock:
An enclosed area, either tidal, where there is no closable gateway, or non-tidal, where a lock gate or caisson (floating gate) is used. On a canal, the basin or dock needs no gate due to the level of water being controlled by the canal's own lock gates. A dock or basin that is tidal and may dry out at low water is sometimes called a camber.

Graving dock:
A dock that can be pumped free of water once the dock gates are shut. Also known as a dry dock.

Patent slipway:
Ramp into the water with rails (or carriageways) for hauling vessels out; this type of slipway having either sliding supports ("[ship's] ways") on those rails

that can be winched up/lowered using wires or chains, or just the wires or chains themselves. In this study, the former will be known as Class 1 and the latter as Class 2. Also known as a patent slip or marine railway (the latter term usually only in North America). Where known, this study will also detail whether the slipways were for sideways or lengthways (fore and aft) hauling of vessels. These will be marked by either "side" or "F&A", respectively.

Slipway:
Ramp into water for hauling vessels out. Also known as a slip or landing slope. Often these slips employ a launching frame or launching trolley on wheels, similar to those that can be attached as trailers to motor vehicles.

Stocks:
Frames built ashore on slipways or sloping beaches (with perhaps a temporary slipway built to facilitate work/launching) to support vessels being worked on. These were often what are called building berths, for which see below. The stocks of such yards as the Belvedere Yard could be set for either sideways or fore and aft arrangements.

Building/repair berth:
A term applied to any slip or other facility that can accommodate new building but in this case an area set aside for the purpose on the quayside. Often a temporary slip has to be built at the site for launching. In other cases, a crane may be used to haul the vessel out of the water and put her back in.

Graving grid:
A secure structure on the foreshore for hauling vessels on to. Also known as a gridiron.

Draw dock:
A partially-enclosed area, essentially like a graving grid with three walls.

Camber (foreshore/beach) Dock:
Often, vessels were simply beached to be worked on during low water or so that they could be hauled further up the beach for work at any tide. The term camber is sometimes applied to a small tidal basin or dock that may dry out at low water.

Sometimes applied to an area similar to the above, wherein a simple dugout is constructed for the building of a vessel, with the launch made possible using channels or gutters sited alongside.

Boathouse:
A building for berthing and repairing vessels, usually with a slipway or patent slipway leading to it, or perhaps covering a (dry) dock/set of (dry) docks (known as a covered dry dock).

Divers:
Diving teams can survey and repair minor damage to hulls of vessels while they are still in the water. Divers can either be helmeted (with an air supply from ashore fed to them in hoses and wearing heavy boots and helmet) or frogmen (with bottles on their backs for air supply and with freedom to swim).

Outfitting berths:
Vessels are fitted out with all the internal furnishings and some ancillary equipment after their launch, usually alongside a jetty, pier or quay(side).

Sheerlegs:
A tripod arrangement of masts for heavy lifting of equipment in shipbuilding and repair, such as engines.

Floating dock:
A towable structure that can be sunk and raised as required to accommodate other vessels. Also known as pontoon docks. Not seen in any of these towns bar Ellesmere Port.

Synchro-lift:
A lowerable platform for raising vessels out of the water on to trams for transport via small railways to a point further inland (such as a boathouse). There may also be a facility just in from the platform for moving the vessel left or right so as to berth several alongside each other. Not seen in any of these towns.

Launching frame:
Either motor vehicle-pulled versions, or part of the slipways and stocks for new-building.

Mobile boat lift/travelift/cradle:
A frame that can be wheeled over two piers to a position over an area of water enclosed on three sides. The frame has slings that are then lowered in order to sit underneath a vessel when she sails in between the piers so as to lift her.

Hydro-lift/floating repair cradle/drive-on dock:
A floating cradle that can be pumped out or filled as required to lower/rise in order to receive boats.

The format of the list is as follows:
Company name:
Nature of maritime business:
Years of business:
Year yard occupied by company: (if different from years of business)
Ship or boat yard name:
Yard location (and facilities):
Further information:
Address: (not including postcode)
Telephone no.: (current firms only)
E-mail address: (current firms only)
Website address: (current firms only)
Also: (Nature of any other businesses involved in.)

Note: If the "nature of business" appears in inverted commas, it is written here as styled by the company itself or by contemporary accounts.

Builders of vessels come under various titles, as follows:

Shipbuilder or ship builder; boatbuilder or boat builder; ship or ship's carpenter (usually a ship-borne artisan but sometimes used to refer to a builder/repairer of vessels); shipsmith, ship smith or ship's smith; shipwright (either the employer or one of his employees; it is often unclear which is being referred to in old census returns).

All ship and boat yards within the old customs port of Runcorn (as listed in this study), launched their vessels into the following waterways with small blue symbols as follows:

M = River Mersey
MM = River Mersey, later Manchester Ship Canal (M.S.C.)
MSC = M.S.C.
B = Bridgewater Canal
T = Trent and Mersey Canal
RW = River Weaver
WN = Weaver Navigation
St = St Helens Canal or Sankey Brook Navigation
Sh = Shropshire Union Canal
* = Launched wherever customer or builder wanted
(taken by road transport)
N/A = Facilities not within the old customs port of Runcorn

There will also be either plain or numbered black asterisks (standard text size) scattered through this work to refer the reader to a list of notes at the end of the book.

All details in red text show currently existing facilities.

All the following were/are builders of wooden sailing ships/boats and "dumb" boats, unless otherwise stated in the section on the nature of their business.

Runcorn
Mersey Road and Old Quay

Company name: William Wright and Charles Hickson
Nature of maritime business: Flat builders?
Years of business: 1802?–?
Ship or boat yard name: "Mersey Street Yard"?, M
Yard location: Mersey Street (now part of "Mersey Road")
(The Mersey Street Shipyard may have had a different name, but none has been found other than reference to its location)
(Stocks; later a patent slipway)

Further information: When this partnership dissolved, Charles Hickson went into business himself as a shipbuilder at Weston Point and later, it seems, at Ellesmere Port. (Information from *Waterways Journal Volume 15, Ship and Boat Building at Ellesmere Port: A History* by Terry Kavanagh.)

Company name:	William Wright
Nature of maritime business:	"Shipbuilder"; flat and wooden paddle steamer builder?
Years of business:	1815?–?
Ship or boat yard name:	As previous listing M
Yard location:	As previous listing

Also: Owner of a sandstone quarry on Runcorn Hill and a tannery in Bridge Street between 1841 and 1851.

Note: *Schooner Port* states that Wright was "building under his name alone" by 1816. The list of locally-built ships at the back of the book shows he launched a 63-ton flat JANE without his former partner in 1815.

Company name:	Dennis Brundrit
Nature of maritime business:	?
Years of business:	?–?
Ship or boat yard name:	As previous listing M
Yard location:	As previous listing

Also: druggist and stone mason/quarry master (owner of the Stenhills Quarry in Runcorn and the mineral rights to the Penmaenmawr Granite Quarry in Wales).

One of the big entrepreneurs of the town, the Brundrit company became the foremost shipbuilder of Runcorn, launching the two biggest vessels built there (one of which was the Dennis Brundrit, which was claimed to be the smallest full-rigged ship in the world).

Dennis Brundrit's former home is now the South Bank Hotel public house. His druggist's shop was at the junction of High and Bridge Streets.

Company name:	Brundrit and Whiteway
Nature of maritime business:	"Stone merchants and shipbuilders"; gentlemen and merchants; flat, ship and wooden screw steamer builders? Ship owners
Years of business:	1823–1869?
Ship or boat yard name:	As previous listing M
Yard location:	As previous listing

Further information: The stocks they had on the foreshore were by now also used for broadside launches into the Mersey, as evidenced by its launch of the WIDDERS in this manner.

Brundrit entered into partnership with Whiteway as both stone merchant and shipbuilder in 1823.

Brundrit's yard had become the largest of the Runcorn yards by 1848 and his facilities were later solely at the Old Quay site.

Note: An 1839 survey of the Port of Liverpool (for the Corporation of Liverpool) recorded the land immediately east of the Railway Bridge was owned by Dennis Brundrit, who had "shipbuilding and other yards" there. Below the present Belvedere Buildings, there were coal and timber yards belonging to Messrs. Brundrit, Whiteway and Forster.

Also: Stone merchants.
Philip Whiteway was a member of the Runcorn Improvement Commissioners and, as a part of that duty, he laid the first stone of the Runcorn Railway Bridge on 12th April 1864.

In 1857, he was noted as one of the chief landowners of Runcorn (along with a Miss Orred) according to a Post Office Directory of Cheshire from that year.

Company name:	John and William Brundrit
Nature of maritime business:	Shipbuilders
Years of business:	1850s/60s?
Ship or boat yard name:	As previous listing M
Yard location:	As previous listing

Further information: Mentioned in *Old Runcorn*; presumably the sons of Dennis Brundrit.
Also: Quarry owners and farmers.

Company name:	Robert C. Whiteway
Nature of maritime business:	Shipbuilder
Years of business:	?–?
Ship or boat yard name:	As previous listing M?
Yard location:	Residential: Irwell

Company name:	Brundrit and Co.
Nature of maritime business:	Wooden and iron sailing and steam ship and two smaller builders and flat and boat builders
Years of business:	1874?–1891

Ship or boat yard name: As previous listing M
Yard location: (Patent slipway [side] slipways [F&A])
Further information: At some point, there began a partnership with someone named Hayes, as this man is mentioned in a couple of sources.

The *London Gazette* gives the answer with the firm of Brundrit and Co. being wound-up in 1891 by partners John Brundrit, William Hayes, and John Higson.

Maps of Mersey Street from the latter 1800s show a sideways patent slip as well as two smaller, longer ones, which must have been for fore and aft hauling of vessels.

Note: Brundrit and Co.'s head office was later on High Street (from at least 1874).

Morris and Co.'s 1874 *Directory of Cheshire* gives John Anderton as the manager for "Brundret and Co.", living at 5, Clarence Terrace. Perhaps he was related to the earlier John Anderton at Castle Rock (see later entry).

Company name: Brundrit and Hayes
Nature of maritime business: Wooden and iron sailing and steam ship and two smaller builders and flat and boat builders?
Years of business: 1886?–1887?
Ship or boat yard name: As previous listing M
Yard location: (Patent slipway [side] slipways [F&A])

Note: Schooner Port and other sources quote the firm of Brundrit and Hayes as builders of the DESPATCH, yet the appendix to the book lists the builder as Brundrit and Co.

Smith's Directory of 1888 gives a listing for "Hayes, Wm., Esq. (BRUNDRIT and CO.), High Street, house, Ashton Heyes, near Chester". Further references exist to "Brundrit and Hayes" (also as "Brindrith and Hayes", which is another error of recording) and so presumably Hayes was a senior man at the company. which it seems he later became a partner in.

Note: Cygnor Gwynedd Council Website (www.gwynedd.gov.uk/DATRhagorolNET/RhestrEitem.aspx?iaith=en&rhif_archif=12&rhif_rhiant=73518&maint_testun=100&cyferbyniad) gives this detail –

CONSENT by Lord Newborough to the assignment of the Lease (13 Dec. 1862) of Gimblet Rock otherwise Carreg yr Ymbyll, pa.[rish] Dyneio [Deneio], by William Wright Brundrit and John Brundrit of Runcorn, quarry proprietors, to John Brundrit William Hayes of Runcorn, merchant, and John Higson of Liverpool, merchants. [N.L.W. Glynllivon 786a].

Thus, it seems the Hayes connection is verified.

Also: Slate merchants.

Note: *Schooner Port* states Brundrit's yard became the public slipway, with the "other part of the yard" being leased out as a repair yard to Stubbs (see entry below). In fact, the M.S.C. Co. rebuilt the main slip at Brundrit's former yard as a public slipway (later leased to Stubbs) and also built another slipway for its own use near to it.

Company name:	Jas. Boot
Nature of maritime business:	Foreman shipbuilder
Years of business:	?–?
Ship or boat yard name:	Cooper Street M?
Yard location:	?

This information is from a *Runcorn Directory* loaned to me by Percy Dunbavand; it follows another piece dated 1860 but it may be from a different year.

I have since read *White's Directory* of 1860, which I believe was one in the same as the above.

Note: Cooper Street was one back from what is now Mersey Road, so if Jas. Boot was a shipbuilder in his own right, he may well have operated from an office in the former and a yard on the latter.

Schooner Port shows a quote naming James Boot as the manager of the Brundrit and Whiteway firm but as he was listed in a commercial, not residential directory, was he later independent?

Note: An article in *Sea Breezes* magazine for December 1971 (*Mainly About Flats* by Frank Ogle) states that there was a Runcorn shipyard, of "three or four slipways… with about 20 shipwrights round each vessel", belonging to Mr. J. Davies. It lists a number of vessels built there from 1877 to 1887, all of which were actually built by the Brundrit company, which was the only firm large enough to have been described as above. I therefore believe that Mr. Davies must have been the manager of that firm in its latter days.

Company name:	Okell
Nature of maritime business:	Shipbuilder?
Years of business:	1821?–1836?
Ship or boat yard name:	Timber yard and smithy M
Yard location:	Adjacent to Brundrit's Yard

Nickson's *History of Runcorn* (written in 1887) gives an account of a "timber yard and smithy owned by Mr. Okell, the site being that now occupied by Brundrit and Co.'s Shipbuilding Yard" existing at what must now be the site of Old Quay Yard.

Company name:	Okell and Webster
Nature of maritime business:	?
Years of business:	1840? - ?
Ship or boat yard name:	Okell's old yard above? M
Yard location:	?

Other sources list the above firm as working in shipbuilding, yet see entry below for the Sotherns.

Perhaps Okell later went into partnership with Webster at another site, or perhaps he continued to use his original site, in conjunction with Sothern and his new partner, above.

Company name:	Thomas Sothern
Nature of maritime business:	Shipbuilder
Years of business:	1814? - ?
Ship or boat yard name:	Okell's old yard above M
Yard location:	?

Starkey's *Old Runcorn* tells of "Thomas Sothern, shipbuilder", and I believe he must have been the father or other relative from whom the work of J. Sothern continued.

Company name:	J. Sothern/Sothern and Co.
Nature of maritime business:	Shipbuilder?
Years of business:	1836?–?
Ship or boat yard name:	As above M

Yard location: ?
Further information: The name is sometimes given as "Southern".

Nickson's *History of Runcorn* states that from 1836, "Messrs. Sothern and Co. (the family of Lord Dunready fame) were carrying on the timber and ship yard of Mr. Okell".

Nickson goes on to say in that book that "Messrs. Brundrit and Whiteway were the occupiers of Sothern and Co.'s ship yard" by the decade, 1841–1851. As the Brundrit Yard was the former Wright and Hickson Yard, the company must have bought the Sothern Yard and added it to its existing facilities and being as no reference exists for a second Brundrit Yard, it may be that the Sothern Yard was adjacent to the Mersey Street Yard and was absorbed into the latter.

Furthermore, Percy Dunbavand has an article "What Runcorn was like in 1838" (author unknown, but given to Percy by John Clark), which states that Runcorn had "four shipyards, The Old Quay Co, The Southern Co, afterwards Brundrit and Whiteway, Samuel Mason, and John Anderton, besides sidings belonging to the Trustees of the late Duke of Bridgewater at the bottom locks".

Company name:	John Stubbs and Sons
Nature of maritime business:	"Shipwrights, blockmakers and makers of masts and spars"; flat builders?
Years of business:	1878?–1922?
Ship or boat yard name:	1. Percival Lane M or B? ?– ?
	2. Belvedere Yard MM
	3. Mersey Road Yard (part of Brundrit's old "Mersey Street Yard") MM or MSC? (1887?)
Yard location:	(Patent slipway and smaller slipway)

Note: An article from the *London Gazette*, dated 7th January 1879 and available on the internet, states that in accordance with the Bankruptcy Act of 1869 and at the County Court of Lancashire held at Warrington, a new firm was to be set up. This firm was under the agreement of John Stubbs of Regent Street, William Shingler Stubbs of Percival Lane, Samuel Stubbs of Belvidere (sic), and James Stubbs of Percival Lane and was designed to allow for them to carry on the "business of Ship, Flat and Boat Builders in copartnership at Percival Lane and Belvidere", under the "style of" John Stubbs and Sons.

The William Shingler Stubbs listed above may well be the man who appears in the censuses for Runcorn as William Stubbs in 1861 as a ship's carpenter (aged 20), in 1881 as a shipwright (40), and in 1891 as a shipwright (50).

It therefore appears that the firm under Samuel Stubbs wound up and went to his son John and these other Stubbs men who were his relatives, most likely siblings.

It also appears the business used the old Belvedere Yard alongside its old premises at Runcorn Docks before moving to the former Mersey Street Yard at Old Quay.

Note: The construction of the Manchester Ship Canal meant the end of true shipbuilding at Runcorn but as a form of compensation, the Manchester Ship Canal Company allowed free passage and right-of-way to vessels up to the slipway the company had re-constructed for public use at Old Quay.

Company name:	Jn. Jas. Stubbs
Nature of maritime business:	"Ship repairer" Boat builder
Years of business:	1934?–1945?
Ship or boat yard name:	Mersey Road (Tel. 187) MSC
Yard location:	(The yard occupied later by F. Stubbs – see entry below – and assumed occupied by John Stubbs, above)

This listing from *Kelly's Directory of Cheshire*, 1934 and 1939, means John James Stubbs was the name the company now operated under. John James Stubbs was the full name of the man who once operated from Percival Lane. He was known as Jack to his friends. Fred Stubbs (see entry below) was the eldest son of John James Stubbs. The younger son Harry died in 1943. These facts have been gleaned from an article for the *Runcorn Weekly News* in Ray Miller's column, written by Ken Stubbs, the son of Fred. The article also makes it clear that the firm carried out work for ships berthed in various ports across the west coast, citing a new section of mast or bowsprit being built and readied for transport to a ship in Holyhead.

There is also mention of a clinker-built dinghy waiting for delivery to a schooner and I take it from that the boat was built at the yard. Ken Stubbs later confirmed his grandfather did indeed build such boats. Mr. Stubbs makes it clear in the above writing that John James Stubbs worked throughout World War II.

Note: The construction of the Manchester Ship Canal meant the end of true shipbuilding at Runcorn but, as a form of compensation, the Manchester Ship Canal Company allowed free passage and right of way to vessels up to the slipway the company had re-constructed for public use at Old Quay (which was actually the rebuilt Brundrit slipway, as *Schooner Port* states this had become the public slipway for the town).

Company name:	Fred Stubbs
Nature of maritime business:	"Shipbuilder"; ship and barge repairer? Schooner and barge repair
Years of business:	?–last days of sail?/1950s?
Ship or boat yard name:	Mersey Road Yard MSC
Yard location:	(Patent Slipway Class 1 [Side] later used by M.S.C. Co. and smaller Slipway [Side], now gone?)

Further information: The main slipway became known as Stubbs's Slip but was the public slipway also known as (Runcorn) Town Slip. (Absorbed into Old Quay Yard)

Note: Schooner Port by H.F. Starkey states Stubbs continued to repair wooden sailing vessels into the 1930s, yet *Images of England: Runcorn, a Century of Change* by the same author shows a picture of the wooden vessel CAMEL under survey at Stubbs's Yard in 1953 (with a caption that repeats the statement above). It appears, therefore, that after the sailing vessels had disappeared the yard continued to repair other wooden (and perhaps steel) vessels until at least the 1950s.

Company name:	Manchester Ship Canal Co. (M.S.C. Co.)
Nature of maritime business:	Building and repair of own barges and tugs

1. Building and repair of own wooden barges and iron tugs (incl. Ship Canal tugs but mainly vessels of the Bridgewater Department of the M.S.C. Co.) Conversions of tugs from steam to diesel
2. Repair of own wooden and iron/steel vessels and building of cock boats Sailmaker Manufacturer of own propellers Conversions of tugs from steam to diesel
3. Repair of own small floating craft
4. See later entry
5. Boat and engine repairs and facilities for users to repair own boats
6. Survey and repair of own vessels

7. Fitting out facility?
8. See entry on Ellesmere Port and ship owners: Manchester Liners Prince
   Line (Owned since 1984? By Peel Holdings)

Years of business: 1885?–present
Ship or boat yard name:

1. Victoria Dockyard ʙ at the former Big Pool. Known as Sprinch Yard
   (Four dry docks [incl. two double dry docks] to accommodate six barges
   and slipway and building berth for temporary slipway [Side] and various
   workshops: boiler, fitting, blacksmith's and wheelwright's shops, cranes and
   sawmill) (1883?–1935?/77?) (Bridgewater Department) (Considered to be
   one of, if not the, finest boatyard in the country)

Yard location: Later extended to include the slipway at the
                                  bottom of Jackson's Lane. Known by the
                                  workforce as Top Yard – see entry for Old
                                  Quay, below.

Note: The yard employed more than 120 shipwrights and was responsible
for the maintenance of 300 flats, twenty narrowboats, floats and maintenance
boats, the maintenance of which transferred from Old Quay Yard in 1890
(although Victoria Yard was opened in 1883, according to *Port of Manchester
Review* for 1978).

Later records refer to the facility as Runcorn Dock Yard.

Ron Turner states the yard also ended up doing repair work on pleasure
craft in its latter days.

Ship or boat yard name (cont):

2. Runcorn Yard of the M.S.C. Co. ᴍsᴄ – the former Old Quay Yard (incorporating all the former Mersey Street/Road Yard – Patent Slipway Class
   1 (Side), which was the public slipway – later taken over by M.S.C. Co.
   from the Stubbs family and rebuilt in the 1950s and 1970s (2ⁿᵈ Nov 1970,
   with a ready-for-service date of 3ʳᵈ Dec 1971, although I have seen a source
   quoting a date of May 1974, which I cannot corroborate) (with seven ways)
   (known by the company as Slipway No.2) – plus another small slipway
   (F&A) along what is now Mersey Road, now gone); another patent slipway
   (side) (Old Quay Slipway, as opposed to the public slipway) (known by the
   company as Slipway No.1 and built on the site of the former Mersey and
   Irwell/Bridgewater slipway and graving dock, but with the gates removed
   to make it a simple access basin such as at Slipway No. 2). This closed and

was filled in in 1970-71 to make way for new workshops, at the same time that the former Stubbs's Slip was modernised. Old Quay Slip was built by the M.S.C. Co. on the former Bridgewater Slip as part of the deal with Runcorn Urban District Council over the granting to the town by the firm, of Mersey Road (with the M.S.C. Co. no longer having to provide the graving dock it at first promised). Travelling cranes (steam). 250-tonne floating crane and other floating cranes, based at Old Quay. (Both the above were used for hauling vessels on to the quayside for repair, as well as for lifting lock gates). (Formerly, graving dock at site of No.1 Slipway – according to several maps – which was gated like a graving dock and allowed access to the slipway). (Last slipway had following specifications: Extreme length 39.62m; length of cradle 30.48m; lifting capacity 178 tonnes over the seven ways/25.4 tonnes per way). The last slipway was also known as (Runcorn) Town Slip and often called Stubbs's Slipway due to its long association with that family. Yard manufactured propellers and other items in its foundry and also had millwrights to repair the yard's own infrastructure. The yard also contained the gate repair shed and facilities where the lock gates for the various canals under the M.S.C. Co. were built/repaired. Yard had a sail loft with a master sailmaker (?), under whom worked any men signed-off sea service for being sick or any men for whom no tug work was assigned. There was also a blacksmith's shop, boilermaker's shop (where the "burners", as they were known on the canal, were based), carpenter's shop, fitting shop, engine house/turning shop, paint shop, sawmill/pattern shop. Known by the workforce as Bottom Yard, as opposed to Top Yard, which was the Victoria Yard – otherwise known as the Sprinch Yard – at the top of the hill and former Sprinch Brook (both yards being the main facilities of the M.S.C. Co. in Runcorn). ?–2003

Note: At its height, the yard employed 280 workers and was the base for the once 27-strong fleet of M.S.C. tugs as well as many other M.S.C. vessels, including the 250-tonne floating crane. The M.S.C. dredging fleet was based at the nearby Runcorn Wall and No Man's Land. Old Quay was responsible for the maintenance of all these vessels, which included a 12-monthly overhaul and boiler clean for all steam vessels and an 18-monthly one for all diesel ones. In 1989, with the decrease in commercial traffic beyond Runcorn the tugs were moved to Eastham, but Old Quay Yard continued to repair vessels and the lock gates of the canal.

Note: The construction of the Manchester Ship Canal meant the end of true shipbuilding at Runcorn, but as a form of compensation, the Manchester Ship Canal Company allowed free passage and right-of-way to vessels up to the slipway the company had re-constructed for public use at Old Quay.

Note: Extract from a Ship Building and Repair Guide – Slipway (Old Quay)

Slipway Repairs

Extreme length	46, 63	-
39. 62m		
Lifting capacity	2, 00	170
178 tonnes		

Length of cradle 30.48m

Lifting capacity quoted is over the seven ways.

Rebuilt 1972.

This is a side slipway and the max. load is 25.40 tonnes per way.

Ship or boat yard name (cont):

3. Engineering Works(hops), Percival Lane MSC (Runcorn Docks)
   2003 (closure of Runcorn Yard)–present
   (Also repair the lock gates of the canal)
   New workshops opened especially in 2003 for transfer of works from Old Quay.
   01928 508550
   01928 567769 (Fax)

4. The facilities of the former Bridgewater Trustees, as the Bridgewater Department of the M.S.C. Co. (see later entry).
   Namely:
   a. Graving grid and dry dock at end of Bridgewater Locks B
   b. Dry Dock at Top Locks B
   ?–Closure of those facilities, respectively in ? and ?

5. Preston Brook Marina B
   Marina Lane
   Tel.: 01928 719081
   (Slipway[s?])
   ?–present

6. M.S.C. Co. divers (both helmeted divers and frogmen). MSC + B
   Based at each of the major locks of the canal: Eastham, Runcorn, Latcham and Mode Wheel. With 4/5 diving boats. Worked at surveying and

repairing lock gates and M.S.C. Co. vessels. ?–2006
7. Fitting-out facilities at Saltport? (*Schooner Port* states there were "two large sheds used as fitting shops and stores"). MSC
8. Facilities at Mode Wheel N/A (Manchester) and Ellesmere Port N/A (see entry on Ellesmere Port). ? - ?
(Manchester Ship Canal Pontoons and Dry Docks Co. Ltd./ Manchester Dry Docks Co. Ltd.).

Note: The former Belvedere Slipway (see entry below) was also a part of an extended Old Quay Yard, stretching-out to the west beyond the former Sea Cadet hut (itself a former workshop of Old Quay). I believe it was not used for ship repair any longer but solely for the storage of the Ship Canal lock gates. The working gear was in place for many years but was removed when the lock gates ceased to be stored there.

Note: Since 1984, the M.S.C. Co. has been owned by Peel Holdings Ltd. When the Runcorn Yard closed in 2003, all remaining M.S.C. Co. staff moved to Runcorn Docks and the slipway remained as the public slipway (and has been used as such since the closure of the yard). In accordance with the 1885 Ship Canal Act, the M.S.C. Co. agreed to provide a public dry dock at Runcorn as compensation for the end of shipbuilding in the town due to the sighting of the ship canal's gantry wall. By 1924 (or 1904?), the promised dry dock had still not been constructed but in that year the M.S.C. Co. handed Runcorn Town Council land it owned on what is now Mersey Road for better access to the transporter bridge (which at that time could only be accessed from Waterloo Road). This land was given on the proviso that the patent slipway on Mersey Road would suffice in lieu of a dry dock for public use. The company built a new slipway at Old Quay as well as re-building the former Brundrit Slipway for use as the public slipway of the town.

A report to the Halton Borough development control committee dated 9th August 2004 admits that "the importance of this proposed residential development ["the Deck"] in encouraging further regeneration of the older parts of Runcorn is considered to outweigh the possible prejudice to the need to facilitate direct use of the ship canal at this point [Old Quay]". This is despite its acknowledgement that the M.S.C. Co.'s original commitment to the town had been to provide two slipways (the refurbished Brundrit Slipway and the new Old Quay Slipway, which was filled in in the 1970s).

The ignorance of the committee to affairs of the canal and its history is evident when it quotes the Old Quay site as having been engaged in "shipbuilding and boat building since 1880", despite much evidence to prove the date is actually at least as far back as 1802. Furthermore, with regard to boat building, that date could go back to the existence of the Runcorn Ferry at Boat House Pool (on the Old Quay site) in the Middle Ages, as the ferry would in all probability have been maintained at the site also. Update (October, 2005): The slipway's infrastructure has been destroyed along with the rest of the once bustling yard, which had been in use by one company or another since at least 1804.

The only pleasing thing about the above report is the statement that, with regard to the former slipway, "if it is possible to incorporate some facility as part of the successful development of the site [Old Quay/the Deck] then this should be welcomed". Perhaps a new but much smaller yard may yet be opened there?

By April 2006, the slipway had seen all its winch gear and blocks removed. Workers building the leisure and residential development at Old Quay site were unaware of any plans to keep the slipway as a feature of the new complex.

The closure of the yard in 2003 meant an end to ship and boat building and repair at the site, which had operated such businesses by different firms since at least 1802 (the first recorded building of a vessel by Charles Hickson) but probably earlier.

Update (August 2006): Peel Holdings, owner of the M.S.C. Co., has made further reductions in staff (around 50), with all remaining divers paidoff and the total number of personnel to run the entire canal being reduced to 70. (See Section on Inland Waterways of the United Kingdom, below).

Company name:	Carmet
Nature of maritime business:	Repair of own tugs and tenders?
	Tug owner/operator MSC
Years of business:	?–1993/4?
Ship or boat yard name:	?
Yard location:	Operator (in the latter days) of the M.S.C.
	Co. tugs (also the slipway?).

Further information: The company has, since 1989, operated the remaining M.S.C. tugs and still operates them, although they are now based at Eastham. Today, it has a shipwright's department involved in repairs to jetties and dolphins, etc. and it also carries out buoy repairs. The firm advertises it can "provide support for" ship maintenance and repair. All of this, however, is from its new base at Westbank, Eastham Locks.

Company name:	Bryant's?
Nature of maritime business:	Ship repairer/builder
Years of business:	? - ?
Ship or boat yard name:	Old Quay Yard/Runcorn Yard of the M.S.C.
Yard location:	Drawing office at Old Quay Yard in one of the lofts.

Ron Turner remembers a drawing office being torn down at Old Quay when the developers came to build the flats and shops there. He was not sure of the name of the firm but believed the office was part of works used by a separate shipbuilder at the site.

Company name:	Bryant's?
Nature of maritime business:	Building and repair of (mainly) own vessels
	Barges only?
	Carriers by water
Years of business:	1804?–1846?
Ship or boat yard name:	Old Quay Yard M
Yard location:	(Patent Slipway at former Old Quay Dock, for vessels up to 200t)

Further information: (Graving dock on site of later gate repair shed of the M.S.C. Co. – two ways, with chains for hauling vessels up to 200 tons out of the dock [which therefore was a wet dock for access to the graving slip rather than a true graving dock although it was gated like one and allowed access to the slipway]).

(Occupying part of the land that later became Old Quay Yard/Runcorn Yard of the M.S.C. Co. and built in an area later partially enclosing the former Boat House Pool or Old Gut, as the Mersey and Irwell Navigation Co. improved its facilities at the terminus of its canal). (1837)

Note: *Schooner Port* cites the Bridgewater Navigation Company and the Mersey and Irwell Navigation Company opposition to the Manchester Ship Canal Bill in 1885, by stating that 204 men were employed at Runcorn, "boatbuilding etc.". Is this solely at Bridgewater and Mersey and Irwell facilities?

The Bridgewater Trustees bought out the Mersey and Irwell Navigation Co.

in 1846, becoming the Bridgewater Navigation Co. Ltd.

Company name: Duke of Bridgewater/Bridgewater Trustees/
                  Bridgewater Navigation Co. Ltd.
Nature of maritime business: Building and repair of own vessels
                  Carriers by water
Years of business: 1785?–1885? (and afterwards as a department
                  of the M.S.C. Co.)

Ship or boat yard name:

1. Dry dock and graving grid at end of old line of locks to Runcorn MM
   Docks/coach lane for repair of own canal boats and building of own river
   flats May also have had the boat yard at the Sevastopol Arm (off the old
   line of locks) as part of this yard at Bottom Locks MM/B
   The above was Duke's Yard, or Bottom Locks Yard, whichever parts were
   used by the duke and trustees (1785?)
   Later part of M.S.C. Co. as the Bridgewater Department.
   The graving grid facility was apparently modified for use after the M.S.C.
   was built (where vessels could be hauled out of the water), and may have
   been used to repair company vessels. This is evidenced by the appearance
   of the grid on later plans and maps, with workshops beside it. The original
   graving grid was outside the wall of the docks, but the later one was inside
   it, north of the locks to the Bridgewater Canal.
   This was later the workplace of the M.S.C. Co.'s resident engineer.
   The graving grid was surrounded on three sides eventually at least (?) by
   walls and so was really a draw dock.
2. Shipbuilding and repair facilities adjacent to the Boat House Pool/Old Gut
   and occupying the remainder of the Boat House Pool after the improvements made to the Mersey and Irwell facilities there by that company
   (later part of the area known as Old Quay).
   Later the Bridgewater Navigation Co.
   Yard, Old Quay. M (1844–1890)
   (Absorbed into Old Quay Yard/Runcorn Yard of the M.S.C. Co.).
3. Packet dry dock B – dry dock in between entrances to old and new lines of
   locks at Top Locks. (Repair of little packets). Later part of M.S.C. Co. as
   the Bridgewater Department.
4. Facilities at Worsley and at Anderton N/A

Note: *Schooner Port* cites the Bridgewater Navigation Company and the Mersey and Irwell Navigation Company opposition to the Manchester Ship Canal Bill in 1885, by stating that 204 men were employed at Runcorn, "boat-building etc.". Is this solely at Bridgewater and Mersey and Irwell facilities? A separate reference in the book states that in 1885, 379 men were in engaged in barge and boat building and repair or as tug or flat crews.

Nickson's History of Runcorn states that, in the decade between 1861 and 1871, "The Bridgewater Navigation Co. employed a large number of men in the building and repairing of boats".

Old Runcorn states that the Duke of Bridgewater set up boat repair facilities at the terminus of his canal; does this include the boatyard at the Sevastopol Arm?

The Bridgewater Navigation Co. Ltd. was bought out by the Manchester Ship Canal Co. in 1885.

Also: Owner of mines at Worsley, near Manchester. Owner of a private railway from the Chester to Warrington Line to the Bridgewater Canal.

Company name:	T. and J. Johnson
Nature of maritime business:	Shipbuilders?
	Ship and boat owners
	Rope makers
Years of business:	1840?–1857?
Ship or boat yard name:	Mill Street M (yard near former steam flour mills in Mersey Street (now part of Mersey Road)
	(Absorbed into Old Quay Yard/Runcorn Yard of the M.S.C. Co.?)
Yard location:	?

Note: Thomas and John Johnson took over the soap works of their father, John Senior (after a brief period in their youth when the factory had been leased to another firm). John Senior had at one time also owned a Rope Walk, but there is no evidence to suggest he was involved in shipbuilding as his sons were. The actual soap works were at the site later occupied by Hazlehurst's soap works and later still, Camden Tannery (on the Bridgewater Canal).

Note: An article by Ray Miller in the *Runcorn Weekly News* states that the yard was opened in 1845.

Also: "Soap and alkali manufacturers" (vitriol/sulphuric acid/soda/chemical producers), colliery owners (coal mine at Laffack near St Helens, suppliers to the Royal Navy – at the time, the largest single consignment of coal to the Navy at home or abroad), limestone quarry owners (in Wales), pyrites mines owners (in Ireland), sulphur mines owners, salt works owners (at Over, near Winsford), rosin works owners and farmers.

According to Starkey in *Old Runcorn*, it was "almost the largest employer in the district".

It was the owner of these facilities across the North-west, Wales and Ireland and of one of the largest commercial fleets on Merseyside. It was the largest exporter of coal, soap and salt to the U.S.A.

The Johnson Brothers were prominent in Runcorn's affairs, setting-up the Runcorn Board of Health and the Runcorn Gas Company; becoming founder members of the Runcorn Board of Commissioners (the forerunner of the Runcorn Urban District Council); helping create and becoming members of the committee to negotiate on port dues, the Highways Board and the Burial Board; giving Parliamentary evidence that helped create the Bonded Port of Runcorn in 1840, which could then go on to become the foremost canal port in the country and later a customs port in its own right; they built Holy Trinity Church and several schools.

The current town hall, Halton Grange, was once Thomas Johnson's home.

Bank House, later owned by Simpson, Davies and Co. (see later in this work) was the home of John (Junior) Johnson.

The yard was, according to Nickson's *History of Runcorn*, taken over by Philip Speakman sometime between 1851 and 1861 (see entry later in this work).

Company name: Frederick John Abbott
Nature of maritime business: "(Foreman) Boat Builder"
                                   Boat owner
Years of business: 1874?–1891?
Ship or boat yard name: Old Quay Mills? M?
Yard location: (Absorbed into Old Quay Yard?)

Schooner Port states the 1874 directory lists Abbott as a "foreman boat builder" and boat owner. It goes on to say that, by 1891, he was in partnership as a boat owner with Walton, operating its craft to Old Quay Mills (see entry on Abbott and Walton, later in this work).

Waterways Journal describes Messrs F. J. Abbott Ltd. as "barge owners of Liverpool and Manchester since 1872, and closely associated with the Bridgewater Canal throughout", so clearly the company was wider established than solely in Runcorn.

Morris and Co.'s 1874 *Directory of Cheshire* lists Abbott as addressed at Heath Road. This may have been a head office, but the yard was at Old Quay.

Note: Morris and Co.'s *Directory of 1874* states there was a John Williamson operating at Old Quay as a smith. Perhaps he may have been involved in marine business at some time.

Note: All the above firms operated at what became Old Quay Yard/Runcorn Yard of the M.S.C. Co. Some also had facilities elsewhere but it is still a busy picture of maritime industry that can be imagined at that one area.

The area of Old Quay originally extended further eastward, beyond the Old Quay Swing Bridge and there were boat houses at the extreme end of the dock complex, as shown in a map of 1873/1874.

Company name:	John Anderton and Co.
Nature of maritime business:	Flat and shipbuilders?
	Ship owner
Years of business:	1810?–1874?
Ship or boat yard name:	"Castle Rock Yard"/"Castlerock Yard" M
Yard location:	Huts, saw pit and area for seasoning wood
	(Founded 1810 with Philip Speakman)

Further information: 1810? (Sole owner by 1840?)–1874? (Speakman said to have taken over Castle Rock Yard in 1860 but the Anderton firm, at least under Jas. B. Anderton, may have continued afterwards).

Note: Referred to in an article in the *Runcorn Guardian* centenary edition as John Anderson.

Research by Terry Kavanagh for his article "Richard Abel and Sons, of Runcorn and Liverpool" (*Waterways Journal Volume 16*), gives various editions of the *Liverpool Mercury* newspaper as source for his statement that John Anderton and Co. had occupied Castle Rock Yard since the mid-1830s.

Company name:	Jas. B. Anderton
Nature of maritime business:	Ship builder
Years of business:	?–?
Ship or boat yard name:	As previous listing? M?
Yard location:	Residential: Albert Terrace

A *Runcorn Directory* loaned to me by Percy Dunbavand states that Jas. B. Anderton, shipbuilder was resident at Albert Terrace; it follows another piece dated 1860, but it may be from a different year.

I have since read *White's Directory* of 1860, which I believe was one in the same as the above.

I believe this may have been the fate of the firm, after the Anderton and LeCouteur incarnation, below.

Company name:	Anderton and LeCouteur
Nature of maritime business:	"Ship and boat builders"
	"All kinds of smiths' and joiners' works"
Years of business:	1855?–1860? (See above)
Ship or boat yard name:	As previous listing? M?
Yard location:	"Patent slip on the premises" according to its plaque.

John LeCouteur married Sarah Anderton, daughter of John Anderton, in 1855. This business partnership may have come before or after the aforementioned marriage. John LeCouteur was my Uncle Frank's grandfather. See entries on Withington and LeCouteur, Withington and Ron Turner below.

Research by Terry Kavanagh for his article, "Richard Abel and Sons, of Runcorn and Liverpool" (*Waterways Journal Volume 16*), gives various editions of the *Liverpool Mercury* newspaper as source for his statement that Anderton and LeCouteur was in business from 1871.

Company name:	Philip Speakman/Philip Speakman and Sons
Nature of maritime business:	Narrow boat and flat, and wooden and iron Steam ship builder
	"Ship, Flat and boat builder"
Years of business:	1810?–1878?
Ship or boat yard name:	

1. "Castle Rock Yard"/"Castlerock Yard" M

   Huts, saw pit and an area for 1810? – seasoning wood. (Founded 1810

with John Anderton and Co.). 1810?–1840?
2. Albion Yard B 1851/1861?–?
   (Both yards occupied simultaneously from 1869).
3. Belvedere Yard M
   Sometime during the decade, 1851–1861? (See later entry)
4. Mill Street Yard M
   Sometime during the decade, 1851–1861? but sold sometime before 1874
   (See earlier entry).
Yard location: ?

Note: Schooner Port states Speakman "took over the Albion and Castle Rock shipyards in 1869".

Nickson's *History of Runcorn* states "Mr. P. Speakman, in addition to working three of the old shipyards (Castle Rock, Belvedere and Mill Street), had established a boat building yard at the Big Pool on the Bridgewater Canal" during the decade, 1851–1861. A map of 1873/1874 shows Albion Yard was on the west bank of Big Pool.

Furthermore, it can be seen from the history of the Mason family at the Belvedere Yard that Speakman's occupation of the site must have been temporary (see entries below).

Morris and Co.'s 1874 *Directory of Cheshire* lists Philip Speakman as being at "Castle rock, Belvedere and Albion Dockyard".

(See entry in section on Runcorn Sailmakers)

Note: According to information from Megan Posnett, cited by Ray Miller in the *Runcorn Weekly News* for 25th December 2014, Speakman finished shipbuilding with the coming of the Manchester Ship Canal. He later sold his home at The Mount to one of Megan Posnett's ancestors, the tanner Robert H. Posnett. It would seem, then, that Richard Abel and Sons (see below) decided to make a go of the Castle Rock Yard for itself, continuing building and repair of smaller vessels there after the larger ships of Speakman's day could no longer be launched from the site.

Note: According to the 1962 *Runcorn Guardian* centenary edition, the Castle Rock Yard, "in its heyday" and up to the 1890s "turned out" schooners, ketches and jigger flats. Look at the list of vessels built in Runcorn to cross-reference this as not all of these vessel types are listed as having been built by the firms operating from Castle Rock Yard.

Company name:	Richard Abel and Sons
Nature of maritime business:	Builders and repairers of barges (some with steel frames)
	Sailmaker
	Chandler (*27)
	Ship? and boat owners, later tug and dredger owners (by then repaired own vessels only)
Years of business:	1850?/1865?–1964?

Ship or boat yard name:

1. Washington Buildings, Top Locks B
2. Castle Rock Yard/Castlerock Yard/ The Dockyard MSC
   (Patent Slipway Class 1 [Side], slipway ship and jetty)
   Ways of the slipway extended 40ft into barge, the water and could accommodate vessels up to 95ft in length.
   October 1894 (*27)–1964?

Yard location: ?

At Castle Rock "by 1890s" according to *Waterways Journal Vol. 14*, "Chester and Liverpool Lighterage and Wharehousing Co. Ltd." By Alan Faulkner. The original yard extended further west than it did latterly, and the patent slip was in the westernmost part of the facility. However, the building of the road bridge to Widnes, right through that part of the yard, necessitated the building of a new slipway in the eastern area, immediately adjacent to the soon-to-be-dismantled transporter bridge. A look at old photographs will show the move from the old to the new slipway, with the bridge reducing the area of the yard. At some point during the 1890s and possibly earlier, there must have been a second slipway, a F&A building berth. This is evidenced from a photo in the "Manchester Ship Canal" article of *Narrowboat* magazine for Winter 2011/2. It shows a vessel under construction at this site, on just such a berth. It is remarkable for the fact I have hitherto never seen any picture or map showing such a facility at Castle Rock. I have no idea when the layout of Castle Rock changed and this was removed. Another photograph of the period shows a set of sheerlegs at the adjacent wharf, and these may or may not have been part of the facilities of Castle Rock. They may otherwise have been for the use of fishing vessels that berthed there. Offices at Washington Buildings, Top Locks (where they were based before moving to Castle Rock Yard? B

Ship or boat yard name (cont):
Residential: 4, Trentham Street (repair yard for own barges and tugs and building yard for own barges).
3. Yard at Clifton, at the former coal dock (Patent Slipway Class 2) (F&A)wn (see Other Building and Repair Facilities of Runcorn).
   ? - ? (Before World War II).
   (Depot and repair yard for own barges/tugs)
4. Repair yard for own barges/tugs at Weston Point Docks.
   (Workshop only? – vessels lay up beside the church).
   Addressed as being at Delamere Dock (Now confirmed from Frank LeCouteur, my father's cousin that the yard was here). msc Lasted after the closure of the main Castle Rock Yard?
5. Depot/Wharf(s) at Liverpool With Head Office eventually at: Canadian Buildings, 7 and 9, James Street, Liverpool 2. Addressed as being at Albert, Canning and Collingwood Docks in Liverpool and with facilities at Sand Wharves North West, Wapping Basin, Liverpool. n/a
6. Depot at Widnes. m
7. Depot at Manchester (including its original berth at Number 8 Dock and latterly, the former William Cooper berth at what was known as 5 Pier in the channel that was the remains of the River Irwell) (*27). n/a
8. Wharf at Birkenhead. n/a
   (All yards and depots occupied simultaneously?)

Note: In 1960, the firm was listed as being at: Albert, Canning and Collingwood Docks in Liverpool and at the dockyard and Delamere Dock, Runcorn (The dockyard was presumably Castle Rock and Delamere Dock is in Weston Point Docks).

Its letterhead stated it was founded in 1869, but this may have been in the latter incarnation of the firm as evidence suggests it was around longer.

It was the last flat builder of all the many yards involved in the business in the area of the River Mersey and beyond, across the North-west of England and North Wales.

According to *Schooner Port*, the yard may also have been the first one operating at Runcorn, although it was supposedly founded in 1810, some years after the first recorded launch of a Runcorn-built vessel.

Also: Barge and dredger owners and dealers in sand. (See entry in section on Runcorn Sailmakers.)

Company name:	Samuel Mason/Samuel Mason and Co.
Nature of maritime business:	"Ship and anchor smith"; flat and builder? Ship owner
Years of business:	1838?–1857
Ship or boat yard name:	

1. Belvedere Building M 1838?–1840?.
2. Belvedere Yard, M below present Belvedere Building (Shortly after 1840). (Yard had stocks [F&A and side]; later a patent slipway [six ways?]).
3. Mill Street M 1850?–?.

Yard location: ?

Did Mason operate from Mill Street (perhaps the former yard of T. and J. Johnson?) or was this address near enough to Belvedere Yard to mean he had an office there but retained the Belvedere Yard?

This may have been the same as the Mason and Co. that became involved in the business in Ellesmere Port.

Research by Terry Kavanagh however (as reported in *Waterways Journal Vol. 15*, "Ship and Boat Building at Ellesmere Port: A History") states this firm proposed to rent the Morton patent slip and yard for £150pa, which the Shropshire Union Canal Company agreed to, only for Mason to then withdraw the offer. So it may well have never occupied the site, despite what my earlier research implied.

Company name:	John Mason and Co.
Nature of maritime business:	?
Years of business:	18??
Ship or boat yard name:	Mill Street M
Yard location:	Residential: Clarence Terrace

This information is from a *Runcorn Directory* loaned to me by Percy Dunbavand; it follows another piece dated 1860 but it may be from a different year.

Again, did Mason operate from Mill Street (perhaps the former yard of T. and J. Johnson?) or was this address near enough to Belvedere Yard to mean he had an office there but retained the Belvedere Yard?

Company name:	Mason and Craggs
Nature of maritime business:	?
Years of business:	1857–Dec 1859

| *Ship or boat yard name:* | Belvedere Yard M |
| *Yard location:* | ? |

Note: A James Mason is referred to in an article in the *Runcorn Guardian* centenary edition as a local shipbuilder. Perhaps he is a son of Samuel Mason who took over the firm from his father or the name is meant to read "John".

Company name:	Mason
Nature of maritime business:	?
Years of business:	1861?–?
Ship or boat yard name:	As previous listing M
Yard location:	?

Note: A James Mason is referred to in an article in the *Runcorn Guardian* centenary edition as a local shipbuilder; perhaps he is a son of Samuel or John Mason who took over the firm from his father.

Note: A Josh Mason is referred to in *White's Directory* of 1860 as a shipbuilder, residential at Vicar Lane.

Company name:	Blundell and Mason
Nature of maritime business:	?
Years of business:	1868?–1879
Ship or boat yard name:	As previous listing M
Yard location:	?

The slips of the Belvedere Yard (or just on the site of it?) were to be seen up until 198? and were used for storing the lock gates/caissons of the Manchester Ship Canal prior to their replacement by the current concrete ones.

After this partnership wound up, Blundell emigrated to Canada and settled beside the Great Lakes. There he worked at Louis Shickluna's Yard at Lakefield, Ontario. He designed and built many ships that traded on the Great Lakes.

A private collector came to own his archive, which contained many plans and specifications from his time as a shipbuilder in Runcorn. The curator of the Marine Museum of Canada, Maurice Smith, pointed out this fact to the late Mike Stammers, then at the Maritime Museum in Liverpool. Mr. Smith arranged for copies of these plans to be sent to the archives int Liverpool, and thus we owe a debt of gratitude for the research and work of these two men in preserving this important piece of our heritage.

The above information concerning Canada is all from *Waterways Journal Vol. 5*, "Building Flats at Runcorn" by Mike Stammers.

Company name:	John Ravenscroft
Nature of maritime business:	"Ship and anchor smith"
	Blacksmith and chain and anchor maker
Years of business:	?–?
Ship or boat yard name:	Church Street M?
Yard location:	?

The *Runcorn Directory* in question was loaned to me by Percy Dunbavand; it follows another piece dated 1860, but it may be from a different year.

Note: Church Street was one back from what is now Mersey Road, so John Ravenscroft may well have operated from an office in the former and a yard on the latter.

Note: Samuel Stock, a Widnes shipbuilder, had his office at Castle Rock in Runcorn and possibly conducted some shipbuilding or repair there.
Note: See entry for Stubbs above.
Note: All the above firms operated along today's Mersey Road (although some had facilities elsewhere also), which was clearly a busy maritime scene (especially at the point where it merged into what became Old Quay Yard/ Runcorn Yard of the M.S.C. Co.).

Big Pool

Company name:	Abbott and Walton
Nature of maritime business:	Repair of own vessels?
Years of business:	?–?
Ship or boat yard name:	Victoria Yard on Big Pool B
Yard location:	(between Victoria Yard [Sprinch] and
	Timmins at the north-east end of Big Pool)
	Slipway (side)
	(See entry on Frederick John Abbott earlier in
	this work)

Company name:	A. Barton Engineering Works
Nature of maritime business:	Boat builders
	Marine auxiliary builders
Years of business:	?–?
Ship or boat yard name:	Victoria Works
Yard location:	Besides Big Pool

Further information: Main Works at St Helens Junction, with other works at Runcorn and at South ? Works, Sunderland. There was also a London office.

According to Ron Turner, the Barton Yard was on the Sprinch, so probably was on Big Pool besides the other works known by the name Victoria.

He remembers the company building boats as well as undertaking heavy engineering, including work for the Navy, such as building winches. (See entry under Marine Engine Builders at Runcorn)

Company name:	Thomas Binns
Nature of maritime business:	?
Years of business:	?–?
Ship or boat yard name:	VHeath Road B?
Yard location:	Besides Big Pool

Further information: (Presumably, if addressed at Heath Road, Thomas Binns' Yard was on Big Pool).

Company name:	Canalside Narrowboats Limited
Nature of maritime business:	Narrowboat Builders
Years of business:	?–Present
Ship or boat yard name:	Presumably operating near Big Pool B?
Yard location:	Off Victoria Road

Company name:	John Clucas
Nature of maritime business:	Shipwright
Years of business:	?–?
Ship or boat yard name:	Ellesmere Street B?
Yard location:	

(Presumably, if addressed at Ellesmere Street, John Clucas' Yard was on Big Pool)

Company name:	John Crippin
Nature of maritime business:	Ship owner
Years of business:	1800?–?
Ship or boat yard name:	Bridgewater Foundry B
Yard location:	?

As he was based at Bridgewater Foundry, perhaps he owned the boatyard at Big Pool next to the foundry (later owned by Abbott and Walton – this being where the sSlipway was as marked on 1905 maps of the town).

Also: Millwright and iron founder; salt and coal merchant; agent to the Bridgewater Trustees; steam tug owner/operator? And by 1850, partner in the Rock Ferry Steam Packet Company.

Note: Nickson's *History of Runcorn* gives the foundry owner's name as "Crippen", who was working the foundry starting sometime between 1841 and 1851.

Note: Bridgewater Foundry was later taken over by E. Timmins (see entry under Marine Engine Builders of Runcorn).

Company name:	Simpson, Son and Davies. Later became: Simpson, Davies and Co./Simpson, Davies and Sons Ltd.
Nature of maritime business:	"Coal and salt carriers and ship brokers" Boat builders (own vessels only?) and repairers of own vessels?
Years of business:	1821–196?
Ship or boat yard name:	High Street B?

1. Bank house and boat yard. B
   Heath Road/end of Victoria Road.
   (Building dock and Patent Slipway Narrow Class 1 [side] [large enough to accommodate two narrowboats or possibly a barge] on the east side of Big Pool). Ron Turner states the yard ended up also doing repair work on pleasure craft in its latter days.
2. Winsford. N/A
3. Wigan. N/A

(All three premises occupied simultaneously)

Yard location: ?

Note: An advert from 1890 shows the firm based at Bank Chambers (same as Bank House?) and having been established in 1821.

Also: Proprieters of Kirklees Colliery, Aspull near Wigan, agents for the Leeds and Liverpool Canal Co. and distributors for the Salt Union Ltd.

Company name:	Philip Speakman
Nature of maritime business:	"Ship, flat and boat builder"
Years of business:	1851/61–?
Ship or boat yard name:	Boat yard on the west side of Big Pool B
Yard location:	Boat house?
	(A map of 1873/1874 shows a boat house beside that yard)
	(See earlier entry)

Company name:	Samuel Taylor
Nature of maritime business:	?
Years of business:	?–?
Ship or boat yard name:	Boatyard on Big Pool B
Yard location:	?

Note: See entry for M.S.C. Co., above and for Ron Turner, below.

Note: All the above firms operated on what was Big Pool (although some had facilities elsewhere also), which was clearly another busy maritime scene.

Top Locks

Company name:	William Bate
Nature of maritime business:	"Coal merchant, flat and boat builder and dealer in building and moulding sand"
Years of business:	?–?
Ship or boat yard name:	Greenway Road/Lowlands Road B?
Yard location:	Coal yard on south bank at Top Locks

Was this the same person as the William Bates who later worked out of Liverpool and for whom Abel's of Runcorn built several vessels?

Being addressed at Greenway Road/Lowlands Road, Bate was probably working from Top Locks.

Company name:	John Hitchmough
Nature of maritime business:	Foreman Shipwright
Years of business:	1874?–?
Ship or boat yard name:	?
Yard location:	39, Greenway Road

Manager for another firm or a shipbuilder in his own right? Being addressed at Greenway Road, he may well have worked at Top Locks.

Company name:	John Rawlinson
Nature of maritime business:	Wooden paddle steamer builder? and block and pump maker
Years of business:	1836–?
Ship or boat yard name:	Top Locks B
Yard location:	?

Further Information: Presumably, the same person as John Rollinson; Block, Mast and Pump Maker of Top Locks mentioned in *White's Directory* of 1860.

Company name:	Peter Stubbs/Peter Stubbs and Co.
Nature of maritime business:	Shipwright/shipwrights
Years of business:	1888?–?
Ship or boat yard name:	1. Waterloo Bridge B
	2. Top Locks B
Yard location:	?

Company name:	Charles Stubbs
Nature of maritime business:	Shipwright
Years of business:	1906?–1922?
Ship or boat yard name:	Top Locks B
Yard location:	?

Company name:	Withington and LeCouteur
Nature of maritime business:	"Shipsmiths"
Years of business:	1906?–1922?
Ship or boat yard name:	Top Locks B

Yard location: ?

Further information: The late Mr. Frank LeCouteur was the great uncle of the author, who had said either his father or grandfather (I couldn't remember which, but think now he said his grandfather) was involved in shipbuilding and his family generally. Since that time, Kelly's Directory of Cheshire (for 1906 and 1910) has proved his memory. I also remember him saying that the family owned Castle Rock Yard and subsequent research shows this too was correct.

John LeCouteur co-owned Castle Rock Yard with John Anderton and later, James Fleury LeCouteur was in partnership with Ira Withington at Top Locks.

See entries for Anderton and LeCouteur above and for Withington and Ron Turner below.

Note: See entries for Bridgewater Trustees, M.S.C. Co. and Richard Abel and Sons, above and for Ron Turner, below.

Note: All the above firms operated at Top Locks, which was clearly another busy maritime scene.

Runcorn Docks

Company name: John Caine
Nature of maritime business: Ship's smith
Years of business: ?–?
Ship or boat yard name: Runcorn Docks? M or B?
Yard location: ?

Further information: John Caine (father of Runcornian author, Sir Thomas Henry Hall Caine), a blacksmith from the Isle of Man who moved to England and retrained at Liverpool as a ship's sSmith, moved to Runcorn after working on a repair job in Runcorn Docks.

Was this working for himself or as an employee of someone else, such as Bridgewater?

Company name: Knowles Brothers
Nature of maritime business: "Ship and general smiths"/"ship smiths"
Years of business: 1874?–1922?
Ship or boat yard name: Percival Lane M or B?
Yard location: ?

Company name: Mick Mills

Nature of maritime business: "Ship and general smiths"/"ship smiths"

Years of business: 2003–present?

Ship or boat yard name: Runcorn Docks Industrial Estate *

Yard location: ?

Further information: Planning to build three 50ft narrowboats to be sold on and fitted out as cabin cruisers. Has enough scrap steel for these and has nearly completed his first. Hopefully more will come.

Company name: Potters

Nature of maritime business: Builders? and repairers of own narrowboats

Years of business: ?–1960s

Ship or boat yard name: Boat yard at Sevastopol Arm? B

Yard location: Graving dock

Further information: Ron Turner remembers this firm having a "dockyard and dry dock" halfway down the locks, so on quizzing him about this, we agreed it must have been at the Sevastopol Arm. Certainly, the company's offices were there.

Company name: Robert/R. Stubbs and Co.

Nature of maritime business: Shipwrights/ship and boat builders

Years of business: 1906?–1924?

Ship or boat yard name:
1. Percival Lane M or B?
   1906?–?
2. James Street ?
   1924?–?

Yard location: Postal Address: 109, Greenway Road

Note: The *London Gazette* for 11ᵗʰ May 1909 ran an article stating Samuel Stubbs (of 109, Greenway Road), Robert Stubbs (of 8, Dale Street), and John James Stubbs (of 9, Lightburn Street), lately carrying on business under the title of Robert Stubbs and Company at James Street, were now out of business. They were "shipwrights and boat builders".

Therefore, it seems this firm I had as R. Stubbs and Co. was preceded by the fuller-named company and then went out business for a time before coming back under a slightly altered name. Again, it appears tthe Stubbs family had several businesses involved in this trade.

It also appears they worked in co-operation, with different members of the family running separate firms from various addresses. For example, Samuel

Stubbs ran his own firm and he lived at 109, Greenway Road, which was the postal address for the firm run by Robert Stubbs.

Company name:	Samuel Stubbs
Nature of maritime business:	"Carpenter"/shipwright
	Shipbuilding?/ship repair
Years of business:	?–?
Ship or boat yard name:	1. Percival Lane
	2. Belvedere Yard
Yard location:	?

Further information: This was the business later taken-over by Samuel Stubbs' Son, John Stubbs, who later moved to Old Quay. See entry for John Stubbs and Sons, above.

Company name:	Ira Withington
Nature of maritime business:	Shipwright
Years of business:	1923?–1933?
Ship or boat yard name:	Percival Lane M or B?
Yard location:	?

Further information: Presumably, the Withington formerly in partnership with LeCouteur (see earlier entry).

Note: See entries for Bridgewater concern and M.S.C. Co., above and for Ron Turner, below.

Note: All the above firms operated on/near Percival Lane (although some had facilities elsewhere also), which was clearly another busy maritime scene.

Due to them having addresses in Percival Lane, it could be the boatyard on the Sevastopol Arm off the New Line of Locks was used by these firms above, or perhaps they leased the graving grid or dock at Bridgewater Docks (all firms bar Mick Mills).

Weston Point Docks/Port Weston

Company name:	Richard Abel and Sons
Nature of maritime business:	Repair of own vessels only?
Years of business:	?–?
Ship or boat yard name:	Weston Point
Yard location:	?

Note: See entry for Richard Abel and Sons, above.

Company name:	Bob Bowes
Nature of maritime business:	Bespoke Narrowboat and barge builder (Incl. Dutch barges)
Years of business:	?–Present

Ship or boat yard name:

1. Yard at Weaver Industrial Estate, Garston. N/A

?–Present

2. Yard at Port Weston, Runcorn. *

?–Present

(Both yards occupied simultaneously from 200?).

Yard location: ?

(All built to order and designed by computer; the plans are given to steel mills for cutting the sections, which are then fabricated at the yards and outfitted with every conceivable modern convenience, from hot-tub to sauna and with master en suite bedroom and up to two more bedrooms).

(Also aids John White – See Addendum to Cheshire Shipyards; List for Garston)

Company name:	Charles Hickson
Nature of maritime business:	?
Years of business:	1815?–?
Ship or boat yard name:	Weston Point
Yard location:	?

Further information: When the partnership of William Wright and Charles Hickson dissolved, the former carried-on at Mersey Street and the latter went into business on his own at Weston Point. He later opened a yard at Ellesmere Port.

Charles Hickson built up a good business in shipbuilding and repair, as well as in the leisure industry. He advertised bath houses and a hotel in Ellesmere Port and chartered some steamers from Runcorn. Unfortunately, one of these steamers sank during a heavy storm in the Mersey in December 1822 and he made great losses. Eight people died, public confidence was shook and passenger numbers were still low when it came to the end of Hickson's lease on the yard in 1823. He went bankrupt and still owed money to the Ellesmere Canal Company. (Information from *Waterways Journal, Vol. 15*, "Ship and Boat Building at Ellesmere Port: A History" by Terry Kavanagh).

Company name: Upper Mersey Navigation Commission
Nature of maritime business: Minor repairs to own vessels?
Repair of buoys and markers
Years of business: ?–?
Ship or boat yard name: Next to Weston Point Docks
Yard location: ?

Further information: The U.M.N.C. had its yard here and may well have conducted minor repairs and routine maintenance to its vessels at the facility alongside its work maintaining the buoys and markers of the River Mersey.

Preston Brook

Company name: ?
Nature of maritime business: Builders of GRP cabin cruisers
Years of business: 1950s/1960s
Ship or boat yard name: The old sheds, Preston Brook
Yard location: ?

My father, Ian, remembers there being a firm here at the old transhipment sheds in the late 1950s or early 1960s and he took a couple of photos of its boats on his Box Brownie camera.

Company name: Claymoore Navigation Ltd.
Nature of maritime business: Boat maintainer/servicer, Emergency repairer,
painter and outfitter
Years of business: 1973–Present
Ship or boat yard name: The Wharf, Preston Brook (Yard) B
Tel.: 01928 717273
Lo-Call 0845 0900180
Yard location: ?

Company name: Inland Waterway Holiday Cruises Ltd.
Nature of maritime business: Boat rebuilder/repairer of own narrowboats
Years of business: 1968?–?
Ship or boat yard name: 1. Railway Shed, Preston Brook B
2. New Shed, Preston Brook B
Yard location: ?

Further information: The late Peter Froud was one of the founders of the Inland Waterways Museum at Ellesmere Port.

Company name: Venture (Venture Canoes and Venture Kayaks)
                              Pyranha Whitewater Kayaks
                              P&H Custom Sea Kayaks
                              Pyranha Mouldings Ltd.

Nature of maritime business: Builders of GRP canoes/kayaks, small boats
and paddles/equipment and boat repairers

Years of business: 1971–present

Ship or boat yard name:

1. Various locations in Warrington (see entry under Warrington)
(1971–June 1979).
2. Marina Village, Preston Brook (Boat yard/factory). B/*
3. Production at Brindley Road, Astmoor Industrial Estate (factory) *
(1986–1990).
4. Marina Village.
5. Rivington Road (Factory) * (1999–2010)
(Office and development based at marina village throughout 1986–2010
period).
6. Unit 1, Premier Point,
Aston Lane South,
Whitehouse Industrial Estate
(Factory) * (2010–present)
Tel.: 01928 716666
Fax: 01928 714399
sales@pyranha.com

Yard location: ?

Note: Sales came under the company name of Kayaks North West, on the
telephone number, 01928 710770.

Pyranha US, Inc. was established in 2002 (at 2004-J Riverside Drive, Asheville,
NC 28804) to promote sales there.

Note: In 2004, Pyranha took over P&H Custom Sea Kayaks of West Hallam,
Derbyshire.

Note: In 2005, Pyranha took over Mobile Adventure, changing name to
Venture, with two sister companies, Venture Canoes and Venture Kayaks.

See www.marygordon.org.uk/marygordon.htm

Company name: Ron Turner

Nature of maritime business: Wood and steel boat builder

Boat owner, Canal carrier
Water can manufacturer
Pottery manufacturer
Years of business: 1966/7?–2003?
Ship or boat yard name:

1. Later site of marina village (co-located with Peter Froud, above?) B
   1966/7? – ?.
2. Packet dry dock, Top Locks B 1968?–?.
2. Stott's Yard B (Former Timmin's Yard (Stott's was a shipping agent) (two/three years?).
3. No. 2 and No. 3 Building, Runcorn Dock estate (Near salt works) * (two years?).
4. Frodsham (At the Old Mill) *
   1980? –?
5. Boat and butty yard B
   1980?–2003?.
   (Welding and launching some boats here that he built in Frodsham as well as doing whole builds at this location).

Yard location: ?

Ron Turner was a motor mechanic at Crosville's bus depot in Runcorn, where he met and befriended then conductor and current author and photographer Roy Gough.

In around 1966, he got involved in boat building at various locations in and around Runcorn. Peter Froud helped him get started on a boat rescued from the Bridgewater Canal and he was originally in partnership with an employee of Froud; a man from London called Peter Shrubs. Later, he worked alone and he built around fifteen boats at various locations.

He later started a canal carrying company and was one of the last men involved in the business, bringing the last four boatloads of salt into Weston Point, among other activities such as running coal between Runcorn, Manchester and Macclesfield. Very keen on canal history (with Jesse Wallwork one of his ancestors), he also became involved in manufacturing watering cans (a business his son now continues) and pottery; both very much canal industries.

Ron Turner started boat building in the days when he remembers four dockyards in Runcorn and the shipwrights would often stop, watch him and pass comment as he worked. He was taught many things such as steam-bending planks by Jimmy LeCouteur, a shipwright who once worked for canal carrier

Jonathon Horsefield and Simpson Davies, and later for Peter Froud. He was a brother of my great uncle Frank.

Ron Turner's wife Hazel's maiden name was Wight and she is from the family who may be cousins to my grandfather, George Ratcliffe. Her aunt married a Bill Ratcliffe, hence the connection. I am still researching the connection to the family of my friends and potential relatives Brian Ratcliffe and Elaine Slevin, who are siblings.

Note: All the above firms operated in Preston Brook, which was clearly another busy maritime scene.

Other Places in Runcorn

Company name:	The Boat and Butty Co.
Nature of maritime business:	Provide facilities for clients to use for repair of own boats? And possibly, narrowboat builders/rebuilders? Sailmaker
Years of business:	Early 1980s–present
Ship or boat yard name:	Ockleston's Wharf
	Ringway Road
	(Yard and slipway? dry dock?) B
	Tel.: 01928 569069/574259 ?
	Mob.?: 0(7)976 303 696
	enquiry@boatandbutty.co.uk or
	boatandbutty@fs2.com?
	Early 1980's–present?
Yard location:	?

Further information: See entries on Ian Riley and the Wooden Canal Craft Trust, in this section, and for Ron Turner, above.

Company name:	Joseph Clarke
Nature of maritime business:	Flat builder?
Years of business:	1867? - ?
Ship or boat yard name:	?
Yard location:	?

Company name:	Drammen Maritime (U.K.) Ltd
Nature of maritime business:	Naval architects and marine engineers
Years of business:	1984?–1987?

Ship or boat yard name:	1. 7, Kirkstone Crescent, Cloughwood 1984?–1985?
	2. Widnes (see separate entry) 1985?–1987?
Yard location:	?

Facilities, know-how and people to provide the following services to owners, large consultants, new-building and repair yards; classification drawings for hull and machinery; hull and steel structure drawings; arrangement drawings, hull and machinery; engine room layout and pipe diagrams including isometrics; accommodation plans and arrangements; ventilation systems; technical surveys for repair and conversion; new-building from specification through to supervision and delivery; outline specifications for tendering purposes; Use of CAD/CAM.

Through association with Norwegian companies Drammen Maritime – Hokksund, Isasco A/S and Drammen Ship Services A/S, can also supply and install all kinds of marine equipment for offshore oil/gas rigs as well as ships.

Company name:	William Dunbavand
Nature of maritime business:	"Ship's carpenter"
Years of business:	1880s/90s?–?
Ship or boat yard name:	?
Yard location:	?

Further information: Percy Dunbavand is a friend of the family of the author, who used to work with the author's grandfather George Ratcliffe on the M.S.C. Co. tugs. His ancestors were involved in shipbuilding and, although styled as a ship's carpenter, William Dunbavand was a shipbuilder or repairer. He later ran the Conservative Club.

Company name:	William Evans
Nature of maritime business:	"Shipbuilder"
Years of business:	1823?–?
Ship or boat yard name:	Probably the same as the "W. Evans" operating in 1840.
Yard location:	?

Company name:	Jones
Nature of maritime business:	Boat builders?

Years of business:	?–?
Ship or boat yard name:	?
Yard location:	?

Further information: Evidence solely an entry on Jim Shead's The Boat Listing website.

Company name:	Tim Leech
Nature of maritime business:	Boat Repairer?
Years of business:	? - Present
Ship or boat yard name:	Dutton dry dock т (the former North Staffordshire Railway dry dock) (see entry on North Staffordshire Railway).
Yard location:	?
	www.hnboc.org.uk/links/services.htm

Company name:	North Staffordshire Railway
Nature of maritime business:	Own tunnel tugs
Years of business:	1846 - 1923
Ship or boat yard name:	Covered dry dock, southern end of repair of Dutton Tunnel т (see entry on Tim Leech)
Yard location:	?

Company name:	William Martin
Nature of maritime business:	"Shipbuilder"
Years of business:	1823?–?
Ship or boat yard name:	?
Yard location:	?

Company name:	Robert Mitchell
Nature of maritime business:	?
Years of business:	1800?–?
Ship or boat yard name:	?
Yard location:	?

Further information: This information is all from *Waterways Journal Vol. 8*, "Sailing Flats on the Chester and Ellesmere Canals" by Terry Kavanagh.

Company name:	G. and J. Reeves
Nature of maritime business:	Boat Repairers?

Years of business: ?–?
Ship or boat yard name: Tel.: 01928 815581
Yard location: ?

Further information: This company was in Warwickshire, but I have found a reference to it under the Runcorn telephone number above.

Company name: William Rigby
Nature of maritime business: Wooden paddle steamer builder?
Years of business: 1816?–?
Ship or boat yard name: ?
Yard location: ?

Company name: Ian Riley
Nature of maritime business: Boat rebuilder/repairer
Years of business: Early 1980s–present?
Ship or boat yard name:
1. Boat and Butty Co.'s Yard B Early 1980s–2001
2. Dutton dry dock? T (according to the Boat and Butty Co.) 2001–?
Yard location: ?

Company name: Scenic Boat Builders Ltd.
Nature of maritime business: Bespoke narrowboat builders
Years of business: ? -?
Ship or boat yard name:
1. 38, Wenlock Road, Cloughwood
2. Boat and Butty Co.'s Yard? B
3. Aqueduct Marina, The Outlanes, Church Minshull, Nantwich N/A
   (Office remains at 38 Wenlock Road)
Yard location: ?

Company name: John Weedall
Nature of maritime business: Flat builder?
Years of business: 1824?–?
Ship or boat yard name: ?
Yard location: ?

Company name: Waterworth Boats Ltd.
Nature of maritime business: Narrowboat builders

Years of business:	?–present
Ship or boat yard name:	130 Boston Avenue
Yard location:	?

Company name:	Wooden Canal Craft Trust/Wooden Canal
Nature of maritime business:	Boat Society Restoration/rebuilding of historic boats
Years of business:	1987?–present

Ship or boat yard name:
1. Boat and Butty Co.'s Yard B (1987?–1999?)
2. Heritage Boat Yard in Stalybridge N/A (1999?–present)
3. Also used Bridgewater Motor Boat Club's Yard (At least for the rebuilding of the narrowboat HAZEL) B
(See entry under Other Building and Repair Facilities of Runcorn, below).

Yard location:	?

Note: The existence of the ferry at Runcorn suggests some sort of boat building experience was known in the town since the medieval period the service started in.

The ferry is believed to have been established in 1178, although this is not confirmed. It is also likely the local barons (Halton and Widnes baronies) kept their own boats for passage across the Mersey.

An earlier ferry may have existed in Roman times, between Ditton and Runcorn. This may instead have been a ford, or may not have actually existed as there seems scant evidence to prove this.

Note: The existence of the ferry at Thelwall suggests some sort of boat building experience was known in the area since the medieval times the service started in; but was this at Runcorn (within which Parish Thelwall traditionally resided) or within what is now the boundary of Warrington (where Thelwall is now a part)?

Note: The existence since at least medieval times of fisheries at Runcorn and nearby again suggests some sort of boat building and repair industry locally in existence. The Mersey was famed for its salmon and also teemed with trout, sparling, herring, lampries, and eels (eel was a popular dish known locally as snig). There were fisheries mentioned in the Domesday Book at Halton, Weston, and Aston. Fish garths (staked nets anchored to the river bed) existed within the Runcorn fishery and two of these belonged to the Abbot of Norton (they were named, Charity and Gracedieu). There was also the granting of rights by the barons of Halton to individuals to fish. One such was Philip de Orreby, who was allowed a boat and one net within the limits of Halton.

Sturgeon were also known to spawn in the upper reaches of the Mersey and, although these were a royal fish and thus to be presented to the king if caught (via the king's steward of Halton Castle for those caught locally), there are legal records concerning those who fished these without giving them up to the sovereign.

Finally, there were shellfish beds in the Mersey Estuary and these might have been as far inland as Runcorn due to the cockle, mussel and oyster shells found during the excavations of Norton Priory.

Note: Old Runcorn states that shipbuilding and repair began in Runcorn in 1790, although the author of that book, Starkey, shows records in his earlier work *Schooner Port* of vessels built there from 1778 and a comment that Runcorn shipbuilding began in the late 18th Century. He also says Runcorn "had no tradition for shipbuilding" prior to 1790, but that undoubtedly "small craft were repaired on primitive slipways" there. The presence of a ferry at Runcorn since medieval times also suggests some boat building and repairing experience, however simple, was to be found locally since that period. The ferry was originally at Boat House Pool (which was at the site of the later Old Quay Docks), but was moved by the Bridgewater Trustees a quarter of a mile upstream to a place which then became known as Ferry Hut. Its service lasted until 1905.

Nickson, writing of the year 1821, states in his *History of Runcorn* that "there must have been some boat building or repairing at this time but the trade does not seem to have been of sufficient importance to merit a notice or to be added to the annual value of the town".

Nickson goes on to say (whilst discussing the shipyard of J. Sothern) that by 1836, "shipbuilding had now become a staple industry of the town, and two other shipyards were under the management of the late Messrs. Samuel Mason and John Anderton respectively".

Later in that tome, Nickson says of Runcorn in the 1880s that "its industries comprise the manufacture of the various alkalies and acids, the making of soap, ship and boat building, the smelting of lead, silver refining, copper extraction, the making of steam engines, gas plant and well sinking apparatus, tanning, the extraction and distilling of glycerine...".

Shipbuilding grew out of an earlier repair industry and became permanent, going on to gain what Starkey calls "something of a national prestige for the building of small coastal craft". Runcorn shipwrights became "widely esteemed for their expertise", according to *Schooner Port*.

Shipbuilding at Runcorn ended with the building of the Manchester Ship Canal from 1888, although ship repair and boat building and repair continued well into the Twentieth century.

Note: Boatyard at end of Sebastopol Arm, Bridgewater Docks: Bridgewater or one of several firms operating at Percival Lane? B

Note: An aerial photograph of this yard shows what appears to be a patent slipway (side).

Were either the graving grid or dock at Bridgewater Docks leased by Stubbs? B/M

Note: It is probable the relatively large number of ship and boat builders/ repairers in the then small town of Runcorn of the late Nineteenth/early Twentieth centuries shared the public slipway at Old Quay (perhaps leasing it for a set period once winning a contract for work) and perhaps other facilities also, such as the packet dry dock at Top Locks.

Note: Percy Dunbavand states some ship repair work was conducted on ships left high and dry at low water, lying in the River Mersey. I am not sure which firms conducted this work. Perhaps several were involved. I have seen at least one photograph of a sailing ship lying alongside the wharf extending west of Castle Rock Yard, looking to be under inspection or repair.

Note: The many local fishing vessels owned and registered locally may well have been repaired in the same manner discussed above, beaching them and awaiting low tide to conduct repairs. A clutch of pictures shows some boats being painted and worked while beached to the immediate west of the Runcorn Ferry waiting room at the end of Castle Rock wharf.

Note: A great deal of investigating still needs to be done but it seems highly likely all the concerns run by men named Stubbs must be related. Charles, Fred, John ("Jack"), Peter, Robert and Samuel Stubbs were all engaged in shipbuilding or repair at various times within the town of Runcorn.

Samuel Stubbs was the father of Jack Stubbs, who in turn fathered Fred Stubbs; the former two worked in business with Robert Stubbs. The remaining two men (Charles and Peter Stubbs) may also be related.

The court agreement that led to the founding of John Stubbs and Sons was signed by himself (John Stubbs of Percival Lane), his father (Samuel Stubbs of "Belvidere"), William Shingler Stubbs of Percival Lane, and James Stubbs of Percival Lane.

Note: The trade union Runcorn Shipwrights was formed in 1871 and joined the Associated Shipwrights' Society in 1892.

Other Building and Repair Facilities of Runcorn

Company name:	Bridgewater Motor Boat Club
Nature of maritime business:	Repair of members' boats
Years of business:	1952–present
Ship or boat yard name:	Victoria Dockyard B
	The former Sprinch Yard (slipway [F&A], crane and dry dock)
	1956?–present.
	The slipway is not a patent slip. It is sited on the former double dry dock at the north of the islet.
	Also, the packet dry dock at Top Locks
	1956–its infilling.
Yard location:	?

Company name:	Public Dry Dock
Nature of maritime business:	Facilities for users to repair own boats
Years of business:	?–1956?
Ship or boat yard name:	The former Sprinch Yard B
Yard location:	?

Company name:	Top Locks
Nature of maritime business:	Facility can be used to repair users' own boats
Years of business:	?–?
Ship or boat yard name:	Small crane and plot of land at site of former Simpson, Davies Coal Yard B
	(crane used to haul boats on to quayside)
Yard location:	?

Further information: I believe some repair of vessels was conducted at Top Locks even into quite recent times (cabin cruisers included) using the old cranes there and with boats hauled on to the quayside.

There is some photographic evidence to support this theory as I have heard at least one person say they had seen such a sight, and I have myself seen a photo from the Waterways Archive (maintained by the Ellesmere Port Boat Museum) that seems to show this.

Company name:	Weaver Motor Boat Club
Nature of maritime business:	Repair of Members' boats
Years of business:	?–present
Ship or boat yard name:	Patent Slipway Class 2 (F&A) and dock, Ashville Point WN (formerly Ashville Industrial Estate) (Clifton) (Sight of Abel's depot and repair yard) (Before World War II–present)
Yard location:	?

Further information: Apparently, the old coal dock for Parker's (?) steel works was bought by Abel's and used as a depot for its sand lighterage business. A slipway (F&A) was built, but was abandoned, as it proved impossible to haul barges out of the water at the steep angle it was built on.

The land now belongs to the Aston Estate but has been leased to the Weaver Motor Boat Club since before World War II. It managed to make a narrower slipway for smaller vessels, using discarded sections of the old railway line that used to run to the steel works. The rails of the old barge slipway can still be seen outside the newer ones.

Company name:	Public Slipway?
Nature of maritime business:	?
Years of business:	?
Ship or boat yard name:	Former Abbott and Walton Yard at Big Pool
Yard location:	?

Further information: Ron Turner remembers at least one vessel being slipped here in the days after Abbott and Walton had closed.

Marine Engine Builders at Runcorn

Company name:	A. Barton Engineering Works
Nature of maritime business:	Marine auxiliary builders

Years of business: ?–?
Ship or boat yard name: Victoria Works
Yard location: Beside Big Pool

Further information: Main Works at St Helens Junction, with other works at Runcorn and at South? Works, Sunderland. There was also a London office.

According to Ron Turner, the Barton Yard was on the Sprinch, so probably was on Big Pool besides the other works known by the name Victoria.

Mr Turner remembers them building boats as well as doing heavy engineering, including work for the Navy, such as building winches, etc.(See entry under Big Pool).

Company name: E. Timmins and Sons Ltd.
Nature of maritime business: Steam engine builders
"Engineer, millwright and ironfounder"
Manufacturer of diving apparatus
Years of business: 1827–1955?
Ship or boat yard name: Bridgewater Foundry and Engineering Works B
Yard location: Heath Road

Further information: According to an article in the Ray Miller column of the *Runcorn Weekly News*, this firm built several marine engines for locally-built vessels.

Note: A *Runcorn Directory* loaned to me by Percy Dunbavand says John Timmins and Co., Engineer was based at Halton Road; it follows another piece dated 1860 but it may be from a different year. Perhaps he had undertaken some marine engineering work in connection with his namesake.

At its height, the company employed more than 200 people.

Ebenezer Timmins took over the foundry from Crippen sometime during the decade 1851 to 1861. According to Nickson's *History of Runcorn*; 1827 is perhaps the date of the foundry's building rather than the Timmin family involvement (see entry for Ship and Boat Builders and Repairers of Runcorn).

Company name: James Troop and Co. Ltd. Group
Nature of maritime business: "Diesel, Gas and dual fuel engineers, remote monitoring of prime movers, generator and pump specialists, spare parts"
Years of business: ?–present
Ship or boat yard name: 1. Liverpool

2. 4 Davy Road, Astmoor Industrial Estate,
WA7 1PZ
Tel.: 01928 566170
Fax: 01928 577314
sales@jamestroop.co.uk
www.jamestroop.co.uk

Yard location: ?

Further information: Group of companies includes: Brooks Diesel Services
Ltd., Gen Power Ltd.

Other Engineering Firms with a Maritime Interest at Runcorn

Company name:	Henry Branch and Sons
Nature of maritime business:	Engineers
Years of business:	1827–1955?
Ship or boat yard name:	Foundry and engineering works at Basin side, Weston Point (beside Wright's Dock) Also at another location in Weston Point, further along the waterfront towards Clifton
Yard location:	?

Further information: The firm conducted repairs to ship's soilers and other
fittings.

Also: Manufacturers of buoys used on the River Mersey (see notes at the end
of the Section on Ancillary Industries at Runcorn).

Branch's may have later been owned or associated with the E. Timmins
and Sons firm, according to recollections of the author's father, George Ian
Ratcliffe.

Makers of Masts and Spars at Runcorn

Company name:	John Rawlinson/Rollinson
Nature of maritime business:	Block, mast and pump maker
Years of business:	?–?
Ship or boat yard name:	Top Locks B
Yard location:	?

(See entry under Ship and Boat Builders and Repairers of Runcorn)

Naval Architects at Runcorn

Company name: Euro Marine Consultants Ltd.
Nature of maritime business: Naval architects and marine surveyors (boats)
Years of business: ?–Present
Ship or boat yard name: Marine Lodge
                              PO Box 22
                              WA7 6FA
                              01928 719566/278
                              surveyors@euro-marine.com
Yard location: ?

Related Industries at Runcorn

Company name: John Pope
Nature of maritime business: Inland craft surveyor
Years of business: ?–Present?
Ship or boat yard name: See Euro Marine, above.
                              01928 719566
Yard location: ?

Company name: Peter Sweet
Nature of maritime business: Boat surveyor/examiner
Years of business: ?–present
Ship or boat yard name: 01932 712260/07803 176382
                              pmsboatsurveysltd@tiscali.co.uk
Yard location: ?

Further information: Other companies were likely to have been involved in some form of survey work on vessels locally for insurance purposes but one such national company working partly in this field was Cornhill Insurance.

The author's father worked for Cornhill for a period and it was during this time he completed survey work on the pleasure boat TENACITY and hence met and befriended her builder and owner, the late Reg Lindop. TENACITY was moored at Preston Brook Marina and hence fell under the area of responsibility of Ian Ratcliffe.

Ancillary Industries at Runcorn
Sailmakers at Runcorn

There were a number of sail-making lofts, and a variety of firms such as:

Company name:	Richard Abel
Nature of maritime business:	"Sailmaker, canvas merchant and general ship chandler"/"sailmaker and canal carrier"
Years of business:	?–?
Ship or boat yard name:	Washington Buildings, Top Locks
Yard location:	?

(See entry under Ship and Boat Builders and Repairers of Runcorn)

Company name:	The Boat and Butty Co.
Nature of maritime business:	"Polypropylene tarpaulins, manmade and natural fibre rope, boat fenders, all kinds of ropework – full splicing service"
Years of business:	?–present
Ship or boat yard name:	As per the entry under Ship and Boat Builders and Repairers of Runcorn Tel. 01928 573028
Yard location:	?

(See entry under Ship and Boat Builders and Repairers of Runcorn)

Company name:	Thomas Chadwick
Nature of maritime business:	?
Years of business:	?–?
Ship or boat yard name:	Top Locks B
Yard location:	?

(See entry in section on Runcorn Rope and Twine Makers)

Company name:	William Cooper
Nature of maritime business:	"Rigger, sail and tent maker, maker of flags and seller of ropes"
Years of business:	?–?
Ship or boat yard name:	
1. High Street 1850?–?	
2. Mill Street 1874?–?	
3. Waterloo Bridge, Top Locks 1892?–?	
Yard location:	?

Company name:	Cooper and Hudson
Nature of maritime business:	"Sail, tarpauling and oil cloth manufacturers"

Years of business: 1834?–?
Ship or boat yard name: ?
Yard location: ?

Presumably, the same Cooper as above and presumably the Hudson as mentioned later in this list (see entry below).

Company name: Robert Davies
Nature of maritime business: Sailmaker
Years of business: 1850?–?
Ship or boat yard name: Top Locks
Yard location: ?

Company name: Greigs
Nature of maritime business: "Tarpaulin makers"/sail makers and fender-makers
Industrial textile manufacturer
Manufacturers of tarpaulins, covers, banners and flags
Years of business: 1923–present
Ship or boat yard name:

1. Waterloo Hotel (rented premises).
2. Waterloo Road Building (rented top loft above Bridgewater Stables/ "Duke's Stables") (Former Canal Horse Stables). Later owned the whole building, which became known as Greig's Buildings. 1923?–1975
2. Robert "Bob" Grieg (former Mariner's Mission)
   The Mariners' Hall,
   Irwell Lane
   1975–present
   Sales and general information: dawn@robertgreig.co.uk
   Production enquiries: dave@robertgreig.co.uk
   Website enquiries: matt@robertgreig.co.uk
   www.robertgreig.co.uk
Yard location: ?

Company name: Fred Hayes
Nature of maritime business: Sailmaker
Years of business: ?–?

Ship or boat yard name: Waterloo Road
Yard location: ?
Also: Grocer

Company name: Hayes and Sproston
Nature of maritime business: Sailmakers
Years of business: 1874?–?
Ship or boat yard name: Ferry slip
Yard location: ?
Further information: Presumably related to the above firm.

Company name: George Hudson
Nature of maritime business: Sailmaker
Years of business: 1850?–?
Ship or boat yard name: Mersey Street
Yard location: ?
Further information: Presumably the same man who at one time was in partnership with Cooper (see entry above).

Company name: William Meadows
Nature of maritime business: Sailmaker, ship chandler
Years of business: ?–?
Ship or boat yard name: High Street
Yard location: ?

Company name: Wm. Mothersill
Nature of maritime business: "Yarn and cloth manufacturer"
Years of business: 1860?
Ship or boat yard name: Heath House
Yard location: ?

Company name: Edwin Pritchard
Nature of maritime business: Sailmaker
Years of business: 1906?–1922?
Ship or boat yard name: 8 Waterloo Road
Yard location: ?

Company name: W and A Pritchard
Nature of maritime business: "Rope and canvas merchants"
Years of business: 1934?–?
Ship or boat yard name: Duke Street
Yard location: ?
Further information: Were they also manufacturers?

Company name: Rathbone and Dutton
Nature of maritime business: Sailmakers
Years of business: 1874?–?
Ship or boat yard name: Top Locks
Yard location: ?

Company name: Samuel Ravenscroft
Nature of maritime business: "Sailcloth manufacturer"
                                       "Sail, stack cover and cart sheet maker"
                                       Ship chandler
Years of business: ?–?
Ship or boat yard name: 8 Waterloo Road
Yard location: ?
Further information: Perhaps related to my cousin Matthew's wife, Helen, but I have not proved this yet.

Company name: The Runcorn Marquee and Sail Co. Ltd.
Nature of maritime business: "Sail makers"
Years of business: 1924?–1939?
Ship or boat yard name: Station Road 1924?–1934?
                                       Waterloo Road 1934?–1939?
Yard location: ?

Company name: William Rhodes
Nature of maritime business: (Sailmaker to the Bridgewater Trustees).
Years of business: ?–?
Ship or boat yard name: Wellington Street
Yard location: ?

Company name: Ann Speakman
Nature of maritime business: ?

Years of business:	?–?
Ship or boat yard name:	Castle Rock
Yard location:	?

Further information: (Wife or daughter of Speakman the shipbuilder?).

Company name:	Wm. Wrench
Nature of maritime business:	"Sail maker"
Years of business:	1834? V ?
Ship or boat yard name:	?
Yard location:	?

Further information: Related to the Wrench family of the author's Aunt Chris?

Christine Wrench married my uncle, (Frederick) Harry Ratcliffe (who incidentally, before going to sea with the N.Z.S.Co., served as lock boy at Old Quay).

Note: According to *Schooner Port*, there were "half a dozen" sailmaking firms in Runcorn in 1859.

Note: According to an article from the *Runcorn Weekly News* of 22nd May 2008 (taken from a talk given by Earle Ryan, the son-in-law of Runcorn sailmaker Bob Greig and a friend and former neighbour of my uncle Harry Ratcliffe), when Bob Greig started in the business of sailmaking in the 1920s, there were "already half a dozen sailmaking lofts in Runcorn".

Riggers

There were also those who rigged newly built vessels as well as repairing them.

Company name:	John Bate
Nature of maritime business:	Rigger
Years of business:	?–1883?
Ship or boat yard name:	?
Yard location:	?

Rope and Twine Makers at Runcorn

There were a number of ropemakers (and apparently three ropewalks/rope-works – including one along the new line of locks from Top Locks to the Bridgewater/Runcorn Docks according to maps of 1873/1874 and 1938).

Company name: Bridgewater Navigation Co.
Nature of maritime business: Steam ropery
Years of business: ?–?
Ship or boat yard name: Top Locks
Yard location: ?
(See below)

Company name: Thomas Chadwick
Nature of maritime business: Residential: Clarence Terrace
Years of business: ?–?
Ship or boat yard name: Top Locks
Yard location: ?
(See entry in section on Runcorn Sailmakers)

Note: According to Nickson's *History of Runcorn* states there was "a new steam ropery now owned by the Bridgewater Navigation Co. at Top Locks" worked by Mr. D. Chadwick of Liverpool.

     Was this originally in the hands of the Chadwick family and then bought by the Bridgewater Navigation Co. or vice versa?

Company name: William Chadwick
Nature of maritime business: ?
Years of business: ?–?
Ship or boat yard name: Bentinck Street
Yard location: ?

Company name: Chadwick, Daniels and Co.
Nature of maritime business: Ropemakers
Years of business: 1850? –?
Ship or boat yard name: Top Locks
Yard location: ?
Related to the above firms?

Company name: William Clarke
Nature of maritime business: Ropemaker, ship owner
Years of business: ? –?
Ship or boat yard name: ?
Yard location: ?

Mentioned in *Schooner Port* as a local ship owner but was he Runcorn-based?

Company name: Charles Harrison
Nature of maritime business: ?
Years of business: ? –?
Ship or boat yard name: Duke's Dock
Yard location: ?

Company name: George Howard
Nature of maritime business: ?
Years of business: 1850?–?
Ship or boat yard name: 1. High Street
2. Waterloo Road – Rope Walk high up the road
Yard location: ?

Presumably related to the above firm.

Company name: William Howard
Nature of maritime business: Ropemaker
Years of business: 1874?–?
Ship or boat yard name: Waterloo Road
Yard location: ?

Company name: John Johnson
Nature of maritime business: ?
Years of business: ?–?
Ship or boat yard name: Waterloo Road
Yard location: ?

Also: Farmer, land owner, soap factory owner, turpentine works owner, slate shop owner.

The executors of John Johnson, Hayes and Ollier, then ran the late entrepreneurs businesses (namely his turpentine works, soap works and the rope works, above) before his sons, John Junior and Thomas, took over in 1821(?).

(See entry on T. and J. Johnson in the section on Runcorn Ship and Boat Builders)

Company name: Hayes, Ollier and Company
Nature of maritime business: ?

Years of business: 1821?–1828?
Ship or boat yard name: As previous entry
Yard location: ?
Also: Soap works owners and rosin and turpentine works owners.

Company name: Johnson and Briddons
Nature of maritime business: ?
Years of business: 1828?–at least 1834
Ship or boat yard name: As previous entry
Yard location: ?
Also: Soap boilers.

Company name: W and A Pritchard
Nature of maritime business: Rope and canvas merchants
Years of business: 1934?–?
Ship or boat yard name: Duke Street
Yard location: ?
Were they also manufacturers?

Note: According to *Schooner Port*, there were four rope-making firms in Runcorn in 1859 and there were rope walks in Percival Lane and Rutland Street, one of which was steam-powered.

There were also:

Anchor smiths and chain makers (such as John Matthew Paul Arran, cable chain manufacturer of Halton Road [who set up business in the old acid works sometime between 1841 and 1851] and John Ravenscroft, cable chain manufacturer of Waterloo Road); block and pump makers (such as Ellen Lovatt of Top Locks); a copper, iron and tin plate worker and "Brass and Other Fog Horn Maker" (R. Hampson) and makers of ship's stoves.

Nickson's *History of Runcorn* says "The chain works had given place to the Ellesmere Lint Company" in the decade 1851 to 1861. Where this chain works was and who operated it is not made clear in the book.

There was, according to Starkey, one firm that supplied (made?) ship's lamps and one that supplied (made?) navigation buoys (was this Walter Barr, the tinsmith mentioned in the main text for building the buoys on the Upper Mersey, or is it in reference to Henry Branch and Sons, whom I also believe to have been engaged in this business?).

Today there is J.L.T. (based at The Heath Business and Technical Park), which provides computer systems for various needs. The firm won a contract in January 2009 to provide rugged computer systems for Plymouth-based mini-submarine builders Marlin Submarines.

Also today, there is Cloudis Limited, another company based at The Heath Business and Technical Park and which provides a system called Cloudis Configuration Managed Project Integrated Capability (C.M.P.I.C.). It advertises this as a system for shipyards to provide a "range of capabilities from design, through installation planning and the management of the initial process".

On top of this, there is a further company at The Heath Business Park called Polymorph Ltd. that produces a system for integration of computers between allied warships.

Wood Group PSN is an international company with a workforce of 28,000. It has a branch in Runcorn, which expanded from 80 staff in 2011 to more than 300 in 2013. It offers a range of services to the on and offshore oil and gas industries, including construction, rigging, pipe-fitting, instruments, mechanical, electrical and plating/welding.

Furthermore, there is Halton Fabrications Ltd., which since 1973 has provided services for Admiralty shipyards, installing and relocating plant equipment.

And on a final note, Daresbury Laboratories has developed technologies to help preserve the ancient timbers of King Henry VIII's former flag ship MARY ROSE.

Hull Cleaners and Ship Painters at Runcorn

There were firms that specialised in these two trades and would have had to use their own or another's slipways or other facilities, such as dry docks.

Company name:	Francis Gallagher
Nature of maritime business:	"Marine artist"
Years of business:	?–?
Ship or boat yard name:	58 Ashridge Street
Yard location:	?

(Was he a painter of pictures or did he gild/decorate ships' figureheads?).

Company name:	Joseph Pegg
Nature of maritime business:	Hull cleaning and painting services to owners

of iron vessels (using "Pegg's Prepared Composition")

Years of business: ?–?
Ship or boat yard name: Loch Street
Yard location: ?
Also a Mersey pilot

Company name: George Yarwood
Nature of maritime business: Painter
Years of business: ?–1883?
Ship or boat yard name: ?
Yard location: ?

Frodsham

Company name: George Edwards
Nature of maritime business: Shipbuilder
Years of business: 1798?–1805?
Ship or boat yard name: Frodsham Bridge
Yard location: ?

This information is all from *Waterways Journal Vol. 8*, "Sailing Flats on the Chester and Ellesmere Canals" by Terry Kavanagh.

Company name: Frodsham Water Sports
Nature of maritime business: Jet ski and boat repairers and converters
Years of business: ?–present
Ship or boat yard name: Frodsham Bridge
(Frodsham side)
(Yard and slipway [F&A]) RW
128 Bridge Lane,
Frodsham,
WA6 7HZ
Tel. and Fax: 01928 733187
Yard location: ?

Company name: William Hayes
Nature of maritime business: "Shipbuilder and slate merchant"; flat and shipbuilders?
Years of business: 1795?–1816

Ship or boat yard name: Frodsham Bridge RW

Yard location: ?

Also: Slate merchant.

Company name: Mulvey and Evans

Later moved from Frodsham and operated from Chester and (then?) Liverpool. Firm dissolved in 1820.

Company name: Ron Turner

Nature of maritime business: ?

Years of business: ?–?

Ship or boat yard name: Old Mill

Yard location: ?

(See entry under Preston Brook)

Company name: John Urmson

Nature of maritime business: ?

Years of business: Early Nineteenth century?

Ship or boat yard name: As above RW

Yard location: ?

Also: Salt works owner with Wm. Crosbie as partner.

Company name: Hayes and Urmson

Nature of maritime business: ?

Years of business: ?–?

Ship or boat yard name: As above RW

Yard location: ?

Company name: William Hayes and John Urmson

Nature of maritime business: "Shipbuilders"

Years of business: 1821?–at least 1834

Ship or boat yard name: As above RW

Yard location: ?

Company name: William Hayes/William Hayes and Co.

Nature of maritime business: "Flat builders?

Years of business: 1837?–1844?

Ship or boat yard name: As above RW

Yard location: ?

Also: Slate and timber merchant.

Company name from *Waterways Journal Vol. 8*, "Sailing Flats on the Chester and Ellesmere Canals" by Terry Kavanagh.

Company name:	William Hazlehurst
Nature of maritime business:	Ship owner
Years of business:	1838?–1856?
Ship or boat yard name:	The Yard, Frodsham Bridge RW
	(Site of today's Frodsham Sailing Club).
	Dock (Now filled).
	Originally described as being of Sutton,
	Frodsham.
Yard location:	?

Also: Coal, slate and timber merchant.

It may be this yard was at the site referred to usually as the dockyard, where today's small port is based, beside the former Aston Arms public house, especially with reference to there being a dock there, which I have heard no evidence for at the other site.

There was a sale of shipbuilding timber and tools at Frodsham Bridge in 1856.

Company name:	Edward Jones
Nature of maritime business:	Flat builders?
Years of business:	1857?–1860/62?
Ship or boat yard name:	As above RW
Yard location:	?

Further information: Said to have been the last Frodsham shipbuilder, which ceased shipbuilding in 1860. However, the last Frodsham launching was of the flat FANNY in 1862.

Company name:	Isaac White
Nature of maritime business:	Flat builder?
Years of business:	1799?–?
Ship or boat yard name:	Frodsham Bridge RW
Yard location:	The yard as above?

Schooner Port states that Isaac White, William Hayes and John Urmson were building vessels at Frodsham Bridge at the beginning of the Nineteenth century.

The Booklet *Discovering Old Frodsham: A Trail to Follow* shows a map with the dockyardat the east bank of the Weaver at today's The Quay, near Frodsham Bridge. The book *Frodsham* states the area known as Quayside, from the bridge to the salt works "included a small shipyard".

The former position for a yard is acknowledged by the book *A Towpath Walkers Guide to the History of the River Weaver Navigation, Volume 2*. This book states there was a boat building yard immediately to the left of the viaduct on the opposite bank; the entrance to its dock being at the end of the piling. This opposite bank is, in other words, opposite Frodsham itself and the former port there (also known as Quayside), which used to have wharves along the west bank of the Weaver beside the former Bridge Inn and then along Ship Street, which previously was at the water's edge of the Mersey before silting led to the creation of the marshes.

Every other reference shows the dockyard to have been on the site of the current Sailing Club. Were there two (or perhaps more) shipyards at the east bank and a further one on the western shore?

The Frodsham Archaeology Assessment by Mike Shaw and Jo Clark states the yard was founded during the Napoleonic Wars.

I have referred to the yard as that at the site of the current sailing club and the dockyard as that which appears to have a graving or dry dock and as shown in a map on the website The Deep History of Folk and Cows in Rural Cheshire (www.themeister.co.uk/hindley/domesticated_animals.htm), at the location of today's small port at Frodsham.

According to the book *Frodsham*, 'it is likely the first crossing [at Frodsham Bridge] was a ferry'. The presence of a ferry at Frodsham would suggest some boat building and repairing experience, however simple, was to be found locally since that period.

Marine Engineers at Frodsham

Company name:	Pilkington Marine Engineering
Nature of maritime business:	"Wide range of services, parts and repairs, main dealers for a wide range of engines and parts, marine heat exchanger and cooler repair and servicing, RYA teaching establishment for diesel engines".
Years of business:	1966–present
Ship or boat yard name:	1. Frodsham Bridge RW (Frodsham side) 1966–1980

2. Newton Abbott, Devon N/A (As PME Ltd.)

Yard location: The yard as above?

Note: Mike Pilkington introduced inflatable boat racing to the U.K. in 1970, with a race on the River Weaver.

Related Industries at Frodsham

Company name: B Hayes
Nature of maritime business: Boat surveyor/examiner
Years of business: ?–present
Ship or boat yard name: 01928 732444/07702 262742
Yard location: ?

Ancillary Industries at Frodsham
Rope and Twine Makers at Frodsham

Company name: James Ellam
Nature of maritime business: "Rope maker"
Years of business: 1834? –?
Ship or boat yard name: ?
Yard location: ?

Company name: Robert Ellam
Nature of maritime business: "Rope maker"
Years of business: 1834?–?
Ship or boat yard name: ?
Yard location: ?

Note: According to *Frodsham: The History of a Cheshire Town* by Frank A. Latham et al, "only one person seems to have engaged in this work at Frodsham at any one time", and "especially between 1790 and 1860" when the port was at its busiest. Furthermore, the book states there used to be a road called The Ropewalks near the railway cutting on The Rock.

Were the two above operating semi-independently as they were probably related?

Helsby

No firms were engaged in marine engineering of any sort at Helsby but it is interesting to note the electrical cable manufacturer BICC built a large part of the PLUTO (Pipe Line Under The Ocean) undersea pipeline to France in World War II. The group was also involved in electrical cable manufacture for ships, certainly at the Erith plant (formerly Callender's Cable and Construction Co. Ltd.) and maybe also at Helsby.

Widnes and Fiddler's Ferry

Company name:	CNM Narrowboats
Nature of maritime business:	Narrowboat (hulls and sailaways) builders
	Mark ?
Years of business:	?–?
Ship or boat yard name:	Golden Triangle Industrial Estate *
	Ditton Road
	07862 242619
	01928 716718 (Runcorn; Place of residence)
	cnmnarrowboats@ntlworld.com
	(Also use the facilities of the Boat and
	Butty Co. in Runcorn and send outfitters to
	Northwich Boat Company to fit out boats)
Yard location:	?

Company name:	Cheshire Boats Ltd.
Nature of maritime business:	Narrowboat builders and repairers
Years of business:	?–present
Ship or boat yard name:	New name for the above.
	Unit 43B
	Golden Triangle Industrial Estate
	Harrison Street
Yard location:	?

Company name:	Brian Coleman
Nature of maritime business:	Narrow Boat and Wide Beam Boat Builder
Years of business:	?–present
Ship or boat yard name:	Unit 10
	Stanley House *
	Ditton Road
	0151 495 9074
Yard location:	?

Company name:	William Cooper and Sons Ltd.
Nature of maritime business:	Wood and steel flat builders?/repairers
	Barge owners

Years of business: 1868?–?
Ship or boat yard name:

1. St. Mary's Road M
   (Two slipways [both side?] and stages, carpenter's shop, joiner's shop and welding shop). 1868?–?
2. Gandy's former yard at Spike Island (Incl. later patent slipway) M or St
   (Repair only). ?–?
3. Depot at West Bank Dock, Widnes N/A
3. Depot at Liverpool N/A
4. Depot at Birkenhead N/A
5. Depot at Warrington M?
4. Depot at Manchester N/A

Yard location: ?

Also: Dealers in sand, gravel and concrete aggregates and quarry owners (quarries at Rossett and Wrexham).

It is interesting to note that in 1918, the manager of the shipwright's department of Messrs William Cooper and Sons was John Joseph Gandy; perhaps related to the former yard owners?

(The author's grandfather, George Ratcliffe, worked for Cooper's on its barges and was skipper of EMILY II).

Company name:	Concrete Seacraft Ltd.
Nature of maritime business:	Concrete ship and barge builders
Years of business:	Winter 1917/18–1920?
Ship or boat yard name:	Fiddler's Ferry M
Yard location:	Yard at site of the wharf by Old Lock
	Five building slipways.

Note: David Long (*28) describes the firm as the Concrete Seacraft Company Limited.

He states it had a workforce of "200-odd".

He says the company also built concrete houses, creating "pre-cast concrete houses" in response to the 1919 Housing Act. A terrace of six houses built by the company still stands in Warrington's Cornwall Street, although they are all brick-clad today and therefore not so obvious.

This endeavour was clearly successful and David Long goes on to state the management of the firm went on to change the name of its business to reflect its own surnames, becoming Williams Tarr Ltd., which today is a major construction company in Warrington.

Company name:	Nigel Dennis Kayaks Ltd.
Nature of maritime business:	Boat builders and repairers
Years of business:	?–present
Ship or boat yard name:	Unit 7
	55/61 Halton View Road
Yard location:	?

Company name:	Drammen Maritime (U.K.) Ltd.
Nature of maritime business:	Naval architects
Years of business:	1984?–1987?
Ship or boat yard name:	Waterloo Centre, Waterloo Road
	(Formerly in Runcorn – see separate entry)
	1985?–1987?
Yard location:	?

Further information: Facilities, know-how and people to provide the following services to owners, large consultants, new-building and repair yards: Classification drawings for hull and machinery; hull and steel structure drawings; arrangement drawings, hull and machinery; engine room layout and pipe diagrams including isometrics; accommodation plans and arrangements; ventilation systems; technical surveys for repair and conversion; new-building from specification through to supervision and delivery; outline specifications for tendering purposes; use of CAD/CAM.

Through association with Norwegian companies Drammen Maritime – Hokksund, Isasco A/S and Drammen Ship Services A/S, can also supply and install all kinds of marine equipment for offshore oil/gas rigs, as well as ships.

Company name:	Ferry Boatyard
Nature of maritime business:	Boat repairs?
Years of business:	?–present?
Ship or boat yard name:	Fiddler's Ferry Yacht Haven
Yard location:	?

Company name:	Edward Gandy
Nature of maritime business:	Flat builders?
Years of business:	1890?–?
Ship or boat yard name:	Yard at Spike Island (Slipways) M or St?
Yard location:	?

Company name: Hill and Grundy
Nature of maritime business: Flat builders?
Years of business: 1877?–1880?
Ship or boat yard name: Fiddler's Ferry St
Yard location: ?

Company name: William Jamieson
Nature of maritime business: Wooden Screw Steamer Builders?
Years of business: 1879?–?
Ship or boat yard name: ?
Yard location: ?

Company name: Samuel Stock
Nature of maritime business: Flat and shipbuilders?
Ship owner
Years of business: 1861?–1875?
Ship or boat yard name: Castle Rock Wharf, Runcorn M (But built his vessels at Widnes)
Yard location: ?

Also: Owner of a colliery at Blackleyhurst, near St Helens. Owner of a private railway from the mine to the Sankey Canal.

Company name: West Coast Marine
Nature of maritime business: ?
Years of business: ?–present
Ship or boat yard name: Stanley House, Ditton Road
Yard location: ?

Company name: Thomas Wilkinson
Nature of maritime business: Flat builders?
Years of business: 1859?–1885?
Ship or boat yard name: Fiddler's Ferry M
Yard location: ?

Company name: W. Wilkinson
Nature of maritime business: Flat builders?
Years of business: 1869?–1882?
Ship or boat yard name: Fiddler's Ferry M
Yard location: ?

Company name: The Wyre Boat Yard
Nature of maritime business: Boat repairs?
Years of business: ?–present
Ship or boat yard name: Chapel Lane, Cronton
Yard location: ?

Note: According to M.K. Stammers in his article, Slipways and Steamchests (as published in the *International Journal of Nautical Archaeology Volume 28, Issue 3*), the "Sankey Canal running from the Upper Mersey Estuary to St Helens had three yards at Fiddler's Ferry, Sankey and St Helens and a repair yard at Winwick in the Nineteenth century".

Ancillary Industries at Widnes
Sailmakers at Widnes

Company name: United Alkali Company
Nature of maritime business: ?
Years of business: ?–Late 1930s
Ship or boat yard name: Sail Loft
Yard location: ?

Further information: The firm maintained a sail loft in Widnes for making and maintaining canvas work for their fleet.*31

Ellesmere Port

Company name: Boat Building Services
Nature of maritime business: Narrowboat, wide beam boat and cruiser builders and outfitters
Years of business: ?–present
Ship or boat yard name: Unit 2, Indigo Road Industrial Estate
Yard location: ?

Company name: George Dawson
Nature of maritime business: Shipwright
Years of business: ?–1819?
Ship or boat yard name: Shipyard at Ellesmere Port M?
Yard location: ?

Further information: May have been a sub-tenant of Charles Hickson as the latter was still engaged in the business at time of George Dawson's activity in Ellesmere Port. George Dawson was from Walton, near Liverpool.

Company name:	Ellesmere Canal Co.
Nature of maritime business:	Repair of own barges
Years of business:	?–?
Ship or boat yard name:	(Slipways at docks) M or Sh or MSC?
Yard location:	?

(When the Ellesmere Canal Co. and others merged to form the Shropshire Union Canal Co., presumably these facilities were turned over to the new company. See entry for Shropshire Union Canal Co., below)

Company name:	Ellesmere Port Boat Museum
Nature of maritime business:	Rebuilders and repairers of river and canal craft
Years of business:	1974–present
Ship or boat yard name:	Dockyard Road/South Pier Road
	0151 3555017
	Fax: 0151 3554
	Fax: 0151 3554079
	www.boatmuseum.org.uk
	(Building halls and slipways [?] and dry dock) MSC + Sh
Yard location:	?

(Now part of the National Waterways Museum, also with sites at Gloucester and Stroud?).

(See entry on North West Museum of Inland Navigation).

Company name:	John Goulden/Goolden
Nature of maritime business:	Shipbuilder?
Years of business:	?–1822?
Ship or boat yard name:	Timber yard at Whitby Locks M?
Yard location:	?

Further information: Chester shipbuilder that may have built vessels in its timber yard at Ellesmere Port.

Information from *Waterways Journal Vol. 15*, "Ship and Boat Building at Ellesmere Port: A History" by Terry Kavanagh.

| Company name: | John Grace |
| Nature of maritime business: | Shipbuilders? Two vessels only? |

Years of business: 1817–?
Ship or boat yard name: ?
Yard location: ?

Company name: William and Richard Haselden
Nature of maritime business: ?
Years of business: 1825–1828
Ship or boat yard name: ? M?
Yard location: ?
Further information: Had a yard on the west side of Salthouse Dock, Liverpool and then also leased the yard at Ellesmere Port. William Hasleden carried on the business after his brother's death in 1826.

Company name: Charles Hickson and Co.
Nature of maritime business: Shipbuilders
Years of business: 18??–1817
Ship or boat yard name: ? M?
Yard location: ?
Further information: Probably the Charles Hickson from Runcorn and later Weston Point was the co-partner in this firm, along with Manley and Co.

It is unclear whether Charles Hickson was a partner of Ralph Manley from the start or whether he joined his successors in the Carrying Firm (Joseph Manley and Jon Sothern) after Ralph Manley's death in 1815. Dissolved by mutual consent in 1817.

Charles Hickson built up a good business in shipbuilding and repair, as well as in the leisure industry. He advertised bath houses and a hotel in Ellesmere Port and chartered some steamers from Runcorn. Unfortunately, one of these steamers sank during a heavy storm in the Mersey in December 1822 and he made great losses. Eight people died and public confidence was shook. Passenger numbers were still low when it came to the end of Hickson's lease on the yard in 1823. He went bankrupt and still owed money to the Ellesmere Canal Company.

Info from *Waterways Journal Vol. 15*, "Ship and Boat Building at Ellesmere Port: A History" by Terry Kavanagh.

Company name: Reg Lindop
Nature of maritime business: Builder of own pleasure cruiser and diesel engine, later replaced by his own steam engine (TENACITY was the cruiser).

Years of business: 18??–1817
Ship or boat yard name: *
Yard location: ?
Further information: The late Mr. Lindop was a friend of the family of the author. Reg Lindop's father was at one time the manager of the pontoon dry dock at Ellesmere Port (at the turn of the 20th century).

Company name: Manchester Ship Canal Company
Nature of maritime business: Ship repair
Years of business: 1922–1923
Ship or boat yard name: Morton's patent slip and yard MSC
Second slipway was adjacent to it and may have been part of the yard.
Yard location: ?
Further information: After 1923, the slip was abandoned.

Company name: Manchester Ship Canal Pontoons (and) Dry Docks Co. Ltd./Manchester Dry Dock Ltd. (After 1906)
Nature of maritime business: Ship repairers and builders
Years of business: 1893–1969
Ship or boat yard name: Eastern end of the docks complex (Seven acre yard, including dry docks and slipways and a floating dock; a frontage of 900ft).
Yard location: ?
Further information: The floating dock, or pontoon (dry) dock as it was known, measured about 300ft long by 70ft wide and was capable of raising a vessel of 5,500 tons carrying capacity and a length of 350ft. MSC

Staff from this yard also carried-out voyage repairs to vessels at Ellesmere Port Docks, Stuart Wharf and Bowaters Wharf, Stanlow, and Eastham and worked on the removal and refitting of masts and funnels at the latter for ships sailing beyond Runcorn that needed to pass under the bridges.

The latter job utilised the sheerlegs once there and the crane currently in situ (the latter being there since the late 1940s, according to *30). (Info from John Huxley in an article in *The Tow Line issue 33*, February 2014).

John Huxley later wrote an article for the Liverpool Nautical Research Society magazine *The Bulletin* entitled, "The Manchester Dry Docks at

Ellesmere Port" in which he gave the maximum capacity of the floating dock as being able to take ships up to 4,000 tons. In this article he also stated workers from the yard undertook voyage repairs on vessels at the QEII Dock in Eastham, and on vessels at Ince and Stanlow.

The company was founded 1891 and continued at Manchester until 1974, when it was sold to Furness Withy. The closure at Ellesmere Port came in October 1969 (1967 according to John Huxley's second article, quoted above), with the loss of more than 150 employees.

The pontoon was taken away and broken up on the Dee at Connah's Quay. (See earlier entry for M.S.C. Co., Runcorn). Information from the Canal Archive (www.canalarchive.org.uk):

The pontoon dock was designed by Alexander Taylor of the Manchester Pontoon and Dry Dock Company, the forerunner of Manchester Dry Docks at the top of the Manchester Ship Canal. The business was set up by Sir George Renwick, a Newcastle businessman, and the pontoon dock was constructed on the Tyne. Some sources say the dock came from Scapa Flow, where it had been used by the Admiralty. Both histories are not mutually exclusive, so there may be truth in both.

For ease, during the listing of vessels built or repaired by this firm, I have used the latter name of the company only.

Company name:	Pontoon Dry Docks Co. Ltd.
Nature of maritime business:	Ship repairers
Years of business:	1924?–?
Ship or boat yard name:	?
Yard location:	?

(Alternate name for Manchester Dry Dock Ltd.?)

Company name:	Ralph Manley
Nature of maritime business:	Barge builder
Years of business:	1810?–?
Ship or boat yard name:	?
Yard location:	?

Further information: A Runcorn man, set up in Chester as a carrier, who in 1810 applied to lease land to build "cottages, workshops, sheds, cranes, etc., and a timber yard for building, repairing and launching flats and small coasters into the river".

In the end this was soon taken over by the Ellesmere Canal Company, which extended the lease for its own works. This was likely to have been on the south side of the tidal (entrance) basin.

Manley, however, eventually got his own yard and built vessels in Ellesmere Port.

Company name:	Mason and Co.
Nature of maritime business:	?
Years of business:	1853?–1853?
Ship or boat yard name:	Leased slipway from Shropshire Union Canal Co. Sh?
Yard location:	?

Further information: This may have been the same as Samuel Mason and Co. of Runcorn.

Research by Terry Kavanagh however (as reported in *Waterways Journal Vol. 15*, "Ship and Boat Building at Ellesmere Port: A History") states that this firm proposed to rent the Morton patent slip and yard for a sum of £150 pa, which the Shropshire Union Canal Company agreed to, only for Mason to then withdraw the offer. So it may well have never occupied the site, despite what my earlier research implied.

Company name:	William Newall
Nature of maritime business:	Flat builder
Years of business:	1873–1882
Ship or boat yard name:	Dockyard in Ellesmere Port
Yard location:	?

Further information: Formerly of Winsford, then Garston Dock.

After nine years at this location, Newall was forced to give it up as he believed the place unsuitable and that it would not pay.

Info from *Waterways Journal Vol. 15*, "Ship and Boat Building at Ellesmere Port: A History" by Terry Kavanagh.

Company name:	North West Museum of Inland Navigation (Later the Ellesmere Port Boat Museum – see separate entry)
Nature of maritime business:	Rebuilders and repairers of river and canal craft
Years of business:	1976–present (under new name)
Ship or boat yard name:	MSC + Sh
Yard location:	?

Company name:	William Parkes
Nature of maritime business:	?
Years of business:	1863–1866
Ship or boat yard name:	Leased the patent slip and yard
Yard location:	?

Further information: Leased the patent slip at Ellesmere Port in 1863 and built at least two ships there.

Built the sloop LORN (69 or 79 tons depending on source), in 1864.

From *Waterways Journal Vol. 15*, "Ship and Boat Building at Ellesmere Port: A History" by Terry Kavanagh. He leased the yard and premises, including use of the patent slip, for £71 pa. Later became a boat builder at Chester.

Son of Joseph Parkes, who at one time was manager of the Dee Bank Shipbuilding Yard. Is Parkes the same person as Peake, below (perhaps a misspelling)?

Company name:	Peake
Nature of maritime business:	?
Years of business:	1863–?
Ship or boat yard name:	Leased slipway from Shropshire Union Canal Co. Sh?
Yard location:	?

Company name:	Shropshire Union Canal Co.
Nature of maritime business:	Repair of own barges?
Years of business:	?–?
Ship or boat yard name:	Same as Haselden Sh
	(Eventually included a patent slipway)
	(Also a floating dock?)
Yard location:	?

Note: Reg Lindop recalled his father telling him the M.S.C. Co. floating dock at Ellesmere Port was originally owned by the Shropshire Union Canal Co. but surely it would have been too big for its needs?

Perhaps there was an older, smaller floating dock at Ellesmere Port before the M.S.C. Co. built its own or was this confused with the patent slip?

(See Section on Inland Waterways of the United Kingdom, below and entry for Ellesmere Canal Co., above)

Company name: William Skinner
Nature of maritime business: Shipwright and boatbuilder
Years of business: 1873–1875
Ship or boat yard name: Yard at Ellesmere Port
Yard location: ?
Further information: Also had a yard in his native Liverpool.

Company name: Stirling Narrowboats Ltd.
Nature of maritime business: Narrowboat and wide beam boat builders
Years of business: ?–present
Ship or boat yard name: North Road Industrial Estate/Thornton Park Industrial Estate
Yard location: ?

Company name: Thomas Telford
Nature of maritime business: ? For self or Canal Co. ?
Years of business: ?–?
Ship or boat yard name: Leased the same land as Ralph Manley
Yard location: ?

Company name: Universal Engineering Co. (Ellesmere Port) Ltd.
Nature of maritime business: General ship smiths
Years of business: 1924?–?
Ship or boat yard name: Grosvenor Street Works
Yard location: ?

Also: Joiners, wheelwrights, coach and motor body builders; boiler makers and repairers; wood and iron turners and fitters; oxyacetylene welders and burners; and shoeing smiths.

Note: When the Ellesmere Port Docks were extended and reopened in 1843 under the Shropshire Union Railway and Canal Company, they came with a Morton patent slip capable of taking vessels of 200 tons Burthen and available for rent. It was 200ft long and came with a range of workshops.

When the Manchester Ship Canal was dug, the slip was extended by 400ft and the workshops demolished and rebuilt in order to accommodate this.

The slip was further extended by 32ft when in 1909 the M.S.C. Co. decided to increase the depth of the canal from 26ft to 28ft. It was still in Shropshire Union

Canal Company hands at that stage, only passing to the M.S.C. Co. in 1922.

Note: The first yard at Ellesmere Port was at the southern end of the tidal basin. Later, there was a yard situated around the patent slip. However, Victoria Arm and South Pier were also used for shipbuilding and repair at various times (possibly using the basin at South Pier and Victoria Arm itself as graving docks?), according to *Waterways Journal Vol. 15*. That magazine shows a photograph of the launch of PRINCESS OF WALES from North Quay in 1904, so the North Pier must also have been used for such work. In 1884 and 1908, patent slips were built at the end of the Victoria Arm for the repair of canal craft. Presumably, this refers to the two slipways into the Ship Canal to the east of the Victoria Arm.

After William Newall vacated the yard, it was agreed by the Shropshire Union Canal Company to let the premises and facilities on a casual basis in between the work needed by the company herself.

Sankey Bridges/Sankey/Sankey Brook

Company name: William Clare, later Clare and Son?
Nature of maritime business: Flat and shipbuilders?
Years of business: 1807?–1831
Ship or boat yard name: Sankey Dockyard st
(Yard with dry dock – on alternate bank from rest of yard – and crane for lifting vessels into boat house and building Berth [side] on quayside [as seen in pictures from Clare and Ridgeway's Yard])
Warrington at Work states that the yard was founded in the early 1800s as Clare and Son, so it seems logical that this name was a later incarnation of the business and that on William Clare's death it continued under John Clare.
Yard location: ?
Also: Ropemakers (as well as flat builders) according to *Warrington at Work*.

Company name: John Clare
Nature of maritime business: Flat and shipbuilders?
Years of business: 1832–1861

Ship or boat yard name: As above St
Yard location: ?

Further information: The Clares built and repaired their own flats between 1807 and 1846, when they also began to build for others.

Company name: Executors of John Clare
Nature of maritime business: Flat and ship and wooden screw steamer builders?
Years of business: 1861–?
Ship or boat yard name: As above St
Yard location: ?

Company name: Clare and Ridgeway
Nature of maritime business: Flat and ship and wooden screw steamer builders/repairers?
Years of business: 1867?–1929?
Ship or boat yard name: As above St
(Sometimes referred to as Clare's Yard).
Yard location: ?

Company name: Richard G. Cross
Nature of maritime business: Shipbuilder
Years of business: 1913?–1913?
Ship or boat yard name: As above St
Yard location: ?

Company name: Winwick Maintenance Yard and Winwick Dry Dock
Nature of maritime business: ?
Years of business: ?–?
Ship or boat yard name: Dry dock and crane/boat house St
(to lift boats into boat house)
of above firm, but yard at opposite Bank. *Yard location:* ?

Further information: The Maintenance yard maintained the Sankey Canal as well as boats and was owned and operated by the canal company.
(See Section on Inland Waterways of the United Kingdom, below).

Note: According to M.K. Stammers in his article "Slipways and Steamchests" (as published in the *International Journal of Nautical Archaeology Volume 28, Issue 3*), the "Sankey Canal running from the Upper Mersey Estuary to St Helens had three yards at Fiddler's Ferry, Sankey and St Helens and a repair yard at Winwick in the Nineteenth century".

Warrington

Company name:	(Warrington) Bridge Foundry Company
Nature of maritime business:	Iron ship and paddle steamer builders?
Years of business:	1840?–1845?
Ship or boat yard name:	Warrington Bridge M
Yard location:	?

Company name:	Graham Mackereth/Pyranha Mouldings
Nature of maritime business:	?
Years of business:	1971–June 1979
Ship or boat yard name:	Work began from the family garage, then moved to Workshop at 23 Poachers Lane, Latchford *, then Osnath Works, Lythgoes Lane (1975–June 1979) * moving to Preston Brook, Runcorn (see separate entry).
Yard location:	?

Company name:	Mailspeed Marine
Nature of maritime business:	?
Years of business:	?–present?
Ship or boat yard name:	16 Greys Court Kingsland Grange
Yard location:	?

Company name:	Tayleur, Sanderson and Co.
Nature of maritime business:	Iron ship and paddle and screw steamer builders?
Years of business:	Shipbuilding 1846–1857 1837–c. 1860
Ship or boat yard name:	Vulcan Foundry or Bank Quay Yard (Patent slipway class 1 – four ways?) (Shipbuilding and boiler yard; wharf crane;

travelling crane; sheer legs; foundry platers' shed; furnace and shed; keel smithy; smithy and machine shop and railway siding to main line). M

Yard location: ?

Further information: According to a layout of the yard in *Cheshire Shipyards*, there were four "ships' ways", leading to the assumption above that the yard had a Patent slipway class 1.

Also: Charles Tayleur founded the Vulcan Foundry at Newton-le-Willows in 1830, later going into partnership with Robert Stephenson, the famous railway engineer, building steam locomotives.

He established the Bank Quay Foundry with George Sanderson and was soon building ocean-going vessels there. He also established a high reputation for building cannon for the Royal Navy.

The foundry made ironwork for railways, including some for the tubular bridges at Conway and across the Menai Straits.

The Vulcan company at Newton-le-Willows was incorporated as the Vulcan Foundry Co. Ltd. in 1864 and went on to manufacture diesel and electric locomotives, as well as tanks during World War II

The company owned Robert and Hawthorns Ltd. (another locomotive business).

Later, the Vulcan Foundry Co. Ltd. merged into the English Electric Co. Ltd., which in turn became part of the General Electric Co. Ltd. (G.E.C.).

Later developments within the group meant that Rushton Paxton Diesels Ltd. (later Rushton Diesels Ltd.) became manager of G.E.C. Diesels Ltd., the then operator of the Vulcan Foundry.

Company name: Tayleur and Co./Tayleur and Company
Nature of maritime business: Iron ship and screw steamer builders?
Years of business: 1853–?
Ship or boat yard name: As above M
Yard location: ?

Company name: Bank Quay Foundry Co.
Nature of maritime business: Iron shipbuilders?
Years of business: 1856–1857
Ship or boat yard name: As above M
     (Known as Bank Quay Foundry)

Yard location: ?
Further information: Bank Quay Foundry went up for sale in the press in November 1857 and from then until January 1860 the shipbuilding equipment was sold off.

Company name:	Whitley and Co.
Nature of maritime business:	Builder of an iron flat
Years of business:	?–?
Ship or boat yard name:	Warrington Bridge Foundry
Yard location:	?

Note: As early as 1830, iron barges had been built locally.

Note: *Warrington at Work* by Janice Hayes and Alan Crosby, gives these details:
• "Warrington was also a minor centre for shipbuilding. For centuries, small river vessels had been constructed here".
• "Several small shipyards and repair yards were established on the river [Mersey] at Bank Quay and on the north bank adjacent to Warrington Bridge, where during the 1840s the Bridge Foundry constructed four iron paddle steamers…".

Related Industries at Warrington

Company name:	M Crompton
Nature of maritime business:	Boat surveyor/examiner
Years of business:	?–present
Contact details:	01928 787333/07831 841108

Company name:	N Hamilton
Nature of maritime business:	Boat surveyor/examiner
Years of business:	?–present
Contact details:	01923 265129/07904 325372

There were ancillary industries at Warrington:
Sailmakers at Warrington

There were numerous Sailmakers in Warrington, and sailcloth was an important local industry. Hemp was grown in the area and used in the manufacture of this material and Warrington had a national reputation as a manufacturing town for sailcloth. Such was its involvement in this trade that *Warrington at Work* by Janice Hayes and Alan Crosby, goes so far as to say that, as well as supplying the merchant ships of Great Britain, "Warrington district provided no less than half the acreage of sails for the fleets [of the Royal Navy] which fought and helped to defeat Napoleon".

The Rylands family were prominent in this trade and a later member of that clan, John Ryland, founded a partnership with Nathaniel Greening in the wire industry.

Unfortunately, the trade slowly withered and died with the cutback the Navy suffered after the defeat of Napoleon (sounds familiar, doesn't it...?), and by 1851 there was only one sailcloth manufactory in the town, based at a yard on the east side of Bridge Street.

Wire and Wire Rope Makers at Warrington

Warrington was a massive centre for metalworking in various forms. There were copper works, ironworks, steelworks, pin-making concerns and all manner of metal industries in copper, brass, iron, and steel.

Included in this list were a number of wire rope manufacturers:

Armitage and Rigby (at Cockhedge)

The British Wedge Wire Co. Ltd. (in Academy Street)

Firth Wire Company

N. Greening and Sons Limited (small factory in Warrington, then at the end of Church Street – see below about partnership with Ryland – then at Bewsey Street)

W.D. Houghton (Wireworks in Tanner Lane, later at the Sankey Wire Mills, Wire Rope and Bright Steel Barworks)

Thomas Locker/Lockers (at Market Street, later at new site in Church and Ellesmere Streets)

The Longford Wire Iron and Steel Company Ltd.

Monks Hall Steelworks

Richmond and Co.

Ryland Brothers Wireworks (works at the end of Church Street – see comments below about partnership with Greening)

The Whitecross Company Ltd. (opened by Frederick Monks and later part of Lancashire Steel Group)

John Ryland and Nathaniel Greening were also partners at one time also (in a works at the end of Church Street), before the former went into business by himself and the latter returned to running his own firm.

There was also the Continuous Mill at Battersby Lane.

There were also firms operating in what today are suburbs of Warrington:

Stockton Heath

Company name:	Cash's Boatyard
Nature of maritime business:	?
Years of business:	?–?
Ship or boat yard name:	London Bridge B
Yard location:	?

Company name:	Thorn(e) Marine
Nature of maritime business:	Boat and engine repairers. Now engine repairs only
Years of business:	?–present
Ship or boat yard name:	London Bridge (opposite the above) B? (Slipway)
Yard location:	?

Lymm

Company name:	Hesford Marine
Nature of maritime business:	Boat builders and repairers (then just repairs). Now engine repairs only
Years of business:	?–present
Ship or boat yard name:	Warrington Lane Agden 01925 65129 (Building hall and slipway) B (Site of an old boatyard, but whose?)
Yard location:	?

Company name:	Lymm Marina/Cheshire Narrowboats Ltd.
Nature of maritime business:	Boat builders and repairers Narrowboat and wide beam boat builders and outfitters
Years of business:	?–present
Ship or boat yard name:	(Slipway and dry dock) B Sales 01925 752945
Yard location:	?

Company name: Northern Fabrications
Nature of maritime business: ?
Years of business: ?–present?
Ship or boat yard name: Warrington Lane
                            (Related to Northern Marine Services?)
Yard location: ?

Company name: Northern Marine Services
Nature of maritime business: Narrowboat and wide beam boat builders/
                            repairers/refitters, outfitters and servicers and
                            engine installers
Years of business: ?–present
Ship or boat yard name: The Old Camp Shop B
                            Warrington Road
                            Lymm
                            john@northernboats.co.uk
Yard location: ?

Company name: Wharfage Boat Company
Nature of maritime business: Boat builders and repairers
Years of business: ?–?
Ship or boat yard name: Agden Wharf B
                            01925 754900
Yard location: ?
Further information: Presumably, on the site of the yard of the firm below.

Company name: Tyrer Marine
Nature of maritime business: Northern Cruiser Centre
                            Engine repairs
                            Slipway and moorings for owners own repairs
Years of business: ?–?
Ship or boat yard name: Agden Boatyard
Yard location: ?

Note
Inland Waterways of the United Kingdom
Note that between 1940 and 1947, the entire network of British canals came
under the jurisdiction of the Ministry of War Transport, making this government

body the ultimate overseer of all the ship and boat building and repair concerns belonging to the canal/waterway-owning companies, such as the M.S.C. Co.

Merseyside

According to the Merseyside Maritime Museum website, "Ships and boats were undoubtedly built on the shores of the Mersey from the earliest times of settlement".

According to the Merseyside Maritime Museum Website, "By 1900, although there was still extensive ship repairing capacity on Merseyside, the only yard to build ships of significance, was Lairds".

APPENDIX A

A List of Vessels Built on the Upper Mersey

This list primarily focuses on local ship and boat building/repair, at Runcorn, Frodsham and Widnes. The main hub of this work will be commercial vessels but, where possible, some of the pleasure craft built in the area will also be listed.

Note: This list will not include a full breakdown of the large number of vessels repaired in the local yards but will mention what little details remain of such works and also more recent repairs and rebuilds completed locally.

Unless otherwise noted, all vessels listed here come from the list provided by H.F. Starkey in his book *Schooner Port*.

Unless otherwise stated, the vessels listed here were of wood construction.

Key

Tonnage Burthen: The old British measure of a ship's size; based upon the number of tuns or casks of wine that could fit in the holds.

The system remained in place until gradually fading from use after the introduction in a 1773 Act of Parliament of the Builder's (Old) Measurement and disappearing by the end of the Eighteenth century.

It was originally calculated as:

$$\frac{L \times B \times D}{100}$$

where L = length, B = breadth and D = depth

In 1694, a law was introduced making it a requirement to mark the waterline on merchant vessels and the formula was now officially adopted, with a slight modification as:

$$\frac{L \times B \times D}{94}$$

Builder's Tonnage or Builder's (Old) Measurement: This system was designed to give a more accurate measurement.

It was calculated by using the formula:

$$\frac{(L - 3/5\ B) \times B \times 1/2\ B}{94}$$

Tons Burthen is approximately equivalent to today's net tonnage.

This system continued until the mid-nineteenth century, although a similar method called the Thames Measurement, continues in some spheres today as a calculation for yachts' size.

Gross registered tonnage (GRT): Under Moorsom's Rule, established to measure a ship's size in the days when iron-hulled steamships were replacing wooden sailing ships (where the old system was inaccurate), the total capacity of a ship's hull under the waterline was calculated in cubic feet and divided by 100. This gave the gross tonnage.

Net registered tonnage (NRT): Tonnage gross did not give a good representation of a ship's carrying capacity, so a second method was established. This was calculated by using the same formula as above to calculate the engine and machinery spaces, crew quarters and facilities, etc, and deducting it from the gross tonnage to give net tonnage.

Register tonnage: Both of the above are known as register tonnage as they are entered on a ship's certificate of registration.

Deadweight tonnage (DWT): This is the measurement of the weight of cargo carried based on the long ton of 2, 240lb (1, 017kg). The calculation is made by reckoning the amount of water displaced by a ship when unloaded but fully loaded with fuel and stores and by the vessel then fully loaded; the difference between the two figures then being expressed in tons (where thirty-five cubic feet of seawater is equal to one ton).

Displacement tonnage: The usual method of calculating naval vessels' weight, this is produced by calculating the weight of the water a ship displaces when it is fully loaded with fuel and stores. Again, it is calculated using the measure of thirty-five cubic feet of seawater to one ton.

In 1969, the International Maritime Organisation adopted the International Convention on Tonnage Measurement of Ships, which was implemented in 1982; it was designed around the Metric System and hence replaced the Imperial System previously used as well as for the first time, seeking to bring all nations under one standard.

The new measures are:

Gross tonnage (GT): A function of the moulded volume of all enclosed spaces of a ship.

Net tonnage (NT): A function of the moulded volume of all cargo spaces of a ship.

All details in red text show vessels that are still in existence.

In the following tables, all vessels are listed with year of build/launch, name, type of vessel, weight (in tons unless otherwise stated) and builder.

Runcorn

1778   Cooper   brig   70t   ?

Schooner Port states in its "The Ship Builders" section of Chapter 3 that "before 1790, ship launches had been an occasional event and the vessels on the slips were mainly river craft but at the turn of the century the local builders were launching genuine sea going ships". Therefore, there must have been more vessels built in this period.

1791   Royal Charlotte   flat   92t   ?

In *Waterways Journal Vol. 5*, "Building Flats at Runcorn" by Michael Stammers, the following details are given:

The first known flat to have been built in Runcorn; a "very large flat and presumably designed for estuary and coastal work".

Described as a "substantial" vessel.

1792   Manchester   brigantine?   139t   ?

Described in *Schooner Port* in separate entries as either a barquentine or Brigantine, respectively.

1792   Worsley   schooner   130t   Bridgewater?

Waterways Journal Vol. 10, "The History of Runcorn Docks: 1773–1914" by

Alf Hayman, gives these details:
  Burthen 130 tons;
  One deck, two masts;
  Length 72ft, breadth 21½ft;
  Depth of hold 10 10/12ft;
  Square-stem schooner;
  Owner: Francis Egerton, Duke of Bridgewater.
This was the first of four coasters the Duke had built for him at Runcorn.

1794   Rochdale   brigantine?   133t   ?
Described in *Schooner Port* in separate entries as either a barquentine or brigantine, respectively.

1798   Sampson   brigantine?   140t   ?
Described in *Schooner Port* in separate entries as either a barquentine or brigantine, respectively.
Note: According to the Historical Merchant Navy, Bibby Line website at: www.red-duster.co.uk/BIBBY8.htm Sampson was 139t burthen, built of wood and brig-rigged; built for local short sea trade;
    Acquired by Bibby and Highfield in 1817 and refurbished in 1818 (and copper sheathed for West Indies or African trade); further refitted in 1822 and given new topsides and reputedly, iron cables; 73ft × 21ft 4in.
    After a further nine years trading; vessel broken up at Dublin in 1831.

1800   Ann   snow   102t?   ?
Described in *Schooner Port* in separate entries as either 120t or 102t, respectively.
    The same book later describes the snow, "Ann" as having been launched "in Runcorn in 1802".

1800   Jane   flat   40t?   John Crippin
Presumably, the vessel described thus: built at Runcorn in 1800 of English oak; a 40 ton Bristol Channel trow (presumably converted from a flat sometime after 1800), the ship spent sixty years as a Mersey flat before being sailed out of Bridgwater by a member of the Smart family, who later sold her on to retired seaman "Captain" Leonard Smart in the early Twentieth century.
    She served during World War I as a government survey vessel in the Bristol Channel and was then sold by Captain Smart to a Bristol merchant for use as

a storage hulk. In 1938 she was believed towed to Lydney to be broken up.

She was the oldest British merchant ship afloat at this time.*1

This seems to be confirmed in *Mersey Flats and Flatmen*.

Note: According to *Cheshire Shipyards* by Antony J. Barratt, she was originally a sloop and later converted to a ketch.

I have been given, by Dave Keenan, an article from the *Runcorn Weekly News* of 21st September 1951 (reporting on the launch of OAKDALE) and this states that a vessel named JANE, working the Bristol Channel, was reported in 1928 as being 129 years of age. The same vessel was apparently dry-docked in 1951 and her timbers were found to be of the state expected of a vessel a quarter of that age; fantastic considering that in 1951 she would have been over a century and a half old!

1800   Edith   flat   60   Robert Mitchell
Length 64.3ft, breadth 14.3ft, hold depth 5.9ft; owned by Coffield and Co.
The Edith was one of a number of flats that were condemned as past repair and sold, in late 1914, to Summers of Shotton. It filled them with stone and sank them in the Dee as part of flood defences.

This information is all from *Waterways Journal Vol. 8*, "Sailing Flats on the Chester and Ellesmere Canals" by Terry Kavanagh.

Note: Old Runcorn states that the Duke of Bridgewater had a dozen barquentines and schooners built for him in Runcorn between 1791 and 1800.

Schooner Port states that the Duke of Bridgewater had a number of "sizeable" vessels built for him at Runcorn: Three brigantines, each of 140 tons, and a snow of 120 tons, all constructed between 1792 and 1800. According to the appendix to *Schooner Port*, there was a snow built in Runcorn in 1800 but she was mentioned in the main text of the book as belonging to someone else, and also recorded in the appendix as being 102 tons.

1802   George and Ann   sloop   95t   ?
In *Waterways Journal Vol. 5*, "Building Flats at Runcorn" by Michael Stammers, the following details are given: "This almost certainly had a flat-type hull possibly with a greater draught and with a different rig, which included a bowsprit and probably a square sail or sails in addition to the normal foresail and gaff main sail of a flat". Described as a "substantial" vessel.

1802   Sarah   flat   57t   Wm. Wright and Chas. Hickson
In *Waterways Journal Vol. 5*, "Building Flats at Runcorn" by Michael Stammers, the following details are given: an "average size for the time". Described as a "substantial" vessel.

1803   Anne   flat   59   Wm. Wright and Chas. Hickson
Waterways Journal Vol. 8, "Sailing Flats on the Chester and Ellesmere Canals" by Terry Kavanagh states that the "Ann" of 57 tons was built in 1804 by William Wright for Coffield and Co.

Is this the vessel listed here and has Terry Kavanagh just gone slightly wrong on the date and tonnage as well as omitting the partnership of William Wright to Charles Hickson?

A company order in November 1873 gave direction to repair and sell this flat.

1803   Hannah   flat   59t   Wm. Wright and Chas. Hickson
1803   Glory   flat   58t   ?
Built in Chester in 1792 and rebuilt in a Runcorn yard in this year.

Schooner Port states that Philip Whiteway was the owner of the flat Glory. Was it this vessel and, if so, was the rebuilding of this vessel completed by Whiteway himself? More likely, it was completed for him by someone else, as Whiteway's first foray into shipbuilding was probably when he went into partnership with Dennis Brundrit.

1805   Elizabeth   flat   56t   Wm. Wright
Owned by Coffield and Co. Later owned by the Shropshire Union Company. A company minute in August 1873 suggested it was not economically viable to repair this flat but, in the end, she was repaired and she continued her service for the firm.

In 1920, the remaining vessels of this company, including this one, were put up for sale. This was one of 58 that remained unsold and they were all left to rot in the Dee Basin in Chester.

This information is all from *Waterways Journal Vol. 8*, "Sailing Flats on the Chester and Ellesmere Canals" by Terry Kavanagh.

1806   Friends   galliot   92t   ?
1806   Rhydland Trader   flat   38t   ?
1807   Bettys   barquentine   132t   ?

| 1808 | Bradshaw | galliot | 108t | ? |
| 1810 | Lady Stanley | sailing packet | ? | Chas. Hickson at Weston Pt |

Eastham Ferry Sailing Packet

Information from *Waterways Journal Vol. 15*, "Ship and Boat Building at Ellesmere Port: A History" by Terry Kavanagh.

| 1811 | John and Ann | flat | 64t | ? |

Owned by William Hazlehurst, coal merchant of Sutton, Frodsham and his brother, Charles.

1812	Commerce	flat	46t	?
1815	Jane	flat	63t	Wm. Wright
1815	Eccleston	flat	52t	Speakman

This information comes from Percy Dunbavand, after researching the Liverpool registers.

He describes ECCLESTON thus:

Wooden one-masted flat, carvel-built with round stern; built 1815?; first registered in 1846; rebuilt by Clare and Ridgeway at Sankey Bridges in 1887; re-registered on 25th April 1887.

Owner: John Clare Ridgeway, Slate Merchant of Sankey Bridges (64 Shares); passed to Clare Lighterage of Sankey Bridges on 23rd September 1902; sold to William Irwell of 53, Irwell Road, Widnes on 10th March 1911; sold to John Lovall, Waterman of Seacombe on 21st July 1920.

64.9ft × 16.8ft x 6.3ft; official number 7059; registration closed 1st December 1930; vessel brokenup.

| 1816 | Duke of Wellington | wood paddle steamer | 59t | Wm. Wright |
| 1816 | Prince Regent | wood paddle steamer | 57t | Wm. Rigby |

Owned by a schoolmaster, an inn keeper, a waiter, a butcher, a seaman and a cabinet maker.

Sunk in a storm off Ellesmere Port in 1822. She was raised and towed to Runcorn but nothing further is known. Perhaps she was repaired there?

1821	Holyhead Trader	sloop	76t	?
1823	Sarah	flat	52t	?
1824	Maria	flat	46t	John Weedall

Owned by Mr. J. Ryley.

1824   Earl of Bridgewater   steam tug   ?   Bridgewater?

This vessel suffered a boiler explosion in this year (the year she was built) and was repaired, but was this at the Bridgewater facilities in Runcorn?

1825   Manchester   wood paddle steamer   40t   ?
1825   Elizabeth   smack   42t   William Martin

Although the above details (bar a builder, who was unknown to Bert Starkey) appear in *Schooner Port*, more information came from *Waterways Journal Vol. 6*, "Mersey Sailing Flats & Flatmen" by Terry Kavanagh:

56ft round-stern flat; built by William Martin of Runcorn; owned by James Cogswell & Co., Carriers to Rochdale and Halifax.

Note: *Schooner Port* states the Mersey and Irwell Navigation Company decided to build three small steamers in 1831, which may have been built at its facility at Runcorn Old Quay.

1833   Ann   flat   42t   Mersey and Irwell?

From *Waterways Journal Vol. 6*, "Mersey Sailing Flats & Flatmen" by Terry Kavanagh: "In 1833 the Old Quay Co. adopted a new design of river flat, recommended by their Runcorn agent James Wylde, which had one-third more cargo capacity than the old sailing flats. A new wooden flat to this design was built at their own yard…".

Taking this evidence and the fact Bert Starkey listed the above vessel as being built in this year (bereft of a builder's name), I have assumed this was the vessel Terry Kavanagh was speaking of and that she was therefore built by the Mersey and Irwell Co.

1834	Patent	flat	45t	?
1834	Rival	wood paddle steamer	50t	?
1836	Tower	wood paddle steamer	47t	J. Rawlinson
1837	James and Sarah	schooner	63t	?
1838	Susan	schooner	?	?
1838	Thomas	schooner	97t	Samuel Mason

Schooner Port lists her as built and owned by Mason, but she is not confirmed as such in the book's appendix.

1838   Thomas Mason   schooner   62t   Samuel Mason

Sixteen shares held by Samuel Mason.

1839	Gem	smack	33t	?
1839	Duke	wood paddle steamer	?	?
1839	Elfleda	schooner	116t	Crippin?

Schooner Port states the schooner ELFLEDA was owned by John Crippin; presumably, it was this vessel. Did Crippin also build her and subsequently maintain her?

1839	Maria and Elizabeth	?	?	?
1840	John	schooner	55t	Brundrit and Whiteway

Forty-eight shares held by Brundrit and Whiteway; sixteen shares held by Robert Owen, her master.

1840	John and Henry	schooner	72t	?
1840	British Queen	schooner	107t	Anderton
1841	Catherine	sloop	50t	?
1841	Princess Royal	schooner	97t	Anderton

Part-owned by John Crippin.

Note: www.fleetwoods-maritime-heritage.info/?tag=coaster gives these details: Schooner rig (coastal trade); Length 63ft; net tonnage 83.

Registered at Liverpool. 1853; sold to Richard Warbrick, William Strobe, James Heron and others of Fleetwood. 1st Jan 1883; owned by William Poole of Fleetwood and registered at Fleetwood.

1841	Margaret	schooner	102t?	?

Described in *Schooner Port* in separate entries as either 64t or 102t, respectively.

1841	Susannah	flat	45t	?

Owned by John Wright, tanner.

1841	Doris	schooner	137t	J. Sothern
1841	Ann Widnell	sloop	36t	?
1842	Alice	flat	49t	?
1842	Ellen	schooner	69t	?
1842	Philip	schooner	72t	Brundrit and Whiteway

Owned by Brundrit and Whiteway (holding equal shares each).

1842	Mersey	schooner	92t	?

Presumably the vessel owned by T. Rigby, coal and salt merchant of Runcorn.

1842	Heir Apparent	schooner	132t	?
1842	Hugh Lupus	schooner	64t	Bridgewater
1843	Commerce	flat	55t	Bridgewater?

Schooner Port details the above vessel but no builder. *Waterways Journal Vol. 4* has an article by Alf Hayman concerning the "Carrying Craft of the Bridgewater Canal, 1773–1974" and it states the above was a Mersey flat launched in 1842 at "the bottom locks yard" of the Bridgewater Trustees.

1843	Mary Jane	schooner	111t	Brundrit and Whiteway
1843	Sarah and Ann	schooner	100t	Samuel Mason
1844	Martha	flat	8t	?
1844	Mountain Maid	sloop	53t	?
1844	Julia	schooner	73t	Brundrit and Whiteway

Owned by Brundrit and Whiteway (holding equal shares each). Possibly the schooner of the same name in which Percy Dunbavand's great grandfather, John Dunbavand, served in as mate from January 1866 to January 1867. John's brother, Tom Dunbavand, was captain.

Note: This may be the schooner of that name rescued by the Castletown RNLI on 8th December 1886, according to the Irish Wrecks website.

Note: This may be the mast flat JULIA that was lost of Penmaenmawr on 19th February 1903, (that wreck being from research by Percy Dunbavand) being under the ownership of William Cooper of Widnes at the time.

1844	Jane	flat	?	?
1845	Fanny	schooner	71t	?
1846	Sarah	schooner	77t	Brundrit and Whiteway

Owned by Brundrit and Whiteway (holding equal shares each).

A schooner of Runcorn by the name of SARAH was caught in a storm off the Balbriggan Coast in February 1873 and her crew was rescued by lifeboat. She was on the way to Bray with coal. About a mile from the SARAH, the lifeboat lost her oars and seven of ten lifeboatmen perished. Is this the same vessel as above?

| 1846 | Ino | schooner | 75t | ? |

She was owned by Brundrit and Co. and foundered in a force nine gale four miles of Beaumaris with all three crew on 20th February 1877. This was while sailing from Penmaenmawr to Dublin with 135t of granite.

1847   Maragret and Martha   schooner   66t   ?
1847   The Port   schooner   65t   Brundrit and Whiteway
Schooner Port lists her as built and owned by the Brundrit and Whiteway partnership (holding equal shares each) but she is not confirmed as such in the book's appendix. Owned by Brundrit and Whiteway.

1847   Rosalie   brig   215t   ?
Built for the Liverpool to West Indies trade and felted and yellow metalled.

1848   Empress   schooner   68t   Anderton
Owned by John Anderton.

1848   Duke   schooner   80t   Brundrit and Whiteway
1848   Spectacular   flat   43t   Samuel Mason
1849   Alice   flat   42t   ?
1849   William Court   schooner   56t   ?
Owned by William Clarke, rope maker. Lost in the Irish Sea in 1853.

1849   Edward and John   sloop   29t   ?
1850   Shamrock   schooner   65t   ?
1850   Ann   flat   50t   ?
1850   Margaret   smack   21t   ?
1850   Ellesmere   schooner   75t   Brundrit and Whiteway
Owned by Brundrit and Whiteway (holding equal shares each). If it was owned by Brundrit and Whiteway, it can be assumed that she was maintained at its yard.

1850   Sandeel   sailing flat   42.35t   ?
Wooden sailing flat; built 1850 in Runcorn; by 20th February 1877, owner: Mersey Docks qnd Harbour Board; vessel abandoned at Birkenhead in 1914, removed and broken up.
    Official Number 76417; registration closed 26th April 1929. *23.

1851   Emperor   schooner   70t   Anderton
Owned by John Anderton.

1851   Emmeline   schooner   70t   ?
1851   Sir Robert   schooner   68t   Brundrit and Whiteway

1851	Eliza	flat	39t	?
1851	Rose and Margaret	sloop	32t	?
1852	May	flat	57t	?
1853	Eva	brigantine	134t	?

Note: May be the EVA described as a schooner of Runcorn in the website, www.old-merseytimes.co.uk/lifeboats1896.html. This vessel had two crew members rescued from her during a storm in late 1896.

Or, this may be the Runcorn fishing vessel of that name mentioned in the website, www.caithness.org, which details recues of some thirty-one lives from a variety of vessels during a storm on 16th June 1878. See EVA of 1877.

1853	Anne Chesshyre	ship	451t	Brundrit and Whiteway

According to Runcova Volume I: The first ship built in Runcorn; carrying capacity of 700t; launched on Monday, 28th February 1853; Mr. William Whiteway appointed captain.

I have a list provided to me by Mr. Ken Stubbs (who himself got the list from his grandfather, Jack Stubbs, the shipwright) that shows a number of significant vessels built by "Messrs. Brundrit and Whiteway... later Brundrit and Hayes".

This list gives the date for this vessel's launch as 1859. It also spells the name "Annie Cheshire" and gives her description as "barque".

Michael Stammers, in his "Building Flats at Runcorn" in *Waterways Journal Vol. 5*, calls this vessel "Ann Cheshyre".

Described in Starkey's "Iron Clipper 'Tayleur'" as the largest vessel ever built at Runcorn but she held that record only up to the point of the launch of DENNIS BRUNDRIT in 1856.

1853	Anne Walker	schooner	128t	Samuel Mason

Felted and zinc-clad. Registered by Lloyd's as A1.

1853	Uncle Tom	flat	52t	?
1854	Brackley	schooner	88t	Brundrit and Whiteway

Note: Mersey Flats and Flatmen states that, according to *Marwood's Register of Liverpool Shipping* (published in 1854), nine flats were completed in Runcorn in 1854.

Therefore:

1854	?	flat	?	?
1854	?	flat	?	?
1854	?	flat	?	?
1854	?	flat	?	?
1854	?	flat	?	?
1854	?	flat	?	?
1854	?	flat	?	?
1854	?	flat	?	?
1854	?	flat	?	?
1855	Alma	schooner	118t	Brundrit and Whiteway

Note: Runcorn Family History Group (and www.curiousfox.com) give some detail of the Alma's fate.

She sank off Anglesey in a storm in 1879 under command of Captain James Patten.

1854	?	flat	?	?
1855	Mary Houghton	schooner	71t	Brundrit and Whiteway
1855	Penmae	sloop	54t	?
1855	Borland	barquentine	141t	?
1856	Edward Whitley	flat	?	?
1856	Dennis Brundrit	ship	462t	Brundrit and Whiteway

Said to be the smallest full-rigged ship in the world.

The list given to me by Mr. Ken Stubbs shows a number of significant vessels built by "Messrs. Brundrit and Whiteway... later Brundrit and Hayes".

This list gives the date for this vessel's launch as 1857. It also spells the name "Denis Brundrit".

1856	Reviresco	brig	114T	?

Felted and zinc-clad. Registered by Lloyd's as A1.

1857	Ellen Owen	brigantine	132T	?
1857	Bertha	schooner	87T	J. and T. Johnson
1857	Cheshire Lass	schooner	85T	?
1857	Squall	sloop	7T	Brundrit and Whiteway
1857	Samuel	flat	67T	?
1857	Selina	schooner	99T	?
1857	Delhi	flat	57T	Anderton
1857	Llanfair	sloop	52T	Brundrit and Whiteway

1857   Agnes   flat   51T   ?

This information comes from Percy Dunbavand, after researching the Liverpool registers.

He describes Agnes thus: Wooden one-masted flat, carvel-built with round stern; registered on 20th February 1860.

Owners: Robert Pierpoint, book keeper of Runcorn (twenty-two shares); Thomas Speakman, coal agent of Runcorn (twenty-one shares); Peter Greenhough, publican of St Helens (twenty-one shares).

65.2ft × 16.7ft × 6.9ft; official number 28185; registration closed 10th July 1885.

1858   Widders   sloop   ?   Brundrit and Whiteway
Launched in July.

My great great grandfather, William Ratcliffe (1829–1890), had a sister called Sarah (born 1819), who married a Richard Widders (born 1824). I am not sure if there is a link to this vessel here.

Starkey states in *Schooner Port* she was launched sideways; in common with others, as he states that, some vessels "were launched broadside into the river".

1858	Robin	flat	43t	?
1858	Gipsey Queen	smack	31t	?
1858	Kingfisher	smack	35t	?
1858	James	sloop	67t	Anderton

Built for Raynes, Upton and Company of Liverpool. Launched on 3rd April; christened by James Raynes.

1858	Gwyder	smack	55t	Brundrit and Whiteway
1858	Star	flat	37t	?
1859	Lymm Gray	brig	123t	Anderton
1859	Jessie Roberts	schooner	69t	Anderton
1859	Alice	schooner	65t	Brundrit and Whiteway
1859	Elizabeth and Ann	flat	55	?
1859	Bertie	smack	61t	Brundrit and Whiteway

Terry Kavanagh states (*27) that this vessel (ON 27945) was bought by Abel Towing Co. (a subsidiary of Richard Abel and Sons) in 1917 from Edward Tyson of Liverpool. Sold on to William Cooper and Sons of Widnes in the late 1920s.

1859   Charles Whiteway   schooner   ?   Brundrit and Whiteway

The list given to me by Mr. Ken Stubbs shows a number of significant vessels built by "Messrs. Brundrit and Whiteway… later Brundrit and Hayes".

This list gives the details provided here for this vessel, which I previously knew nothing about.

1860	Duck	smack	34t	?
1860	Quanita	brig	190t	Anderton
1860	Aggravator	steam tug	54 grt	John Mason

69.3ft × 17ft × 6.6ft; two cylinder, 18 nhp engine by unknown builder. Owned at some point by Weston Point Steam Towing Co. Ltd.?; 1873, sold to George Rodrigues of Liverpool; wrecked in 1899 at Port Neigwl, South Caernarvonshire.

Info from Tug Talk.

1861	Priory	schooner	88t	Brundrit and Whiteway
1861	Lancashire Lass	schooner	56t	?
1861	Swan	flat	36t	?
1861	Ada	sloop	36t	?
1862	Rival	schooner	106t	Mason
1862	Barlochan	barque	227t	Anderton
1862	Francis	schooner	55t	?
1862	?	narrowboat	?	Speakman
1862	?	narrowboat	?	Speakman
1862	?	narrowboat	?	Speakman

All three launched on 6th December

1863	Phoebe	schooner	123t	Mason
1863	Eclipse	schooner	78t	Brundrit and Whiteway
1863	Sandfly	flat	19t	?
1863	Julia	flat	40t	?

Note: This may be the schooner of that name rescued by the Castletown RNLI on 8th December 1886, according to the Irish Wrecks website.

1863	Hannah	flat	53t	?
1863	Jessie	flat	32t	?
1863	Laffak	flat	42t	

1864   Alice   wood paddle steamer   107t   ?

Later taken over by the M.S.C. Co. and broken up in the early 1900s (info care of *Tugs of Manchester Ship Canal* by W. B. Hallam).

1864   Oak   flat   42t   William Bate?

Terry Kavanagh's article, "Richard Abel and Sons, of Runcorn and Liverpool" (*Waterways Journal Vol. 16*), gives this information:

OAK OF RUNCORN, 42 tons, built in Runcorn in 1864; ON80288; rebuilt 11 years later while belonging to William Bate; acquired by Richard Abel and Sons in October 1886; registry cancelled in December 1895.

Was she one and the same with this vessel, and was she built and rebuilt by William Bate?

1864	Listers	flat	50t	?
1864	Frances Mary	flat	44t	?
1865	Eliza	flat	62t	?
1865	Jessie	schooner	132t	Anderton
1865	Swift	flat	66t	Brundrit and Whiteway
1866	Parker	smack	58t	?
1866	William	sloop	63t	?
1867	Preston	wood screw steamer	42t?	Brundrit and Whiteway

Note: Schooner Port states that, according to the annual statements of the Navigation and Shipping of the United Kingdom (compiled by H.M.S.O.), one steamer of 28t was completed in Runcorn in 1867.

Note: According to www.steamershistorical.co.uk/steamers_bridgewater_tugs.htm:

69' x 14' 6"; two cylinder engine giving 25hp; built for Bridgewater Trustees, passing to Bridgewater Navigation Co. in 1872 and to the Upper Mersey Navigation Commission in 1885 (who used her for buoy maintenance); broken up 1929.

1867   Comet   flat   56t   Joseph Clarke

Note: Schooner Port states that, according to the annual statements of the Navigation and Shipping of the United Kingdom (compiled by H.M.S.O.), seven sailing vessels to a total of 421t were completed in Runcorn in 1867.

Therefore:

1867	?	topsail schooner	?	Anderton
1867	?	sailing vessel	?	?
1867	?	sailing vessel	?	?
1867	?	sailing vessel	?	?
1867	?	sailing vessel	?	?
1867	?	sailing vessel	?	?

Note: A picture in *Images of England: Runcorn, a Century of Change* by Bert Starkey shows two sailing vessels at Castle Rock shipyard, with a quote stating that "schooners and river flats are being repaired", although only two vessels seem visible.

A Pictorial History of the Mersey and Irwell Navigation by John Corbridge shows the same picture, with a quote stating: "a topsail schooner being built, and another under repair".

Therefore:

1867   ?   schooner   ?   Anderton?
Repair only.

And see first of the six vessels listed above.

1868   Redtail   schooner   80t   Blundell and Mason
Described in *Schooner Port* in separate entries as either "Redtail" or "Red Tail", respectively.

Percy Dunbavand gives her details as:

Redtail; two-masted; 91t; launched by Sarah Dunbavand, wife of Thomas (Tom) Dunbavand (Percy Dumavand's great grandfather's brother) on 23rd July 1868; Tom Dunbavand signed on to this vessel on 24th July and sailed with her for the next fifteen years until discharge on 3rd March 1883 to join a new schooner FOX.

Tom's eldest son, John, joined the Redtail as a boy in July 1878 and the following year was promoted to cook. At sixteen (presumably in 1880 as he was born in 1864) he was an ordinary seaman.

Redtail was sunk by a submarine in 1917 while carrying a cargo of coal.

1868?   ?   ?   ?   Blundell and Mason
1868?   ?   ?   ?   Blundell and Mason
Note: The above two vessels were either built or repaired by Blundell and Mason; they may have actually launched/relaunched later than 1868. The

information is solely from a photograph (dated 1867) of "Red Tail" on the stocks at the yard, along with the other two.

1868?   Swallow   smack   67t   Brundrit and Whiteway
Terry Kavanagh states (*27) this vessel (ON 62003) was bought by Abel Towing Co. (a subsidiary of Richard Abel and Sons) in 1917 from Edward Tyson of Liverpool.
    Sold on to William Cooper and Sons of Widnes in the late 1920s.

1868   Rival   lightship   ?   ?
Repaired at Runcorn in this year for the Upper Mersey Navigation Commissioners.*17

Note: "Schooner Port" states that according to the annual statements of the Navigation and Shipping of the United Kingdom (compiled by H.M.S.O.), nine sailing vessels and two steamers to a total of 565t and 134t, respectively, were completed in Runcorn in 1868.
    Therefore:

1868	?	sailing vessel	?	?
1868	?	sailing vessel	?	?
1868	?	sailing vessel	?	?
1868	?	sailing vessel	?	?
1868	?	sailing vessel	?	?
1868	?	sailing vessel	?	?
1868	?	sailing vessel	?	?
1868	?	steam vessel	?	?
1868	?	steam vessel	?	?
1869	Emily	?	?	Speakman
1869	Pride	flat	79t	Blundell and Mason

Waterways Journal Vol. 5, "Building Flats at Runcorn" by Michael Stammers describes this vessel as being of similar dimensions to the iron flat detailed below but says she was a foot wider in the beam.
    She was owned by Blundell and Mason, who took all the shares, suggesting she was built as a speculation. Most shares were later sold to William Deakin.

1869   ?   iron flat   ?   Blundell and Mason
Waterways Journal Vol. 5, "Building Flats at Runcorn" by Michael Stammers

talks about an interesting vessel. It states that Blundell and Mason signed a contract on 29th September 1868 with William and Thomas Deakin and A.E. Ackerly for the building of an iron sailing flat. The price agreed for the fully completed iron-hulled vessel, fully outfitted with spars and sails was £800. Stammers was uncertain as to whether this vessel was ever completed, but states that the contract stipulated the launch was to be by April 1869.

I have no later record of any work completed by this partnership other than "Pride", above, and as Stammers says, "Blundell and Mason do not appear to have produced any more vessels after this one" that he describes here. Presumably then, this is the last vessel the company built and, although no name is recorded for her anywhere, she may well have been omitted from the registers because of her being limited to inland trade only.

Stammers describes her dimensions as this:
Specified as "for the river trade" and larger than the average flat (which tended to be around 63ft long and 14ft 6in in beam); length 70ft on the keel; extreme breadth of 18ft'; depth of Hold 8ft 2in; very strong, "judging by her dimensions and her wrought iron components"; keel, stem and stern posts were best bar iron, 6in × 2in; frames were 2½in angle iron; plating was 3/8in thick with 7/16in for the bilge strake; three keelsons inside the hull, the centreline one being 10in wide and ½in thick with two angle irons riveted on top for extra strength, the two bilge keelsons were of double angle iron on either side.

A heavy stringer slate 12in deep and 3/8in thick supported the deck beams and strengthened the sides; iron bulkheads at each end of the hold; iron rudder;

The waterways, deck planking, hatch coamings and headledges and deckhead of the hold were all of best quality timber. For example, the deck planks were 6in × 2½in yellow pine and the deckhead was elm to withstand heavy bulk cargoes; timber heads actually made of cast iron.

The whole hull to be given three coats of paint, the cabin and forecastle to be fitted-out "as usual" and grained and varnished; mast of pitch pine and spars of spruce; sails and everything else needed for trading were to be provided.
1869 William Bowden schooner 130t Brundrit and Whiteway
Described in the main text of *Schooner Port* as "William Boden" but in the appendix as above.

1869 Spectacular wood screw steamer 32t ?
1869 Speculator steam tug 32 grt ?
65.2ft × 12.6ft × 6.8ft; 2 cylinder, 32 NHP engine by unknown builder; owned at some stage by Weston Point Steam Towing Co. Ltd.?; 1869: owned by

Richard Clark (harbour master of Weston Point) and others; 1872: sold to Portugal.

Information from Tug Talk, where the "ATOR" end of names was specifically discussed, as it was associated with the Weston Point Steam Towing Co. Ltd., so I believe this is a separate vessel to the one above, and not a typo.

Note: Schooner Port states, according to the annual statements of the Navigation and Shipping of the United Kingdom (compiled by H.M.S.O.), eleven sailing vessels and three steamers to a total of 734t and 45t, respectively, were completed in Runcorn in 1869.

Therefore:

1869	?	sailing vessel	?	?
1869	?	sailing vessel	?	?
1869	?	sailing vessel	?	?
1869	?	sailing vessel	?	?
1869	?	sailing vessel	?	?
1869	?	sailing vessel	?	?
1869	?	sailing vessel	?	?
1869	?	sailing vessel	?	?

Plus, either one more sailing vessel or one more steamer:

1869	?	sailing/steam vessel	?	?

Note: Schooner Port states, according to the annual statements of the Navigation and Shipping of the United Kingdom (compiled by H.M.S.O.), four sailing vessels and four steamers to a total of 779t and 484t, respectively, were completed in Runcorn in 1870. In the main text of the book however, it states four sailing vessels were completed in this year, but this is likely to be a typing error.

Therefore:

1870	?	sailing vessel	?	?
1870	?	sailing vessel	?	?
1870	?	sailing vessel	?	?
1870	?	sailing vessel	?	?
1870	?	sailing vessel	?	?
1870	?	sailing vessel	?	?

1870	?	sailing vessel	?	?
1870	?	sailing vessel	?	?
1870	?	sailing vessel	?	?
1870	?	sailing vessel	?	?
1870	?	sailing vessel	?	?
1870	?	sailing vessel	?	?
1870	?	sailing vessel	?	?
1870	?	sailing vessel	?	?
1870	?	steamer	?	?
1870	?	steamer	?	?
1870	?	steamer	?	?
1870	?	steamer	?	?

Note: Schooner Port states, according to the annual statements of the Navigation and Shipping of the United Kingdom (compiled by H.M.S.O.), two sailing vessels to a total of 185t (and no steamers) were completed in Runcorn in 1871. In the main text of the book, however, it states four small vessels of an average displacement of 61t were launched in that year.

Therefore:

1871	?	sailing vessel	?	?
1871	?	sailing vessel	?	?
1871	?	sailing vessel	?	?
1871	?	sailing vessel	?	?
1872	John Ellis	flat	flat	Bridgewater?

Note: According to the main text of *Schooner Port*, no sea-going vessels were built in Runcorn in 1872.

Schooner Port had no details for a builder or type of vessel, but Alf Hayman states in *Waterways Journal Vol. 4* that she was a Mersey flat launched in December 1872 and implies she was built by the Bridgewater Trustees.

1873 Traffic wood screw steamer 83t? Speakman and Co.
Launched 22nd September 1872; Owner: began working life as a baggage and stores tender at Liverpool; sold to Liverpool Lighterage Co. for port duties in 1896; converted to a dumb barge with engine removed in 1919; sunk on 5th May 1941 in Liverpool Docks during the May blitz by the Luftwaffe; later raised and returned to service until 1955.

155GRT; service speed eight knots; 101ft 10in × 23ft × 7in; broken up on Tranmere Beach in 1955.

Note: Schooner Port states, according to the annual statements of the Navigation and Shipping of the United Kingdom (compiled by H.M.S.O.), one steamer to a total of 45t was completed in Runcorn in 1873.

Note: According to the Historical Merchant Navy, White Star Line website at www.red-duster.co.uk/WSTAR4.htm, TRAFFIC was 155 GRT, 101ft 10in in length, 23ft 7in beam; launched on 22nd Sep, 1872. In 1919, her engine was removed and she served as a "dump barge" (dumb barge?). She was sunk in 1941 in a bombing raid by the Luftwaffe but was raised again and continued to serve until being broken up at Tranmere in 1955.

Note: According to www.titanic-titanic.com/traffic_1.shtml, "TRAFFIC I" was built for the White Star Company and spent her entire career at Liverpool.

Gross tonnage 155t; 101.8ft × 23.6ft; single propeller; one × two cylinder single expansion engine; two decks; one funnel; one mast.

Note: Schooner Port states, according to the annual statements of the Navigation and Shipping of the United Kingdom (compiled by H.M.S.O.), four Sailing vessels to a total of 309t (in the main text, it says a total of 354t) were completed in Runcorn in 1873.

Therefore:

1873	?	sailing vessel	?	?
1873	?	sailing vessel	?	?
1873	?	sailing vessel	?	?
1873	?	sailing vessel	?	?
1874	James	flat	34t	Anderton
1874	Runcorn	wooden motor tug /little packet *2 / *17	?	Bridgewater (Old Quay)

Note: Waterways Journal Volume of May 1999 describes Runcorn thus: 63ft × 9ft'; 14HP steamer from Plenty and Sons, with 12in" bore single cylinder and 16in stroke, water-cooled from the canal by pump and with 80 psi exhausted steam to atmosphere; four-bladed propeller of 36in diameter and 200 rpm.

Authorised 2nd February 1874 and delivered in August. *Note:* According to www.steamershistorical.co.uk/steamers_bridgewater_tugs.htm, delivered October 1874;

63ft × 9ft or 68ft × 10ft 6in; 9HP engine costing £350.

1875   John   iron screw steamer   65t   Speakman
Note: Percy Dunbavand describes JOHN thus: wooden screw steamer with one mast, sloop rig, carvel-built with elliptical stern.

Registered Runcorn, 23rd June 1875; owner: Joseph Andrew Keales, Merchant of Liverpool (64 shares).

74.8ft × 18.6ft × 7ft; 19t then 25t (presumably rebuilt/refitted?); 25 H.P.; official number 70953; registration closed 30th July 1931; vessel broken up.

1875   Rose   flat   44t   Speakman
Note: Percy Dunbavand describes ROSE thus: built 1858; single-masted barge, yawl rig with square stern; owner: Philip Speakman of Runcorn.

76.1ft x 15ft x 5.9ft; 40t; official number 97225.

Foundered off Llandulas, 21st October 1894.

1875   Oak (of Runcorn)   flat   42t   William Bate?
rebuild only.

Rebuilt in this year when under ownership of William Bate, so presumably at his yard. *27

1876   George B   flat   78t   Speakman
This information comes from Percy Dunbavand, after researching the Liverpool registers.

He describes GEORGE B. thus: wooden one-masted flat, carvel-built with elliptical stern;

Registered on 22nd August 1876; owner: Thomas Thompson, coal agent of Liverpool (64 shares); sold to Liverpool Lighterage Co. 9th September 1896.

73.7ft × 19ft' × 8.1ft; official number 74539; registration closed 3rd March 1938; vessel broken up.

1877   St Helens   flat   68t   Speakman
Note: Schooner Port does not give a builder's name for St Helens but Percy Dunbavand describes her thus: wooden one-masted flat, carvel-built with elliptical stern; built by Speakman; Registered 28th September 1882; owner: The Liverpool and St. Helens Lighterage Company (64t); sold to Liverpool Lighterage Co. 12th September 1896.

67ft x 17ft x 8ft'; official number 86227; sank in the Mersey, 23rd November 1911.

1877   Florinda   flat   71t   Speakman

Note: Schooner Port does not give a builder's name for FLORINDA, but Percy Dunbavand describes her thus: mast flat with elliptic stern; registered Runcorn, No. 5/1877; owner: Philip Speakman of Runcorn.

72.5ft × 18.2ft × 7.5ft; official number 67165; foundered off Hoyle Bank, 3rd January 1890. Possibly, she was built by Speakman for his own fleet.

1877   Clara   flat   84t   Speakman

Note: Schooner Port does not give a builder's name for CLARA but Percy Dunbavand describes her thus: wooden one-masted flat, carvel-built with elliptical stern; built by Speakman; Registered 21st January 1878.

Owners: Richard Muspratt, chemical manufacturer of Flint; Edmund Knowles Muspratt, chemical manufacturer of Liverpool; John Kingsby Huntley, chemical manufacturer of Liverpool; (joint owners until Richard Muspratt died 18th August 1885); vessel sold to United Alkali Co. on 16th July 1891.

74.6ft x 18.8ft x 8ft; 84t then 73t (presumably rebuilt/refitted?); official number 78742; registration closed 5th March 1921; vessel sunk off Hale Head 12th February 1921, a total loss.

1877   Amazon   flat   88t   Speakman

This information comes from Percy Dunbavand, after researching the Liverpool registers.

He describes AMAZON thus: wooden one-masted flat, carvel-built with round stern; Registered on 28th March 1899; owner: Liverpool Lighterage Co. (64 shares).

76.2ft × 19.2ft × 8.6ft; official number 110550; registration closed 12th December 1958; vessel burned and completely destroyed.

Note: Schooner Port states, according to the annual statements of the Navigation and Shipping of the United Kingdom (compiled by H.M.S.O.), three sailing vessels to a total of 233t (and no steamers) were completed in Runcorn in 1877.

This is one sailing vessel fewer than detailed above.

1877   Eva   flat   ?   Brundrit and Whiteway

I have a list provided to me by Mr. Ken Stubbs (who himself got the list from his grandfather, Jack Stubbs, the shipwright) that shows a number of significant vessels built by "Messrs. Brundrit and Whiteway… later Brundrit and Hayes".

This list gives the details provided here for this vessel, which I previously knew nothing about.

Note: May be the EVA described as a schooner of Runcorn on the website, www.old-merseytimes.co.uk/lifeboats1896.html. This vessel had two crew members rescued from her during a storm in late 1896. Another contender is the Brigantine built in 1853 but this flat may well have been schooner-rigged like many of her contemporaries and thus better fit the bill.

Or, this may be the Runcorn fishing vessel of that name mentioned on the website, www.caithness.org, which details recues of some 31 lives from a variety of vessels during a storm on 16th June 1878.

Note: Frank Ogle decribes this vessel as a barge.*31

See EVA of 1853.

1878   Martyn   ketch   67t   Brundrit and Co.

Presumably, the same as the 55t ketch "Marten" or "Runcorn" built in Runcorn in 1878 and later owned by persons in Kirkcudbright.*3

The list given to me by Mr. Ken Stubbs shows a number of significant vessels built by "Messrs. Brundrit and Whiteway… later Brundrit and Hayes".

This list states that the vessel was a ketch.

Terry Kavanagh references the Runcorn-built ketch MARTEN (ON67167) (*27).

Frank Ogle calls her "Martin"; a schooner.*31

1878   A.M. Brundrit   schooner   112t   Brundrit and Co.

Wrecked off Black Island, Labrador, in 1885. The list given to me by Mr. Ken Stubbs shows a number of significant vessels built by "Messrs. Brundrit and Whiteway… later Brundrit and Hayes". This list gives the launch date for this vessel as 1879, and also gives the name as "A. N. Brundrit".

Frank Ogle gives the launch date as 1882.*31

1878   Agnes   flat   48t   John Stubbs and Son
1878   Widnes   flat   51t   Speakman

Note: Schooner Port does not give a builder's name for Widnes but Percy Dunbavand describes her thus: wooden one-masted flat, carvel-built with elliptical stern; built by Speakman; Registered 28th September 1882; owner:

The Liverpool and St. Helens Lighterage Co. (64 shares); sold to Liverpool Lighterage Co. on 12ᵗʰ September 1896.

    70ft × 15ft × 6.1ft; official number 86229; registration closed, 9ᵗʰ October 1936; vessel broken up at Runcorn.

1878	William and Alice	flat	90t	John Stubbs and Son
1878	Fiona	flat	54t	Speakman

Note: Percy Dunbavand describes Fiona thus: year built unknown; mast flat with square stern; registered Runcorn, No. 7/1878; owner: Philip Speakman of Runcorn.

    63.4ft × 17.2ft × 6.3ft; 53t; official number 67170.

    Stranded off Mostyn and became a total wreck, 19ᵗʰ December 1884.

1878	Fanny	flat	?	Brundrit and Co.

Frank Ogle describes FANNY as a jigger flat.*31

    The list given to me by Mr. Ken Stubbs shows a number of significant vessels built by "Messrs. Brundrit and Whiteway… later Brundrit and Hayes".

    This list gives the above details, that I previously knew nothing about.

Note: Schooner Port states, according to the annual statements of the Navigation and Shipping of the United Kingdom (compiled by H.M.S.O.), ten sailing vessels to a total of 808t (and no steamers) were completed in Runcorn in 1878.

    Therefore:

1878	Widnes	flat	51t	Speakman
1878	?	sailing vessel	?	?
1878	?	sailing vessel	?	?
1878	?	sailing vessel	?	?
1879	Harvest King	schooner	100t	Brundrit and Co.

Note: Schooner Port does not give a vessel type for HARVEST KING, but *Schooner Sunset* describes her thus: wood, auxiliary-engined three-masted schooner; registered Londonderry.

    91.3ft × 21.7ft × 10.5ft; 119t gross, 81t net; official number 80290; Signal hoist EIGN.

Note: Coastwise Sail describes HARVEST KING as being "today a cut down three-masted auxiliary schooner", and makes clear the ship was a later conversion to auxiliary.

Note: www.waterfordcountyimages.org describes the ship as being a "two-masted schooner" that was later converted to "three-pole masts" when she was engined.

Note: The Irish newspaper *Independent* tells us that the ship was, by 1899, owned by Richard Kearon of Arklow. She was later sold to Arklow Pottery Ltd. At the age of 75, she voyaged to Youghal, Cork, to appear in the 1956 film *Moby Dick*, appearing as the TIT BIT. The year after filming (1955 according to the article), HARVEST KING was stripped of all useful equipment and beached at Porter's Rocks (this was apparently a common means of avoiding scrapping fees).

I have a photocopy of a picture of this vessel given to me by Mr. Ken Stubbs (grandson of Jack Stubbs the shipwright) and on the back Ken has written she was built by Brundrit and Whiteway. She also features on the list of vessels built by "Messrs. Brundrit and Whiteway... later Brundrit and Hayes" he gave to me.

This ship is also one listed by Frank Ogle.*31

1879   Bryan   flat   87t   ? *Note:* Percy Dunbavand describes this vessel, which he called, "Brynn" thus: wooden one-masted flat, carvel-built with elliptical stern; registered Runcorn, No. 7/1878.

Owners: Thomas Thompson, colliery agent of Liverpool (32 shares); Henry Hall Crippin, colliery agent of Liverpool (32 shares); vessel sold to Liverpool Lighterage September 1896.

75.1ft × 18.9ft × 8.5ft; 86t; official number 81301.

Registration closed 7th April 1971; vessel broken up.

1879   Garston   flat   68t   Speakman *Note: Schooner Port* does not give a builder's name for GARSTON but Percy Dunbavand describes her thus: wooden one-masted flat, carvel-built with elliptical stern; built by Speakman; registered 28th September 1882.

Owner: The Liverpool and St Helens Lighterage Co. (64 shares); sold to Liverpool Lighterage Co. on 12th September 1896; sold to Port of Liverpool Stevedoring on 6th February 1925; sold to United Grain Elevators on 11th May 1934.

67.8ft × 17ft × 8ft; 67t; official number 86230.

Registration closed 15th November 1934; vessel broken up.

1879   Willie   flat   69t   Brundrit and Co. *Note: Schooner Port* states, according to the annual statements of the Navigation and Shipping of the United Kingdom (compiled by H.M.S.O.), seven sailing vessels to a total of 663t (and no steamers) were completed in Runcorn in 1879.

Therefore:

1879	?	sailing vessel	?	?
1879	?	sailing vessel	?	?
1879	?	sailing vessel	?	?
1880	Edward Whitley	barge	?	Brundrit and Co.

Percy Dunbavand says Brundrit's were working on a barge called EDWARD WHITLEY prior to building SNOWFLAKE. Was she a sailing barge? If so, she should maybe be included in the list of sailing vessels built in Runcorn in 1880, below.

The list given to me by Mr. Ken Stubbs shows a number of significant vessels built by "Messrs. Brundrit and Whiteway... later Brundrit and Hayes".

This list details this vessel as a flat and states that she was launched in 1886. Frank Ogle states that EDWARD WHITLEY was a jigger flat.*31

1880   Snowflake   schooner   96t   Brundrit and Co.
Note: Schooner Sunset describes SNOWFLAKE (or "Snow Flake") thus: wood, two-masted schooner; Flat's stern, or Irish Sea stern as it was otherwise known; Registered Runcorn.

88.2ft × 21.8ft × 9.7ft; 109t gross, 88t net; official number 80298; Signal hoist MDMJ.

Note: "Days of Sail on the Upper Mersey", an article in *Port of Manchester Review* for 1975 (by William E. Leathwood), describes the above dimensions and weight, with the exception that the net tonnage is given as 84. It further states the ship had a Lancashire stern.

Note: The original article from which the above seems to have been taken, was a same-named essay in *Sea Breezes* magazine for June 1974.

Note: Coastwise Sail describes SNOWFLAKE (or "Snow Flake") thus: topsail schooner, later fore-and-aft auxiliary schooner.

The list given to me by Mr. Ken Stubbs shows a number of significant vessels built by "Messrs. Brundrit and Whiteway... later Brundrit and Hayes".

This list gives the launch date for this vessel as 1881.

Frank Ogle also lists the SNOWFLAKE.*31

The auctioneers Bonham's had for sale in 2006 a model/diorama of Snowflake by Brian Williams that sold for £180.

1880   Hannah and Joseph   flat   57t   Speakman Built in Northwich in 1828 and rebuilt by Speakman in this year.

This information comes from Percy Dunbavand, after researching the Liverpool registers.

He describes HANNAH and JOSEPH thus: wooden one-masted flat, carvel-built with elliptical stern; first registered in 1846, then on 16th December 1880; owner: Philip Speakman of Runcorn (64 shares); later sold.

66.3ft × 16.8ft × 6.7ft; official number 8848.

Foundered five miles south by west from North West Lightship in Liverpool Bay, 17th January 1892.

Note: Schooner Port states, according to the annual statements of the Navigation and Shipping of the United Kingdom (compiled by H.M.S.O.), seven sailing vessels and one steamer to a total of 640t and 180t, respectively, were completed in Runcorn in 1880.

Therefore:

1880   ?   sailing vessel   ?   ?
1880   ?   sailing vessel   ?   ?
1880   ?   sailing vessel   ?   ?
1880   ?   sailing vessel   ?   ?
1880   ?   sailing vessel   ?   ?
1880   ?   sailing vessel   ?   ?
1880   ?   steamer   ?   ?

Frank Ogle lists "Two Mud Hoppers" as built in 1880 by "J. Davies", whom I believe to be the manager of Brundrit's. These must be two of the above sailing vessels.*31

1880   Faraway   schooner   ?   ?

Schooner Port states: "Faraway dragged her anchor and she was swept into the path of a large steamer to suffer a broken bowsprit and foremast. Accidents such as these and the repair of lesser injuries kept Runcorn shipyards busy…".

Can it be assumed that repairs to this vessel took place in Runcorn?

1881   Reginald   screw steamer/ steam flat   116t   Brundrit and Co.

She also features on the list of vessels built by "Messrs. Brundrit and Whiteway... later Brundrit and Hayes" given me by Ken Stubbs, who received this list from his grandfather, Jack Stubbs, the shipwright.

A few years later, she was sold to J. Jorgensen of Bergen and her name changed to BREMNAES.

Frank Ogle also lists this steamer.*31

Note: Schooner Port states, according to the annual statements of the Navigation and Shipping of the United Kingdom (compiled by H.M.S.O.), six sailing vessels and four steamers to a total of 440t and 301t, respectively, were completed in Runcorn in 1881.

Therefore:

1881	?	sailing vessel	?	?
1881	?	sailing vessel	?	?
1881	?	sailing vessel	?	?
1881	?	sailing vessel	?	?
1881	?	sailing vessel	?	?
1881	?	sailing vessel	?	?
1881	?	steamer	?	?
1881	?	steamer	?	?
1881	?	steamer	?	?
1881	Abstainer	schooner	?	?

Damaged in that year and towed to Runcorn for repairs.

1881 Robert schooner ? Samuel Stubbs Repair only. www.plimsoll.org/resources/SCCLibraries/WreckReports/ 14622.asp gives the evidence for this.

1882 Lilly Heaps flat 56t Brundrit and Co.
The list given to me by Mr. Ken Stubbs shows a number of significant vessels built by "Messrs. Brundrit and Whiteway... later Brundrit and Hayes".

This list details this vessel as "Lily Heaps" and states she was launched in 1885.

Terry Kavanagh (*27) states this vessel (ON86182) was a mast flat launched for master Mariner James Heaps and was later bought by Richard Abel and Sons. She was broken up in December 1925.

Frank Ogle calls this vessel "Lily Heaps" and describes her as a jigger flat.*31

Note: Schooner Port states, according to the annual statements of the Navigation and Shipping of the United Kingdom (compiled by H.M.S.O.), eight sailing vessels and one steamer to a total of 600t and 86t, respectively, were completed in Runcorn in 1882.

Therefore:

1882	?	sailing vessel	?	?
1882	?	sailing vessel	?	?
1882	?	sailing vessel	?	?
1882	?	sailing vessel	?	?
1882	?	sailing vessel	?	?
1882	?	sailing vessel	?	?
1882	?	sailing vessel	?	?
1882	?	steamer	?	?
1883	Sunbeam	Schooner	135t	Brundrit and Co.

The list given to me by Mr. Ken Stubbs shows a number of significant vessels built by "Messrs. Brundrit and Whiteway… later Brundrit and Hayes".

This list details this vessel as a three-masted schooner.

Frank Ogle also lists this vessel.*31

1883   Fox   schooner   100t   Brundrit and Co.

Percy Dunbavand describes FOX thus: built by John Brundrit; three-masted. 127t; 96'4ft overall length × 22ft 5in beam × 10ft 2in depth of hold; carried about 220t of cargo.

Launched by one of Tom Dunbavand's daughters (the relation of Percy mentioned earlier as Captain of Redtail) on 7th April 1883.

Tom Dunbavand signed articles for her on 14th April and sailed with her for nearly twenty-seven years. His son, John, joined the ship with him as an ordinary seaman in 1883. In September 1884, John was promoted to mate, leaving the FOX on 23rd June 1888 only to re-join as mate on 24th September that year until discharged at London on 21st May 1890.

The FOX left Cowes on the Isle of White on 18th December 1909 and arrived at Southampton in January 1911 (?). While at anchor in Fishguard Bay, a gale sprang up and her cables parted; she was cast ashore on Saddle Point. The crew were rescued by the coastguard with rocket apparatus. The ship was broken up where she lay.

The captain at the time was John Richard Janion, a man from another famous Runcorn seafaring family (friends of ours also) who was a distant cousin of Percy Dunbavand's grandfather.

The list given to me by Mr. Ken Stubbs shows a number of significant vessels built by "Messrs. Brundrit and Whiteway… later Brundrit and Hayes".

This list details this vessel as a three-masted schooner.

The launch report from the *Runcorn Guardian* newspaper gives the following info: Designed by yard manager Mr. John S. Davies; launched on Saturday, 7th April 1883; built for Thomas Cooper and Co..

Frames, deck framing and top sides of English oak; keelson of pitchpine; outside bottom planking up to the bilges is of rock elm; decks of yellow pine.

Registered tonnage 99 71.100; expected to carry 220t of cargo; 90ft 6in on the keel, 22 ½ft beam, 10ft 3in depth of hold.

Classed 12 years A1 by Lloyds; rigged by Mr. John Bate; full suit of sails supplied by Mr. S. Ravenscroft; all painting and decorative work by Mr. George Yarwood; figurehead and stern carvings by Mr. Clotworthy of Liverpool.

Frank Ogle also lists this vessel.*31

Note: *Schooner Port* states, according to the annual statements of the Navigation and Shipping of the United Kingdom (compiled by H.M.S.O.), three sailing vessels and six steamers to a total of 290t and 730t, respectively, were completed in Runcorn in 1883.

Therefore:

1883	?	sailing vessel	?	?
1883	?	steamer	?	?
1883	?	steamer	?	?
1883	?	steamer	?	?
1883	?	steamer	?	?
1883	?	steamer	?	?
1883	?	steamer	?	?
1884	Elizabeth Bennett	Schooner	154t	Brundrit and Co.

I have a photocopy of a picture of this vessel given to me by Mr. Ken Stubbs (grandson of Jack Stubbs the shipwright) and on the back Ken has written she was built by Brundrit and Whiteway.

The list given to me by Mr. Ken Stubbs shows a number of significant vessels built by "Messrs. Brundrit and Whiteway… later Brundrit and Hayes". This list details this vessel as a three-masted schooner.

The auctioneers Bonham's had for sale in 2009 a painting of this ship by John Russell Chancellor. It sold for £16,800.

Its website gave this information: topsail schooner; owned by Allen Green

and Co. of Liverpool; 162t gross (150 net); 104ft in length; 23ft beam.
Frank Ogle also lists this vessel.*31

1885   Alert   schooner   147t   Brundrit and Co. **Note:** *Schooner Sunset* describes Alert thus: wood, three-masted schooner; registered Falmouth.
103.8ft × 23.6ft × 11.1ft or 31.64m × 7.19m × 3.38m; 163t gross, 133t net; official number 83511; Signal hoist MJBK;
Photos of her deck gear taken by the late Dan McDonald have been copied and are in the National Maritime Museum.

Note: "Days of Sail on the Upper Mersey", an article in *Port of Manchester Review* for 1975 (by William E. Leathwood), describes the vessel as follows: 104ft × 23.5ft' × 11ft'; 165t gross.

Note: The original article from which the above seems to have been taken, was a same-named essay in the *Sea Breezes* magazine for June 1974. This article goes on to say that in 1938 Alert became a yacht before eventually being broken up.

Note: http://ballastblog.blogspot.co.uk/2009_09_01_archive.html gives the following details: top sail schooner; 143 net register tons; registered throughout her life at Runcorn, Fowey, Baumaris, Falmouth.

Note: A listing for an item for an internet auction by Dix Noonan Webb mentions the "topsail schooner" ALERT, of eight crew. However, there is no mention of the ship on its website and I can only imagine the item was sold.
The artist Anne Barrell advertises some earthenware tiles and plates with a picture of Alert on them. I have some of these items in my possession.
Frank Ogle also lists this vessel.*31
David R. MacGregor, in his book *Schooners in Four Centuries*, states there is a model of a three-masted schooner called ALERT in the Parker Gallery. Furthermore, he shows a photograph in the book and says he believes this to be the vessel built in Runcorn.

1885   ?   flat?   ?   Mason?
Either built or repaired at the Belvedere Yard, as evidenced by a famous photograph of the waterfront from this year. One example is to be found on page 12 of *Starkey's Images of England: Runcorn, a Century of Change.*

1885   Ada   yacht   22grt   William Roberts of Chester
Engine (C2cy 14nhp 70ihp 10kn) built by E. Timmins of Runcorn.

Note: David Asprey on the Tug Talk Website describes ADA thus: wood; 55ft
× 10ft × 6ft; 22grt, 15nrt; official number ON 96117.

Owners: built as yacht for William Ringrose Atkins, Cork (reg. Cork);
1897, George Elliot Pyle and Ernest Elliot Pyle, London; 1899, Walter Beavis,
Bristol; E. J. Agius and Co. Ltd., Southampton, converted to tug (21grt, 6nrt);
1906, The Great Yarmouth Transport Co. Ltd., Great Yarmouth (manager
Blake and Palmer) (reg. Yarmouth); 16th July 1918 hired by the Ministry of
Shipping for service with US forces canal transport in France, based in Le
Havre; 19th September 1919, lost off St.Valery-en-Caux (probably on return
to UK).

1885   ?   "Brierley Boat"   ?   Brundrit and Co.
1885   ?   "Brierley Boat"   ?   Brundrit and Co.
Listed by Frank Ogle.*31
1886   Despatch   schooner   145t   Brundrit and Co./ Brundrit and
                                                    Hayes?
Launched 4th May

Schooner Port and other sources describe DESPATCH as being built by
Brundrit and Hayes, yet the appendix to the book states that Brundrit and Co.
was the builder.

The list given to me by Mr. Ken Stubbs shows a number of significant
vessels built by "Messrs. Brundrit and Whiteway... later Brundrit and Hayes".
This list details this vessel as a three-masted schooner.

Mike Stammers' "Building Flats at Runcorn" in *Waterways Journal Vol. 5*
gives the exact date of launch.

Frank Ogle lists this vessel as "Dispatch".

The ship is described as "HMS" DESPATCH in a couple of books but I
have found no evidence to support the notion she was ever a commissioned
ship of the Royal Navy (much to my regret, as that would have been fantastic).

1886   Mars   lightship   ?   Brundrit and Co./ Brundrit and Hayes?
And another Lightship called "Runcorn"?

Mersey Docks Fleet List 1850–1980 describes Mars thus: lightship, Iron
schooner; owner: Mersey Docks and Harbour Board; converted to barge in

1912; vessel broken up.

70ft × 17ft × 7.9ft; 69.66t; official number 93706; Registration closed, 4th October 1927 (scrapped in this year).

I have a photocopy of a picture of this vessel given to me by Mr. Ken Stubbs (grandson of Jack Stubbs the Shipwright) and on the back Ken has written that she was built by Brundrit and Whiteway.

The list given to me by Mr. Ken Stubbs shows a number of significant vessels built by "Messrs. Brundrit and Whiteway… later Brundrit and Hayes".

This list contains details of this vessel.

1886   Edward   flat   ?   Brundrit and Co.

The list given to me by Mr. Ken Stubbs shows a number of significant vessels built by "Messrs. Brundrit and Whiteway… later Brundrit and Hayes".

This list contains details of this vessel, which I previously knew nothing of. Frank Ogle also lists this vessel.*31

Note: Schooner Port states, according to the annual statements of the Navigation and Shipping of the United Kingdom (compiled by H.M.S.O.), four sailing vessels and one steamer to a total of 352t and 70t, respectively, were completed in Runcorn in 1886.

Therefore:

1886	?	sailing vessel	?	?
1886	?	steam vessel	?	?
1887	Percy	flat	85t	? and Co./ Brundrit and Hayes?

Note: www.cotswoldcanalsheritage.org.uk gives Percy as: originally a schooner; wood.

73.4ft × 19.5ft × 8.5ft; 104g/t; 36r/t; official number 83518.

A 20hp engine was put in her in 1912 and she was owned by the Steam Flat Percy Co. Ltd. Of Liverpool; registered at Runcorn but at one time "evidence [to suggest she was] owned at Severnside".

The list given to me by Mr. Ken Stubbs shows a number of significant vessels built by "Messrs. Brundrit and Whiteway… later Brundrit and Hayes". This list contains details of this vessel.

Frank Ogle describes this vessel as a steamer.*31

Note: Schooner Port states, according to the annual statements of the Navigation and Shipping of the United Kingdom (compiled by H.M.S.O.), one sailing vessel and one steamer to a total of 89t and 135t, respectively, were completed in Runcorn in 1887.

Therefore:

1887　?　steamer　135t　?

Note: Schooner Port states, according to the annual statements of the Navigation and Shipping of the United Kingdom (compiled by H.M.S.O.), two steamers (and no sailing vessels) to a total of 225t were completed in Runcorn in 1888.

Therefore:

1888　?　steamer　?　?
1888　?　steamer　?　?

However, Percy Dunbavand describes the EDWARD as follows:

1888　?　sailing flat　?　Brundrit

Built for George Harrison Bolton, chemical manufacturer of Widnes; sold 1890/1 to United Alkali Co./I.C.I., then in 1937 to the Mersey, Weaver and Ship Canal Carrying Co., along with JOHN and WILLIAM. Both vessels had by this time been cut down to dumb barges.

EDWARD sank while in tow by Abel's LITTLEDALE; she was struck by KINSHASA. Later raised and beached at Stone Delph Quarry (Sandy Cove), she was subsequently broken up.

However, the above must not have included dumb barges, as:

1888　Oakdale　barge　46t　William Bate
ON143721.

Later bought by Richard Abel and Sons. Removed from Liverpool register in October 1922.
*27

1889　?　flat　?　Anderton?*22
1889　?　flat　?　Anderton?*22

Note: Schooner Port states, according to the annual statements of the Navigation and Shipping of the United Kingdom (compiled by H.M.S.O.), one sailing vessel (and no steamers) of 80t was completed in Runcorn in 1890.

Therefore:

1890   ?   sailing vessel   80t   ?

Note: Schooner Port states, according to the annual statements of the Navigation and Shipping of the United Kingdom (compiled by H.M.S.O.), three sailing vessels (and no steamers) to a total of 259t were completed in Runcorn in 1891.

Therefore:

1891   ?   sailing vessel   ?   ?
1891   ?   sailing vessel   ?   ?
1891   ?   sailing vessel   ?   ?

An article, "Manchester Ship Canal" in *Narrowboat* magazine for Winter 2011/2 shows a fantastic photo of Runcorn's waterfront that I had previously not seen. It shows a vessel under construction at Castle Rock but is undated.

However, more or less the same background scene is repeated in a photo from the opposite perspective in *Images of England, Runcorn: Second Selection* by Starkey. It shows the gantry wall in the same early stages of build and even shows a flat beached to the west of Belvedere Yard, just as in the "new" picture. It is dated 1891.

Therefore, it may well be that the ribs of the vessel being built on the berth at Castle Rock is one of these above. It may of course be an entirely separate vessel. This picture is the one that shows the construction of the vessel in question on a fore-and-aft berth I previously knew nothing about. Furthermore, the beached ship may well be awaiting repair.

Note: Schooner Port states, according to the annual statements of the Navigation and Shipping of the United Kingdom (compiled by H.M.S.O.), two sailing vessels and two steamers to a total of 139t and 88t, respectively, were completed in Runcorn in 1892.

Therefore:

1892   ?   sailing vessel   ?   ?
1892   ?   sailing vessel   ?   ?
1892   ?   steamer   ?   ?
1892   ?   steamer   ?   ?

However, the above must not have included dumb barges, as:

1892   George Dawson   barge   48t   William Bate
Later bought by Richard Abel and Sons and renamed WINIFRED ABEL (ON140550).

Rebuilt by Abel's 30 years later and worked until "beyond practicable repair" and sunk in the Flashes at Northwich in August 1946.
*27

1892   Laura Bate   barge   48t   William Bate
Later bought by Richard Abel and Sons and renamed SWALEDALE (ON140605).
Rebuilt by Abel's in 1918, her registry was closed in July 1947.
*27

Note: *Schooner Port* states, according to the annual statements of the Navigation and Shipping of the United Kingdom (compiled by H.M.S.O.), one steamer (and no sailing vessels) of 77t was completed in Runcorn in 1893.
    Therefore:

1893   ?   steamer   77T   ?
1896   Rival   lightship ?   ?
Repair only.
Damaged when a flat being towed rammed her. Her mooring chain was slipped to prevent her foundering and she was towed to Runcorn for repairs. Nothing more is said by Starkey as to where and by whom.

1896   Heathdale   flat   55t   Richard Abel and Sons
Dumb Barge, registered at Liverpool (ON140575) sometime between 1914 and 1939.
*27

1897   Rival   lightship   ?   ?
Repaired at Runcorn in this year for the Upper Mersey Navigation Commissioners.*17

1898   Rival   lightship   ?   ?
Repaired at Runcorn in this year for the Upper Mersey Navigation Commissioners. *17

1900   -----   steam engine   -----   E. Timmins and Sons Ltd.
Engine built for the Manchester Ship Canal Co.'s firefighting paddle launch FIREFLY (or FIREFLY II). The hull was built by W. Roberts of Chester as a

steam yacht, with firefighting equipment provided by Merryweather and Co. Ltd. of London.

1902   Bee   flat (temporary lightship)   ?   Richard Abel and Sons

(Repair only)
Flat owned by M.S.C. Co. but hired by Upper Mersey Navigation Commissioners at the time and involved in a collision with one of Abel's boats.*17

1902?   Thames   knobstick   ?   ?
Registered in Runcorn in 1902 "and probably built there".*8

1904   ?   barge/flat?   ?   Mason?
Either built or repaired at the Belvedere Yard, as evidenced by what looks like a barge or flat in a photograph of the waterfront from this year. It can be found on page 20 of Starkey's *Images of England: Runcorn, a Century of Change.*

1906   Helen Bate   schooner   68t net   Charles Stubbs
Two-masted wooden schooner built in Runcorn and registered in Liverpool (Official Number 145946; no signal hoist).

Abel's vessels were registered in Liverpool and many had the "Bate" family connection, so I had assumed it built this vessel (*18). However, Terry Kavanagh's research reveals the builder was Charles Stubbs and the vessel was indeed 68t (*27).

He goes on to state Abel's renamed her HAWKESDALE (ON145948) and her registry was closed fifty years after she was built.

1906   Clarence   flat/barge   ?   Bridgewater (Victoria)
Repair only.*25

1907   Richard Abel   flat   69t   Richard Abel and Sons
Composite Dumb Barge; N1073; master Joseph Abel, brother of the late Richard Abel. Registered at Liverpool Custom House ON 140547 ten years later.
*27

1911   Coronation   flat/barge   ?   Bridgewater (Victoria)
Damaged beyond repair by a ship in Manchester in 1947. *Colours of the Cut* gives her number as 1099.

1913   Empire   flat/barge   ?   Bridgewater (Victoria)
1913   Carrier   flat/barge   ?   Bridgewater (Victoria)
Mike Stammers gives the date for this vessel as 1911 (and this source gives the date of launch as 21st June that year) but then goes on to say that next came two more between 1911 and 1913, then stating that a picture in his *Waterways Journal Vol. 5* article shows Carrier and Empire under construction "about 1912-13". Therefore, I believe his initial statement is a typo.

In the article he describes the flats as being unusually built (focusing on the vessel in the foreground of the picture he shows), with the bottom planking in place despite being only partially framed. Furthermore, it had a much smaller keelson than usual without the rider keelson on top and "sister" keelsons on either side. Apparently, these flats had a unique form of planking where the bottom ones were cross-boarded as they are in a *narrowboat*.

1914   Mull   narrowboat ?   Simpson, Davies and Co.
1914   Emuraffe   flat   2t   Richard Abel and Sons
Dumb Barge, registered at Liverpool (ON137430) sometime between 1914 and 1939. Registered under the Abel Towing Co., one of the subsidiary firms of the Abel empire. Became a total loss following sinking in a collision in January 1919.
*27

1915   ?   flat   ?   Richard Abel and Sons*6
1916   Nidderdale   barge   61t   Richard Abel and Sons
Rebuild only. ON143596. Bought by Abel's and rebuilt in this year. Disposed of twenty-one years later.
*27

1917   Dunsdale   flat   41t   Richard Abel and Sons
Dumb barge, registered at Liverpool (ON140580) in 1917. Sunk in dock in December 1936 and had to be raised and then broken up.
*27

1918   Swaledale   barge   48t   Richard Abel and Sons
Rebuild only.
*27

1920?   Keskadale   jigger flat   ?   Richard Abel and Sons
Rebuilt by the above company from the jigger flat, "Herbert".*

1920   Liberator   sloop/flat   74t   Richard Abel and Sons
Rebuild only.
Built at Winsford in 1874 and bought by Abel's, who rebuilt her this year.
She was renamed by that firm as ARMADALE, and later STAINTONDALE,
presumably the latter straight after rebuild, following purchase. Registry was
closed twenty-four years later.
    STAINTONDALE was beached near Frodsham Bridge and became the
headquarters of the sailing club there for many years before being recently
scrapped
*27

1921   Wharfedale   barge   39t   Richard Abel and Sons
Rebuild only.
Built at Stretford by Henry Rathbone in 1890 (ON14322) and bought by
Abel's, who rebuilt her this year.
*27

1921   Tobin   schooner   171t   Richard Abel and Sons
Rebuild only.
ON7882 as TOBIN, belonging to the North British Railway Co., Glasgow.
Built in Liverpool in 1850 and converted to a barge by Abel's when they
bought her. Renamed GARSDALE. Her registry was closed in 1971.
*27

1922   Winifred Abel   barge   48t   Richard Abel and Sons
Rebuild only.
*27

1922   Sleddale   barge   49t   Richard Abel and Sons
Rebuild only.
Built at Stretford by Henry Rathbone in 1892 (ON145933) and bought by

Abel's, who rebuilt her this year. Her registry was closed in January 1949.
*27

1922   Bracadale   barge   46t   Richard Abel and Sons
Rebuild only.
Built by an unknown builder around 1894 as EPSILON (ON137094) (owned
by Harris Bros.) and bought by Abel's, who rebuilt her this year. She was
broken up in August 1953.
    Wooden dumb barge but became a composite vessel after the rebuild when
Abel's gave her steel frames.
*27

1923   ?   narrowboat   ?   Simpson, Davies
Build or Repair?
Information solely from a photograph of a boat on the slipway from that year.

1923   Vencedora   barge   67t   Richard Abel and Sons
Rebuild only.
Built as a sailing flat at Northwich by Cornelius Gibson in 1875 (ON78774) and
converted to a lightship by the Upper Mersey Navigation Commission. Later
bought by Abel's, who rebuilt her this year, renaming her LITTONDALE.
*27

1924   Baysdale   barge   54t   Richard Abel and Sons
Rebuild only.
ON45909. Built as the wooden steam flat PETER by J. Venables and Co. of
Northwich in 1863 for Bagots of Liverpool. Bought by Abel's and rebuilt in
this year, her registry being closed thirty years later.
*27

1926   Straight Tip/Bedale   flat/barge   93t   Richard Abel and Sons
Rebuild only.
The sailing flat STRAIGHT TIP was built by William Newall at Ellesmere
Port in 1878 and owned by William Beckett Hill of Liverpool until sale to
Abel's. It rebuilt her in 1926 and renamed her BEDALE.
    Registry closed in March 1959 after she was partially broken up. She could
still be seen beached at Wigg Island until at least 1975.
    Information from *Waterways Journal Vol. 15*, "Ship and Boat Building at

Ellesmere Port: A History" by Terry Kavanagh.

In a later article (*27), Terry Kavanagh describes the STRAIGHT TIP as: mast flat; built 1877; 95t; ON78760 when BEDALE; registered as such in May 1926.

1927   Stockton   packet tug   ?   Bridgewater (Victoria or packet dry dock?)
Converted from steam to diesel engine in or from this year.*19
1927   Walton   packet tug   ?   Bridgewater (Victoria or packet dry dock?)
Converted from steam to diesel engine in or from this year.*19
Waterways Journal of May 1999 states that it was a conversion to "semi-diesel".
1927   Lymm   packet tug   ?   Bridgewater (Victoria or packet dry dock?)
Converted from steam to diesel engine in or from this year.*19
Lymm was later sold to Abel's and renamed Dovedale.*24
1927   ?   packet tug   ?   Bridgewater (Victoria or packet dry dock?)
Converted from steam to diesel engine in or from this year.*19
1927   ?   packet tug   ?   Bridgewater (Victoria or packet dry dock?)
Converted from steam to diesel engine in or from this year.*19
1927   ?   packet tug   ?   Bridgewater (Victoria or packet dry dock?)
Converted from steam to diesel engine in or from this year.*19
1927   ?   packet tug   ?   Bridgewater (Victoria or packet dry dock?)
Converted from steam to diesel engine in or from this year.*19
1927   ?   packet tug   ?   Bridgewater (Victoria or packet dry dock?)
Converted from steam to diesel engine in or from this year.*19
1927   ?   packet tug   ?   Bridgewater (Victoria or packet dry dock?)
Converted from steam to diesel engine in or from this year.*19
1927   ?   packet tug   ?   Bridgewater (Victoria or packet dry dock?)
Converted from steam to diesel engine in or from this year.*19
1927   ?   packet tug   ?   Bridgewater (Victoria or packet dry dock?)
Converted from steam to diesel engine in or from this year.*19
1927   ?   packet tug   ?   Bridgewater (Victoria or packet dry dock?)
Converted from steam to diesel engine in or from this year.*19
1927   ?   packet tug   ?   Bridgewater (Victoria or packet dry dock?)
Converted from steam to diesel engine in or from this year.*19
1927   ?   packet tug   ?   Bridgewater (Victoria or packet dry dock?)
Converted from steam to diesel engine in or from this year.*19
1927   ?   packet tug   ?   Bridgewater (Victoria or packet dry dock?)

Converted from steam to diesel engine in or from this year.*19

1927 ? packet tug ? Bridgewater (Victoria or packet dry dock?)
Converted from steam to diesel engine in or from this year.*19

1927 ? packet tug ? Bridgewater (Victoria or packet dry dock?)
Converted from steam to diesel engine in or from this year.*19

1927 ? packet tug ? Bridgewater (Victoria or packet dry dock?)
Converted from steam to diesel engine in or from this year.*19

The above vessels were to be converted along with the entire twenty-six miniature tug fleet of the Bridgewater Department but in the end seven were scrapped and only the above nineteen were changed to diesel.

1928 Liddisdale flat 43t Richard Abel and Sons
Dumb barge, registered at Liverpool (ON161063) in 1928.
*27

1928 Lothersdale steamer 114t Richard Abel and Sons
Rebuild only.
Built by Ann Deakin of Winsford in 1877 as CYNOSURE (wooden dumb barge ON86226) and converted to steam by about 1880. Bought by Abel's from the Salt Union in October 1926 and renamed LOTHERSDALE.

22hp steam flat; 84.2ft × 20.5ft × 8.8ft; two cylinders of 11in × 12in stroke; marine type boiler at 120psi.

Broken up in May 1957.
*27

1931 Fanny Crosfield three-master 119t gross Stubbs
Repair only.*26

1933 Mossdale flat ? Richard Abel and Sons
The flat RUBY, built c.1860 by unknown builders, was bought by Abel's in 1921, and renamed, MOSSDALE. This is a rebuild of that flat. According to Terry Kavanagh (*27), she was "completely rebuilt down to the hog".

Built around 1863 of carvel construction of oak, elm and pitch pine; extensively rebuilt and deepened by Abel's; 71ft 11½in × 14ft 3in × 5ft 6in.

Mainly used to carry grain between Liverpool, Birkenhead, Ellesmere Port, Runcorn and Manchester; found abandoned in Ellesmere Port in 1970 and now preserved at Ellesmere Port Boat Museum.

c. 1935?   Irish Minstrel   schooner   154t   ?

Possible conversion only. The ship was converted to a barge around 1935 in the Mersey and, being as she wintered for three months every year at Runcorn, it may well have been there that she was cut down.

1936   Mary Sinclair   barge   ?   Richard Abel and Sons

Conversion only?

The above vessel was a sailing ship that collided with the Bar light ship in 1936 and was subsequently in the employ of Abel's as a barge.*26

Was she converted to a barge by that firm?

1936/7   Ralph Brocklebank

Daniel Adamson   tug tender   ?   M.S.C. Co. and John Brown and Co.

Refit only.

In this year, major modifications were made to this famous vessel at Runcorn by the M.S.C. Co. and personnel from John Brown's on the Clyde. The men from John Brown's must have used the facilities and workers of the Old Quay Yard at Runcorn, as that was the principle repair facility of the M.S.C. Co. for its tugs, etc.

The following is from the article, "The Tug/Tender Ralph Brocklebank and its Conversion to the Daniel Adamson" by Tony Hirst, from *Waterways Journal Vol. 15*:

The work involved two periods on the pontoon dry dock at Ellesmere Port for survey and repair of the hull and sea cocks, as well as general cleaning and painting, before she was brought to Runcorn.

A letter from the mechanical engineer in charge of Old Quay Workshops, H.G. Pringle, gives the following estimated costs for the work:

Bridge deck, £303 10/-;

Main deck, £399 10/-;

Saloon, £175;

Galley, £35;

Aft cabin, £38.

The overall cost therefore would have been £951 (£50,000 today): Much less than the expected £17,000 + in old money a new vessel would have cost;

Heaton Tabb and Co. of Liverpool did most of the design and work for the fitting out; Willow and Garing of Manchester provided the saloon furniture; Henry Wood and Co. of Chester completed the repairs to the anchor and cable;

canvas gear was provided by Robert Grieg's of Runcorn; Class 3 lifeboat of 14ft in length supplied by Rutherford's of Birkenhead at a cost of £42; "Neptune" floating seats also supplied by Rutherford's; firefighting gear supplied by Pyrene Co. Ltd. (today's market leader, Chubb);

Work began at Runcorn on 24th February 1936 and finished in May 1937. Following the correction of the items found to be in need of attention by the Board of Trade, the job was signed off as completed on 2nd June 1937.

As Tony Hirst puts it, "No record of the final cost has come to light but reading the conversion correspondence and noting the additional work undertaken beyond that specified in the estimate of the 27th November 1935, it is likely that it exceeded the original estimate but still a long way short of the cost of a new vessel. It is amazing that from initial discussions about a new director's launch, to completing the conversion of the RALPH BROCKLEBANK for this role, took less than 11 months, a time that it is unlikely to be matched today".

1937   Foredale   steam barge   183t g   Richard Abel and Sons
Repair only.
Composite steam barge built in 1920 by W.J. Yarwood and Sons of Northwich as BOUNTY (ON143662).
95.9ft × 21.9ft × 9.7ft; 27hp compound direct acting inverted engine (with cylinders of 12in and 27in × 17in stroke) by Cochran and Co. of Birkenhead.

Bought from William Cooper and Sons of Widnes by Abel's in 1937 and renamed FOREDALE; in a collision in 1933 on the Manchester Ship Canal at Ellesmere Port with the Steamer SENTRY. Possibly repaired by Abel's but no reference to this found.

Sunk again four years later in another collision on the Ship Canal, and this time repaired by Abel's before being re-registered at Liverpool later that year.

Registry closed for good in 1962.
*27

1938   Mary Sinclair   schooner   ?   Stubbs
Overhaul by Jack Stubbs at his yard. He regularly repaired a number of locally-owned sailing vessels.

Information from an article in the *Daily Express* of that year, an extract of which was given to me by Mr. Ken Stubbs, the grandson of shipwright Jack Stubbs.

See entry for this ship in 1936.

1939   Fred Abel   barge   ?   Richard Abel and Sons
According to *27: Flat/dumb barge, registered at Liverpool (ON16627) in 1939.

1940?   Surveyor No.2   wooden motor launch   11.42t   Richard Abel
                                                                    and Sons
Built by J.S. White and sold from the Mersey Docks and Harbour Board to Richard Abel and Sons on 9th December 1939 and converted by that firm to a tug. Renamed, presumably on completion of the conversion, LITTLEDALE on 24th January 1940.
Single screw; 45.2ft × 9.6ft × 4.6ft; 11.42t and 5.16t (?).
Sold to Thos. Hodges on 10th August 1954.
*23

1944   Aviator   tug   66t   Richard Abel and Sons?
Refit Only.
According to *Waterways Journal Vol. 7*, this was the tug's third refit.
     She was built in 1876 for the Weston Point Towing Co. by Preston Iron and Steel Co.; Registered in 1911 as AVIATOR and was bought by Abel's after an earlier refit at Yarwood's in Northwich.

1944   Pride o' th' Weaver   weaver packet   178t g   Richard Abel and
                                                                    Sons
Conversion only.
Built as a weaver packet (ON110530) in 1898 for Henry Seddon of Middlewich.
     Bought by Abel's and then converted to a dumb barge, giving her the name of PATTERDALE when re-registering her in July 1944.
     Broken up in the 1960s.
     *27

1947?   Lymm   little packet   15t g   Richard Abel and Sons
Refit only.
Built by Richard Smith at Preston in 1875 as an iron-hulled motor tug. Bought by Abel's in 1947 and given a modern squat funnel and wheelhouse as well as the new name, DOVEDALE (ON183745).
     50bhp two-cylinder Widdop semi-diesel engine installed in 1927/8. Broken up at Ellesmere Port around the mid-1960s.
     *27

1947   ?   barge   ?   Richard Abel and Sons
Repair or build?
Evidence from a photograph from Britain from the Air website.

?   HEATHDALE   barge/flat   ?   Richard Abel and Sons
See entry below for OAKDALE. This vessel must have been built sometime before OAKDALE.

1950/1   Oakdale   barge/flat   63t   Richard Abel and Sons
Built of composite construction (wood and steel) to a design similar to those built by Abel's in the 1850s;
　　　Lister HA3 diesel engine; 72ft 6in × 15ft 9in × 3ft.
　　　Once berthed at Merseyside Maritime Museum, then beached at Lytham St Annes on the way to Cumbria for repair, she is now undergoing restoration at Duddon Estuary in Cumbria by her owner, Mr. David ("Dave") Keenan.
　　　One website (www.pittdixon.go-plus.net) describes her as being built in 1957 (by which time Abel's had shut the Castle Rock Yard). I believe this may be a confusion from the apparent fact that the current engine was built in that year, in accordance with www.nationalhistoricships.org, which also states: 72.5ft × 15.75ft; depth 3ft; gross tonnage 66, but Terry Kavanagh gives this as 63t (*27).
　　　Built "of composite construction" "to the same pattern as boats built by Abel's in the 1850s", with a Lister HA3 diesel engine.
　　　According to Michael Stammers, in his "Building Flats at Runcorn" from *Waterways Journal Vol. 5*, this and the RUTH BATE were built "to the same design which is considerably different in shape to the traditional form" being for example, "almost as square in the bow as the Humber keels". They were designed by Mr. Albert Andrews, the manager of the yard, and he "incorporated a great deal of steel into the framing".
　　　There were three steel keelsons instead of the usual one centreline one as this reduced the amount of the hold taken up by large timber pieces, which would reduce cargo capacity. Straight side frames rolled from steel and the framing timbers at the bow and stern were "fashioned in the traditional way". Additionally, the hatch coamings were also of steel, instead of the traditional timber. All of this gave these vessels great strength. She was built for the company's own fleet.
　　　Her current owner has converted her hold and fitted an engine and a small mast capable of carrying a gaff mainsail and jib.

Dave Keenan wrote an article for the Winter 1990 edition of *The Slabline* (journal of the Humber Keel and Sloop Preservation Society) in which he gave the following details:

He bought the vessel many years before (in about 1975, according to a later article in the *Runcorn Weekly News* dated 25th September 2014) for £300 (or £400 according to the *Runcorn Weekly News*) and went about the surviving barge companies to buy the necessary spares.

In 1929, materials were bought by Abel's to build five flats, but then came the Great Depression and such plans were shelved for the time being. It built FRED ABEL in 1936 (named after Frederica Abel, the owner's mother) and then World War II interrupted expansion plans again. By the end of the war, a steel shortage delayed the next vessel and hence OAKDALE was not started until 1949. It was eventually launched on Saturday, 15th September 1951 by Mrs. F. Abel (with 1930s-built frames). RUTH BATE and HEATHDALE were also built from these materials but what happened to the remaining fifth set of frames is a mystery. This paragraph is all from Dave Keenan's research.

OAKDALE worked for Abel's until 1963 when the company ceased trading and was sold to Rea's. Rea's sold her in 1966;. She was then sold to a man who wished to make her into a floating restaurant but the plans fell through and Mr. Keenan bought her;

The *Runcorn Weekly News* article mentioned above states the barge had been bought by Mr. Keenan when she was lying in deep mud at Burscough near a pub, whose landlord was trying to open her as a restaurant. Dave Keenan took her to Brunswick Dock in Liverpool and later refitted her at the Bootle Barge Company;

72ft 6in × 15ft 9in × 6ft 6in moulded depth; 66 reg tons gross, 63 reg tons net, 52 tons displacement in working order, cargo capacity 120t, official number 183820, but Terry Kavanagh gives it as 183829 (*27);

Composite construction, with iron frames running the length of her parallel body and wood frames from the forward and aft bulkhead. A greenheart bottom and from the turn of the bilges to deck level she is of oak, with her decks of Oregon pine.

Terry Kavanagh describes her as a composite dumb barge with steel frames and wood planking, belonging to William Bate and Co. of Runcorn (*27).

1950/1　?　flat/barge　?　Richard Abel and Sons
A picture in *Waterways Journal Vol. 6* shows the launch of OAKDALE "circa

1950" and there is another flat on the slip in the foreground, presumably under repair.

1953   Ruth Bate   flat/barge   60t   Richard Abel and Sons
Launched 18th May. See entry for OAKDALE, above.

Built for William Bates and Co. but when the company folded in the early 1960s, the Ruth Bate was bought by the Maghull branch of St John's Ambulance Brigade and used as its base on the Leeds and Liverpool Canal. Later in private hands in the mid-1980s, she was left to sink at Burscough. Later raised and taken to Widnes West Bank with a view to restoring her, she was sunk at the basin there until funds became available. She was later raised and broken up in 1999 when those funds were not forthcoming.

ON 185464 and tonnage from research by Terry Kavanagh, who also gives the launch date as March 1953 (*27).

Terry Kavanagh describes her as a composite dumb barge with steel frames and wood planking, belonging to William Bate and Co. of Runcorn (*27).

There is a photograph from the Britain from the Air website showing a barge on the slip at Abel's Yard; I am not sure if it was this vessel or another.

1953   Camel   ?   ?   Stubbs
On Slip at Stubbs's yard for survey after being holed and sunk in collision with ACUITY in April of that year; presumably repaired by the company.*10

1954   Eva   tug   33t   Bridgewater (Runcorn Docks)
Repair only.*20

1956   ?   flat/barge   ?   Richard Abel and Sons
A picture in *Waterways Journal Vol. 5*, "Building Flats at Runcorn" by Michael Stammers shows a "wooden flat under repair at Abel's Castle Rock Yard in 1956".

1958   Silver Jubilee   narrowboat   ?   Simpson Davies
Seen on the slipway for survey (and perhaps repair also?) in a photograph from *Runcorn Through Time* by Roy Gough.

A further narrowboat is tied-up alongside the slipway and another one is seen alongside a cabin cruiser, further north of it. Other vessels can be seen in the picture but they appear to be amongst those abandoned on the Big Pool around this time.

1959   Jonathon   narrowboat   ?   Simpson Davies
Repair only.
One of Jonathon Horsefield's boats, she was captured in a photograph in April
of this year under repair at the yard. The picture is part of the Waterways
Archive maintained at Ellesmere Port Boat Museum.

1959   ?   cabin cruiser   ?   ? at packet dry dock
Repair only?
A photograph from the Waterways Archive (maintained at the Ellesmere Port
Boat Museum) shows this vessel on the packet dry dock in April of this year,
presumably under repair.

1960   MSC Stanlow   tug   ?   M.S.C. Co.
Refit only.
Conducted at Old Quay as evidenced by a photo and comments on Ship's
Nostalgia website.

1960   ?   ?   ?   M.S.C. Co.
Repair only?*14

1960?   ?   barge   ?   Richard Abel and Sons
Quite a well-known picture of Abel's Yard used in various publications, for
example *Waterways Journal Vol. 5*, shows this barge on the slip being worked
on "about 1960". There is also another barge alongside at the yard.

There are other shots available in local books showing a barge at Abel's
with the Runcorn-Widnes Road Bridge (Silver Jubilee Bridge) at around the
same stage of construction.

1961   Mary P Cooper   steamer   1,250dwt   M.S.C. Co.
Salvage Work only.
The vessel was sunk in a collision with the coaster FOAMVILLE and had to be
salvaged and removed from the canal. A massive undertaking was thus begun,
involving Admiralty tugs and pontoons as well as resources from across the
M.S.C. Co.

Divers were used to take measurements and also to conduct subsequent
fitting work for the gear required in the lifting process. Head office engineers
designed two hatch covers to seal the holds. These were then constructed at
Old Quay, each in two sections of nine tons, and measuring 22ft × 20ft ×

2ft. Greenheart timbers were required for supporting the sides of the salvage vessel, DISPENSER, which had been brought in by the Liverpool and Glasgow Salvage Association to support the operation. These will have no doubt been machined at Old Quay also.

1962/3   M.S.C. Arrow   tug   ?   M.S.C. Co.
Converted from steam to diesel engine at Old Quay Yard in this period.*10

1962?   Southam   narrowboat   ?   ?
Launched in 1936 but not built in Runcorn; fitted with an engine there.*7
(See later entry on Southam, below)

1966?-?   Rita?   narrowboat   ?   Ron Turner (Preston Brook) (Top Locks)
(Rebuild only and later? Worked on her at Top Locks)

1966?–?   Adele   Narrowboat (steel)   60ft   Ron Turner
(Preston Brook)
Ron Turner's first steel boat. (Still in existence, Ron believes, in London).

1966?–?   ?   narrowboat (oil boat)   70ft   Ron Turner
(Preston Brook)
(A Rebuild of an old Clayton's oil boat, after which only one original plank remained).

?   Bargus   narrowboat   ?   Ron Turner (Top Locks)
(This job was a request from someone to put in a steel deck to replace the original wooden one for the owner. The owner didn't get enough steel, so just the fore-end was done)

1966?-?   Charlotte   narrowboat   ?   Ron Turner (Timmins' Yard)
(Still in existence, Ron believes, in London).

1966?-?   Sundance   narrowboat   ?   Ron Turner (Timmins' Yard)
1966?-?   Owl   tug   ?   Ron Turner (Timmins' Yard)
1966?-?   ?   narrowboat   ?   Ron Turner (Runcorn Docks)
1966?-?   ?   narrowboat   ?   Ron Turner (Runcorn Docks)
1970   M.S.C. Puma tug   ?   M.S.C. Co.
Percy Dunbavand describes an incident where the PUMA, of which Percy was

captain, was struck by the Sand Hopper, WILLIAM COOPER. PUMA suffered a small split in the hull and a fractured water pipe. She was unable to use her engines and had to be towed to Runcorn by the tug UDINE. Presumably, she was then repaired at Old Quay.

1971   46   barge   ?   M.S.C. Co.
First vessel to slip at the newly rebuilt slipway at Old Quay (on 17 December). Information from Percy Dunbavand.

1972   Worcester   motor tug   ?   North Western Museum of Inland Waterways/Navigation (Today's Ellesmere Port Boat Museum)
Rebuilt only.
Evidence from a picture in *Waterways Journal Vol. 7*, showing the vessel in the "dry dock at Dutton" – presumably the covered dry dock at Dutton.

1974   M.S.C. Dainty   tug   ?   M.S.C. Co.
Repair only.*12
The first vessel to use the newly opened facility (after the May 1974 construction) – according to official M.S.C. Co. Records. This obviously contradicts what Percy Dunbavand recollects and I would rather believe him than the company records.

1975?   June   Yorkshire keel   ?   Peter Froud?
(Repair/rebuild only?)
Iron Yorkshire keel; built in late 1880s probably for the Aire and Calder Navigation Co.
57ft × 13ft 10in.
    This vessel was, in 1988, under the ownership of a Mr. Chris Topp. He bought her from Peter Froud in 1975 after the latter had dug her out of a rubbish tip in Preston Brook.
    It is probable the repair work done to this vessel was undertaken by Peter Froud as that is what he used to do at Preston Brook. Evidence from *Waterways World* magazine from April 1988.

1979?   Piper A   oil rig   ?   M.S.C. Co.
The gate repair shed at Old Quay Yard made a contribution to modernising the oil rig above by machining seventeen greenheart logs ranging from 35ft to 44ft in length for use in the construction of a helicopter landing platform.

1980   ?   narrowboat (steel)   70ft   Ron Turner (Boat and Butty)
(Built in two halves at Frodsham Old Mill and welded/launched at Boat and Butty Yard).

1980   Hereward   narrowboat (steel)   50ft   Ron Turner (Boat and Butty)
(Built in two halves at Frodsham Old Mill and welded/launched at Boat and Butty Yard).

?   Hazel   narrowboat (steel)   70ft'   Ron Turner (Boat and Butty)
(Built in two halves at Frodsham Old Mill and welded/launched at Boat and Butty Yard)
(Named after Ron's wife)

?   May   narrowboat (steel)   70ft   Ron Turner (Boat and Butty)
(Built in two halves at Frodsham Old Mill and welded/launched at Boat and Butty Yard)

?   ?   narrowboat (steel)   50ft   Ron Turner (Boat and Butty)
(Built in two halves at Frodsham Old Mill and welded/launched at Boat and Butty Yard)

?   Ant   narrowboat   ?   Ron Turner
(Old working boat that had been converted to a pleasure craft. Ron Turner stripped her ready for use as a carrier again and used her for salt transport. Ron Turner carried the last four boat loads of salt to Weston Point)

?   Axe   narrowboat   ?   Ron Turner
(Old working boat that had been converted to a pleasure craft. Ron Turner stripped her ready for use as a carrier again and used her for salt transport. Ron Turner carried the last four boat loads of salt to Weston Point)

1981?   Daphne   saloon launch   ?   Pyranha
            (35ft' "beaver-tailed" mid-1920s pleasure craft)
Rebuild/repair only.*19

1987?   ?   ?   ?   M.S.C. Co.
Repair only.*13

1992? Southam narrowboat ? Wooden Canal Craft Trust/ Wooden Canal Boat Society
Repair only.
Launched in 1936 by Walker of Rickmansworth. Bought in 1992 by British Waterways and sold to the Wooden Canal Craft Trust (now the Wooden Canal Boat Society). It took her to Runcorn for extensive refit and the installation of an engine. (See entry for Southam above)

On the National Historic Ships Register.
1994 Davenham Brunner ? Old Quay Public Slipway
Repair only.
This vessel is one specifically named by Peel Ports commercial controller Joe Blythe as having been worked on at Old Quay after the return to commercial ship repair in 1989 (dates and details of work unknown).

1994 Queen narrowboat ? W.C.C.T.
Repair only.
This 1917-built vessel (by unknown builders) was sunk and left at Denham in 1993, bought by British Waterways and then donated to the Wooden Canal Craft Trust in 1994. It then raised her and took her to Runcorn for preservation, I believe at the B.M.B.C. Dry Dock.

On the National Historic Ships Register.
2001 James Jackson Grundy Brunner ? Old Quay Public Slipway
Slipped by new owners, Frodsham Lighterage Company, prior to commencing operations with her after being bought from Northwich Sea Cadets.

2002 Spain? knobstick motor boat Ian Riley
Rebuilt by the above company, after the vessel, believed to be the SPAIN, was rescued from the flashes at Whatcroft on the Trent and Mersey canal.*4

2003? Ivy Wallwork narrowboat 65ft Ron Turner (Boat and Butty)
(When I spoke to Ron Turner on 29th April 2009, he said he built this boat around 5½ years ago).
I saw an advert in the Ellesmere Port Boat Museum when I visited with my mother, father and son Billy in August 2013. It stated IVY was for sale and that she was the last boat built by Ron Turner of Runcorn in 2001. It described her as a 65ft' traditional narrowboat with a Kelvin K2 vintage engine from 1932.

2003/4?	?	steel narrowboat (hull only)	?	Mick Mills
2003/4?	?	steel narrowboat (hull only)	?	Mick Mills
2003/4?	?	steel narrowboat (hull only)	?	Mick Mills
2004	?	dumb barge	?	Old Quay Public Slipway
2004	?	motorised barge	?	Old Quay Public Slipway

The above two vessels were spotted by Ian and Rita Ratcliffe as being repaired at Old Quay after the closure of the Runcorn Yard, sometime in 2004, probably October.

And also:

Before 1850?   Edward   flat   ?   Brundrit and Whiteway

Schooner Port lists her as built and owned by the Brundrit and Whiteway partnership (holding equal shares each), but she does not appear in the book's appendix.

The information that this flat was built and owned by the partners is from the Runcorn Shipping Register of 1847–1850.

If she was owned by Brundrit and Whiteway, it can be assumed she was maintained at its yard.

Before 1890   Jenny Lind   schooner?   ?   Bridgewater (graving grid)
Repair only.*17

?   Gleaner   schooner   ?   ?

According to the Runcorn and District Historical Society Calendar of 2010, this vessel was Runcorn built.

Early 1900s   Pioneer   steam barge   63t   Richard Abel and Sons
Conversion only.

Iron vessel built by John Thompson and Sons of Northwich in 1882 for the River Weaver Trustees.

ON10863. Bought by Abel's in early 1900s. Converted to dumb barge, presumably by Abel's, before sale to James Sheils of Belfast with her Runcorn registry closed in March 1909.
*27

?   Mary Wilkinson   schooner?   ?   Stubbs?
?   ?   flat?   ?   Stubbs?
Repair only.

The above two vessels I have a picture of on what was Stubbs's Slip, by the look of it. They seem to be under some sort of repair, but I have no further details.

?   Mary Ann Mandel   two-master   ?   Stubbs?
Described as having broken her back and then "afterwards she lay beside Stubbs's Yard at Old Quay for a long time before going to the breakers". Did the Stubbs firm try to repair her? *26

?   ?   ?   ?   John James Stubbs
Repair only.
A new section of mast or bowsprit made for a vessel in Holyhead. From the reminiscences of Ken Stubbs, grandson of John James Stubbs.

?   ?   dinghy   ?   John James Stubbs
Clinker-built dinghy for a schooner, I believe was built by Stubbs. From the reminiscences of Ken Stubbs, grandson of John James Stubbs.

?   ?   schooner?   ?   Stubbs?
Repair only?
A picture on the Britain from the Air website shows Old Quay Yard in perhaps the 1930s, with the last dock yet to be filled in, in the days before the construction of the gate repair shed. It shows the two slipways, and on what was then Stubbs's slipway, a schooner or other vessel under repair or survey.

1930s   Volant   schooner   ?   Stubbs
Repair only (new keel fitted)
Schooner Sunset describes her thus: 86.8ft × 21.7ft × 10.3ft (or 26.46m × 6.614m × 3.14m); 113t gross.

Late 1930s   M.E. Johnson   schooner?   ?   Stubbs
Repair only.
Damage to her bows was repaired here.

?   M.S.C. Stretfordlittle packet   ?   M.S.C. Co. (Bridgewater)
                                           (Victoria Dockyard)
Repair only? *15

? ? narrowboat ? M.S.C. Co. (Bridgewater) (Victoria Dockyard)
Evidence from a photo of her launch posted on the Runcorn Photos page on
Facebook.

Inter-War Carmenta schooner 143t Richard Abel and Sons
Rebuild only.
Built in Thurso, Norway, in 1879 and converted to a Barge by Abel's when it
bought her. Renamed LONGDENDALE (ON134965). removed from shipping register in 1947.
*27

Inter-War Concordia schooner 203t Richard Abel and Sons
Rebuild only.
Built in Thurso, Norway, in 1914 and converted to a Barge by Abel's when
it bought her. Renamed WEARDALE (ON147360). Removed from shipping
register in 1954.
*27

? Herbert jigger flat 79t Richard Abel and Sons
Rebuild only.
Built as a two-masted flat at Winsford in 1878 for Thomas Marshall of Widnes
and bought by Abel's. She was then rebuilt and her mizzen mast removed.

She apparently still sailed well only a short main boom and could out-sail
steam packets at times.
*27

? Lunesdale barge 562t g Richard Abel and Sons
Conversion only.
Built as LAGA (ON84973) at Kinderdyk, Holland in 1901.
Bought by Abel's, presumably in 1956, the year her name changed to
LUNESDALE. Her previous owners were the London, Midland and Scottish
Railway Co. and she was registered at Lancaster (where Abel's kept her
registered).

Originally a sand hopper, and later converted to a dredger, but by whom
I am not sure. Possibly by Abel's, but maybe before it owned her (she is
described as a dredger under her former name in the same article from where
this information is drawn).
*27

? M.S.C. Dart ? ? M.S.C. Co. (Runcorn Docks – graving dock)
Information from Facebook page "You know your (sic) from Runcorn when…"
conversation thread comments by Mr. John Lunt.

Early 1960s Saxondale hopper 367t g Richard Abel and Sons
Refit only.
Built by Wm. Simons and Co. of Renfrew in 1877 as NO7 OF LIVERPOOL,
this 65hp iron-hulled vessel was bought by Abel's from the Mersey Docks and
Harbour Board and renamed SAXONDALE (ON78747).

Original Compound Steam Machinery replaced with an oil engine, and a
new and modern funnel fitted. Broken up at Garston in 1968.
*27

? Rossendale hopper 372t g Richard Abel and Sons
Refit only.
Built as RESTORER at Renfrew in 1926. Oil-fired twin screw Paxman Ricardo
engines.

Bought by Abel's and renamed ROSSENDALE (ON165570), she had no
dredging equipment. This was fitted later, along with an enclosed wheelhouse.
Was this done by Abel's?
*27

Late 1970s/ M.S.C. Ince bucket dredger ? M.S.C. Co. (Old Quay)
Early 1980s
Repair only.
A chatroom on the Ship's Nostalgia website featured a discussion by a member
named "Kevver", who said he had worked in M.S.C. INCE and M.S.C.
IRWELL during the late '70s and early '80s. He mentioned working on INCE
at Old Quay to change the bottom "tumbler" or bucket.

1980s? ? dredger? ? M.S.C. Co. (Old Quay)
Repair only.

1980s? ? pilot launch? ? M.S.C. Co. (Old Quay)
Repair only.
The above two vessels can be seen slipped at Old Quay in a photograph avail-
able on the Ship's Nostalgia website.

1980s?   M.S.C. Dainty   tug   ?   M.S.C. Co. (Old Quay)
Repair only.
The above vessel can be seen slipped at Old Quay in a photograph available on the Ship's Nostalgia website.

1980s?   Beaver Gem   tug   ?   M.S.C. Co. (Old Quay)
Repair only.
From photographs published on the COBWEB page on Facebook by Jennifer Wilson.

1990s?   Pushdale H   barge   ?   M.S.C. Co. (Old Quay)
Repair only.
The above vessel can be seen slipped at Old Quay in a photograph available on the Ship's Nostalgia website.

     This vessel is one specifically named by Peel Ports commercial controller Joe Blythe as having been worked on at Old Quay after the return to commercial ship repair in 1989 (dates and details of work unknown).

1980s/ 90s?   Iris Abbott   launch   ?   M.S.C. Co. (Old Quay)
Repair only.
The above vessel can be seen slipped at Old Quay in a photograph available on the Ship's Nostalgia website.

     This vessel is one specifically named (using her alternate name of BLACK ABBOTT OF MERSEY) by Peel Ports commercial controller Joe Blythe as having been worked on at Old Quay after the return to commercial ship repair in 1989 (dates and details of work unknown).

1980s?   ?   launch   ?   M.S.C. Co. (Old Quay)
Repair only.
The above vessel can be seen slipped at Old Quay in a photograph available on the Ship's Nostalgia website.

1980s/ 90s?   ?   pilot launch?   ?   M.S.C. Co. (Old Quay)
Repair only.
The above vessel can be seen slipped at Old Quay in a photograph available on the Ship's Nostalgia website.

1990s?   M.S.C. Dawn   tug   ?   M.S.C. Co. (Old Quay)
Repair only.
The above vessel can be seen slipped at Old Quay in a photograph available on the Ship's Nostalgia website.

1990s?   ?   ferry boat   ?   M.S.C. Co. (Old Quay)
Repair only.
The above vessel can be seen out of the water on the quayside at Old Quay in a photograph available on the Ship's Nostalgia website. It may or may not be being repaired.

?   Zebu   schooner?   ?   M.S.C. Co. (Old Quay)
Repair only.
According to pictures and text posted on the Facebook website by Frank Brown.

Early   SD Severn   dredger   ?   M.S.C. Co. (Old Quay)
2000s?
Repair only. Repair work needed on the in-line pump for the suction pipe.
   Evidence from a photo and post on Facebook by Frank Brown and comments by Tony Dowling.

?   Barley Fly   narrowboat   ?   ?
Evidence solely an entry in Jim Shead's The Boat Listing Website, which states: "built by RUNCORN"; length 10.66m (35ft); beam 2.083m (6ft 10in); Draft 0.01m; metal hull; Power of 999bhp; registered with Canal and River Trust as Number 67599 and as a powered vessel.

?   Rip Curl   narrowboat   ?   ?
Evidence solely an entry in Jim Shead's The Boat Listing Website, which states: length 10.66m (35ft); beam 2.083m (6ft 10in); metal hull; registered with Canal and River Trust as Number 67599 and as a powered vessel.

?   Cleo   narrowboat   ?   Jones
Evidence solely an entry in Jim Shead's The Boat Listing Website, which states: length 11.278m (37ft); beam 2.08m (6ft 10in); Draft 0.01m; metal hull; power of 999bhp; Registered with Canal and River Trust as Number 70955 and as a powered vessel.

? Richard motor boat ? Simpson, Davies and Co.
(narrowboat? – converted from a horse boat)*8

? Dovedale little packet ? Richard Abel and Sons
Converted to a motor tug by the company.*

? Mary Gordon electric boat/ launch ? George MacKereth
Converted to a saloon launch by the company.*9

?	Aggie (510685)	powered narrowboat	?	G. and J. Reeves
?	Alchemy (53584)	powered narrowboat	?	G. and J. Reeves
?	Always Adagio (501449)	powered narrowboat	?	G. and J. Reeves
?	Walton	packet tug	?	Bridgewater
				(Victoria?)

(Repair Only – evidence from a picture of the vessel in dry dock for repairs to
the hull and boiler casing).

? Saxondale ? ? Abel's (Delamere Dock)
(Conversion from steam to diesel engine – evidence from the memories of
Frank LeCouteur, my father's cousin. He believes this may have been the last
job Abel's carried out at Delamere Dock)

Note: Jack Stubbs at Old Quay built wooden boats/dinghies.

Note: According to *Mersey Flats and Flatmen*, "at least two hundred" flats
were built in Runcorn over the years.

Note: Bert Starkey's figures (as given in both *Schooner Port* and in an article in
Waterways Journal Vol. 5 by Mike Stammers) show 733 vessels were built in
Runcorn between 1778 and 1887. Of these, fifty-nine were flats, fifty-five schoon-
ers, fourteen sloops, twelve square-riggers, twelve steamers, and ten smacks.

Mike Stammers goes on to say that "the figure for flats was probably higher
because vessels that were confined to inland waterways did not have to be
registered with the Registrar of Shipping and therefore are difficult to track
down". He also goes on to say that after schooners had ceased to be built in
the town, flats were built intermittently until the 1950s and that in any case, the
bread and butter of the yards was repair work.

The Runcorn Historical Society Website has a page, titled "A Town to be proud of" (sic.), on which it states that: "From Old Quay swing bridge to the dock area [Runcorn Docks, formerly Bridgewater Docks] was once a thriving ship building industry and it is interesting to note that over one thousand vessels were built in the shipyards that once surrounded this part of the river and Ship Canal".

My total for vessels built or repaired in Runcorn from 1778–2004 in the list above is 525 (although some larger figure may have been arrived at since due to subsequent research), and the number for Widnes (1836–1920s) is sixty.

So there is clearly much more research to be done!

Note: Although only one of the little packets (Runcorn) was built locally, others may have been assembled in Runcorn after transportation from elsewhere.*17

Note: A number of cock boats were built at the Runcorn Yard of the M.S.C. Co. (Old Quay Yard).

A number of steel motor and dumb flats were built by the Bridgewater Department of the M.S.C. Co. After World War II; was this at Runcorn?

Note: Runcorn ship owners such as Abel, Brundrit and Whiteway, Mason, Speakman, and Wright and Hickson, presumably maintained their own fleets at their own yards, as did the M.S.C. Co. with its vessels at Old Quay Yard and other facilities in Runcorn.

For example, Thomas Hazlehurst was joint owner of the vessel RANGER, along with William Wright and Charles Hickson. There was a William Hazlehurst who had a shipyard in Frodsham after the years Wright and Hickson was in business, so it is more than probable that this vessel was maintained at the Mersey Street Yard.

Also, all the locally-owned sailing vessels still working out of Runcorn in the early 20th century were maintained by Jack Stubbs and his father Samuel before him. This is evidenced from paperwork given me by Jack Stubbs' grandson, Ken, which included part of a newspaper article that gives this information.

I have seen lots of pictures of vessels being slipped at Old Quay (tugs such as DAINTY, for example) but not necessarily with any dates for these operations.

Note: Terry Kavanagh states (*27) that "in the inter-war period Richard Abel and Sons converted a number of sailing vessels, including schooners, to sand carriers and hopper barges".

Note: "Potter and Son", an article in *Narrowboat* magazine for spring 2012 states that in earlier years the Potter business "was very much Runcorn-focused and probably his boats were built at Runcorn, which had a thriving boat-building industry".

I should imagine that the many boats of this firm registered at Runcorn would be a good bet for being locally-built. These include SPEEDWELL, first registered in Runcorn in 1895; ADA, ANNIE, GEORGE, MARY, SHOT, SPECK, and SWIFTSURE, all registered in 1879; SHANNON, and SUCCESS, registered 1896; SNOWDROP, 1899; and SURVIVOR, 1905.

Note: The following vessels:

1892	Bollin	bucket dredger	?	M.S.C. Co.?
1893	Irk	bucket dredger	?	M.S.C. Co.?
1893	Medlock	bucket dredger	?	M.S.C. Co.?

Vessels were pre-fabricated on the Clyde and shipped in pieces to the site of the M.S.C. They weres assembled on the excavated bed of the canal, the first between Warburton and Hollins Green (at Millbank, Partington) and the latter at the site of Salford Docks.

Was this with the help of Runcorn's shipbuilding artisans? Being as the nearest shipyards were at Warrington, Widnes or Runcorn, this is not an unreasonable assumption.

Note: Runcorn tradesmen were the first to recognise the potential of the steamer and were to finance and build the first paddle steamers to be built on the Mersey.

Note: Schooner Port states there was a falling-off of ship repair in 1873 and that within fifteen years of that date, the industry "would become extinct leaving only a remnant of its expertise to be employed in barge building and repair". This would seem to be at odds with the continued existence (for at least 100 years) of Old Quay Yard and its various occupants, maintaining tugs, coasters and schooners; as well as other yards.

Note: William Leathwood states that "repair work however continued until after the Second World War on vessels both afloat and raised high and dry on the Runcorn Slip".*26

Note: Work by Drammen Maritime (UK) Ltd. included – full drawings for a complete rig built by Fincantieri at Genoa for Micoperi, incorporating all deck plans and loading for these and the cranes, etc. (the full specification for the project); Drawings for offshore boats for India.

Note: Public facilities and club members' facilities are still widely used in the town of Runcorn for individual boat owners to clean, paint, and repair their vessels. For example, if you look at the various boat owner websites you can find details such as that the narrowboats CORDELIA, RAKAIA, and TAMAR were dry-docked at the Bridgewater Motor Boat Club for painting in the summer of 1987, and that CORDELIA did so again in February 2000.

Note: Lock gates were also built and repaired in Runcorn. The Bridgewater Navigation Company at Old Quay built the gates for the lock between the Runcorn and Weston Canal and Fenton Dock. The M.S.C. Co. Yard at Old Quay was where that company built and repaired its own lock gates. *The Port of Manchester Review 1974* gives details of some work in this field completed for others. Specifically, this was the first half of a contract for two greenheart heel posts for a pair large lock gates being repaired by R.H. Green and Silley Weir Limited of London. The work involved machining four five-tonne logs, each 56ft × 24in × 17in.

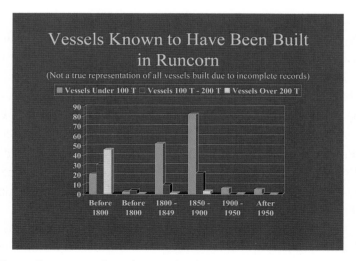

Note: These figures are based on only those vessels whose tonnage details have been discovered. Therefore, they are not representative of the whole product of the shipbuilding industry of Runcorn.

Frodsham and Frodsham Bridge

1728	Armitage	sloop	40t	?
1737	Ann	brigantine	35t	?

Known to have voyaged to Barbados and Virginia.

1746	Benin	brig	50t	?

Registered at Liverpool. At an unknown date, she was captured as a prize of war.

1748	Vine	sloop	30t	?

Presumably, the vessel in which William Hayes and Andrew Ellis of Frodsham held shares and which was involved in the slate trade.

1760	Peggy and Mary	barquentine	83t	?
1786	Mentor	flat	71t	?

Owned by Charles Buchanan and William Horabin of Frodsham. Presumably, the same as the vessel later owned (in 1795) by the widow Catherine Horabin.

1786	Molly	dogger	92t	?
1786	Mary	dogger	92t	?

Quoted from *Mersey Flats & Flatmen*. Is she meant to be "Molly"?

1787	Sutton	flat	74t	?
1788	Olive	flat	71t	?
1788	Swan	flat	54t	?
1791	Ellens	flat	71t	?
1791	Hornet	flat	74t	John Urmson?

Presumably, the vessel owned by William Crosbie and John Urmson. If it was owned by Crosbie and Urmson, it may be she was built at Urmson's yard.

1792	Frodsham Trader	flat	42t	?

Owned by John Hazlehurst of Frodsham.

1793	Friends	flat?	60t	?

Described in *Schooner Port* in separate entries as either a galliot or a glat, respectively.

Note: According to the Historical Merchant Navy, Bibby Line website at www.red-duster.co.uk/BIBBY7.htm, Friends was of 63t burthen; built of wood and galliot-rigged; acquired by Bibby and Co. in 1805 for coastal trading; 67ft 4in × 14ft 6in;

Lost in 1806 on the north-west Welsh coast approaching the River Mersey.

1793	John and William	flat	74t	?
1793	Wilderspool	flat	76t	?
1794	Mills	flat	73t	William Hayes?

Owned by John Pickering, William Hayes and William Mills of Frodsham. Engaged in salt trade and also registered for the slate trade to Caernarvon and Bangor. If it was part-owned by Hayes, it may be she was built at his yard.

1795 Betsey flat 48t Wm. Hayes

Presumably, the vessel quoted as "Betsy" in the main text of *Schooner Port* and under the part-ownership of William Hayes and Andrew Ellis of Frodsham.

1798 Patrick flat 63t George Edwards

This information is all from *Waterways Journal Vol. 8*, "Sailing Flats on the Chester and Ellesmere Canals" by Terry Kavanagh. He gives the following details: owner was Coffield and Co.; typical square-sterned flat.

1799 Ann flat 75t Isaac White

She was wrecked on St Tudwal's Islands on 18th October 1858. Her master cried for divine help, says *Schooner Port,* and his ordeal is remembered in folk songs still sung in Welsh schools to this day.

1800	Nelson	flat	73t	?
1801	Supply	flat	74t	?
1802	Alice and Ann	flat	59t	? at Frodsham Bridge
1802	Stag	flat	77t	?
1802	Mary Ellen	flat	80t	?
1802	Peggy and Mary	flat	?	?
1802	Earl	flat	57t	George Edwards

This information is all from ***Waterways Journal Vol. 8***, "Sailing Flats on the Chester and Ellesmere Canals" by Terry Kavanagh. He gives the following details: length 64.2ft, breadth 14.2ft, hold depth 5.25ft; owner was Coffield and Co. later owned by the Shropshire Union Company.

A company minute in August 1873 suggested it was not economically viable to repair this flat, but in the end, she was repaired and she continued her service for the firm.

In 1920, the remaining vessels of this company, including this one, were put up for sale. This was one of fifty-eight that remained unsold and they were all left to rot in the Dee basin in Chester.

1803   Merry Harrier   flat   78t   ?
According to *Mersey Flats and Flatmen,* she was 76t.

1803	Tom	flat	69t	?
1804	Young James	flat	78t	?
1805	Penketh	flat	76t	?
1805	Isaac	pilot launch	?	?

According to Alan Scarth of the Merseyside Maritime Museum, this vessel was built at Frodsham Bridge and a model or photo of her is in the Science Museum, London.

1805   William   flat   61t   George Edwards
This information is all from *Waterways Journal Vol. 8,* "Sailing Flats on the Chester and Ellesmere Canals" by Terry Kavanagh. He gives the following details: length 64.33ft, breadth 14.4ft, hold depth 5.2ft; owner was Coffield and Co. Later owned by the Shropshire Union Company.

A company minute in August 1873 suggested it was not economically viable to repair this flat, but in the end, she was repaired and she continued her service for the firm.

In 1920, the remaining vessels of this company, including this one, were put up for sale. This was one of fifty-eight that remained unsold and they were all left to rot in the Dee basin in Chester.

1808   May   flat   24t   ?
1811   Mary Ann   schooner   75t   William Hazlehurst?
Owned by William Hazlehurst, coal merchant of Sutton, Frodsham; and also built by him? If it was owned by Hazlehurst, it may be she was built at his yard.

1812	Lydia	sloop	50t	?
1814	Frances Mary	sloop	87t	?*
1815	Sparling	sloop/flat?	62t/61t?	?

Presumably, the vessel mentioned in the main text of *Schooner Port* as the 61t flat (despite being listed in the appendix to that book as a 62t sloop) owned in shares as follows: 21 to Thomas Ellison; 21 to Thomas Wilkinson, innkeeper of Liverpool; and 22 to Joseph Wagstaffe, gentleman of Warrington.

1815   Waterloo   schooner   61t   William Hazlehurst?
Owned by William Hazlehurst, coal merchant of Sutton, Frodsham; and also built by him? If it was owned by Hazlehurst, it may be she was built at his yard.

1816   Kent   galliot   100t Wm. Hayes
1816   Jane and Ann   schooner   68t   ?
1818   Mary   flat   42t   ?
In 1841, MARY was solely-owned by Joseph Crosfield, Soap Manufacturer of Warrington.

1821   Isabella   schooner   74t   Hayes and Urmson
1824   Collins   sloop   39t   ?
1826   St. George   flat   54t   ?
Is this the schooner part-owned by John Crippin of Runcorn?

1831   Frances   schooner   95t?   ?
Described in *Schooner Port* in separate entries as either 94t or 95t, respectively.
    A Frances described in *Schooner Port* had a cargo hold 7ft 9in in depth; is this the vessel built in Frodsham?
    In the 1830s and '40s, FRANCES was owned in equal shares by John Ellison, Linen Draper and Thomas Ellison.

1835   James   schooner   84t   ?
1837   Briton   flat   53t   Wm. Hayes
16 shares held by Joseph Forest, corn merchant of Warrington; 12 shares held by John Hobson, miller; and further shares held by Joseph Crosfield, soap manufacturer of Warrington.

1838   Sarah/Sara   schooner   68t   William Hazlehurst
Owned by William Hazlehurst, coal merchant of Sutton, Frodsham.

1838   Eliza   flat   44t   Wm. Hayes
Information from *Waterways Journal Vol. 8*, "Sailing Flats on the Chester and Ellesmere Canals" by Terry Kavanagh.

Further: length 63.7ft, breadth 12.8ft, hold depth 5.9ft; square-sterned flat, built by William Hayes and Co. for Tilston, Smith and Co. and transferred to the Ellesmere and Chester Company when the former ceased carrying.

1839   Kendal Castle   schooner   85t   ?
A website about Amlwch Port gives this vessel's details as follows: Kendel Castle; captain William Thomas; bought in 1851 by N. Treweek. the captain after that sale was William Thomas.

1839   Importer   schooner   69t   ?
Note: According to the Mighty Seas website at www.mightyseas.co.uk/ marhist/solway/new_importer.htm. New Importer was built in Frodsham in 1839; she was 41 92/100 gross tons; presumably she is the same vessel.

1839   Pearl   schooner   66t   William Hazlehurst?
Owned by William Hazlehurst, Coal Merchant of Sutton, Frodsham; and also built by him? If it was owned by Hazlehurst, it may be she was built at his yard.

1840   Rigby   schooner   72t   ?
Presumably, the vessel owned by T. Rigby, coal and salt merchant of Runcorn.

1844   Hero   flat   57t?   Wm. Hayes
Described in *Schooner Port* in separate entries as either 56t or 57t, respectively.
    Built for Joseph Forest, Corn Merchant of Warrington, who, in 1847 sold shares in the vessel as follows: 16 to John Hobson, miller; 10 to James Sheppard, maltster; and 10 to James Fairclough, miller of Newton-le-Willows.

1847   Lydia   flat   48t   ?
1851   Mary Ann   schooner   ?   William Hazlehurst?
Owned by William Hazlehurst, coal merchant of Sutton, Frodsham; and also built by him? If she was owned by Hazlehurst, it may be she was built at his yard.

Note: Mersey Flats and Flatmen states, according to Marwood's Register of Liverpool Shipping (published in 1854), nine flats were completed in Frodsham in 1854.
Therefore:
1854   ?   flat   ?   ?

1854	?	flat	?	?
1854	?	flat	?	?
1854	?	flat	?	?
1854	?	flat	?	?
1854	?	flat	?	?
1854	?	flat	?	?
1854	?	flat	?	?
1854	?	flat	?	?
1856	Emily Constance	schooner	65t	?
1857	Hannah	flat	38t	Edward Jones
1858	Edward	flat	64t	Edward Jones
1858	Vixen	flat	54t	Edward Jones
1858	Alice and Mary	flat	54t	?
1858	Mary Bollind	schooner	100t	?

Described in **Schooner Port** in separate entries as either 99t or 100t, respectively. Lost off the Norfolk coast whilst laden with coal "two years later", according to *Schooner Port*.

1860	Mersey	flat	50t	?
1862	Fanny	flat	40t	?

According to Terry Kavanagh's article, "Richard Abel and Sons, of Runcorn and Liverpool" (*Waterways Journal Vol. 16*), this vessel was: 43t; ON80295; almost entirely rebuilt by Wm. Bracegirdle and Sons of Northwich in 1878; owned by Richard Abel and Sons of Runcorn, then sold to Robert Jones of Grosvenor Mills, Bagillt, Flintshire, in December 1880; later sold to new owners in Fleetwood in April 1895; broken up in Fleetwood in July 1911.

1980	?	narrowboat	70ft	Ron Turner (Boat and Butty)

(Built in two halves at Frodsham Old Mill and welded/launched at Boat and Butty Yard).

1980	Hereward	narrowboat	50ft	Ron Turner (Boat and Butty)

(Built in two halves at Frodsham Old Mill and welded/launched at Boat and Butty Yard).

?	Hazel	narrowboat	70ft	Ron Turner (Boat and Butty)

(Built in two halves at Frodsham Old Mill and welded/launched at Boat and Butty Yard).

(Named after Ron's wife).

? May narrowboat 70ft Ron Turner (Boat and Butty)
(Built in two halves at Frodsham Old Mill and welded/launched at Boat and Butty Yard).

? ? narrowboat 50ft Ron Turner (Boat and Butty)
(Built in two halves at Frodsham Old Mill and welded/launched at Boat and Butty Yard).

Note: When the yard at Frodsham Bridge was put up for sale in May, 1856, among the items for sale were a "partly-finished ferryboat, a pleasure boat 13ft long with 4ft 10in. beam". Were they later completed by the new owner (Edward Jones, presumably)? *5

Note: Schooner Port states fifty-eight vessels were built at Frodsham between 1728 and 1862, yet the appendix lists fifty-nine.

Note: William Crosbie and John Urmson (Shipbuilder at Frodsham) were salt works owners who owned the following flats: ANT, BEE, FLY, WASP, FRODSHAM, and JOHN AND THOMAS. Possibly, some of these were built by Urmson at his Frodsham shipyard and likely, they were maintained there. Other local owners such as William Hazlehurst likely also maintained their own vessels.

Note: The supposed existence of the ferry at Frodsham Bridge suggests some sort of boat building experience was known in the town from the time that service started.

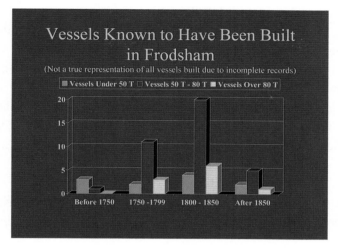

Note: These figures are based on only those vessels whose tonnage details have been discovered. Therefore, they are not representative of the whole product of the shipbuilding industry of Frodsham.

Widnes and Fiddler's Ferry

1836   Shamrock   flat   ?   ?
1859   Bream   flat   72t   T. Wilkinson
Vessel had a single mast and one deck, was flat-rigged, carvel-built on a wooden frame and had a round stern.

1861   Lilly   schooner   57t   Samuel Stock
Presumably, a replacement for the flat of the same name, noted on the Runcorn Register of Shipping (1847–1850) (or it may be a source quoting his financial position in 1859) as owned by Samuel Stock. If she was owned by Samuel Stock, it can be assumed she was maintained at his yard.

1863   Flora   flat   50t   Samuel Stock
Presumably, a replacement for the Flat of the same name, noted on the Runcorn Register of Shipping (1847–1850) (or it may be a source quoting his financial position in 1859) as owned by Samuel Stock. If she was owned by Samuel Stock, it can be assumed she was maintained at his yard.

1865   Mus   flat   80t   T. Wilkinson
Vessel had a single mast and one deck, was flat-rigged, carvel-built on a wooden frame and had a round stern.

1867   Vendace   flat   68t   T. Wilkinson
Vessel had a single mast and one deck, was flat-rigged, carvel-built on a wooden frame and had a round stern.

1867   Hilda   schooner   72t net?   Samuel Stock
Note: Schooner Sunset describes Hilda thus: wood, two-masted schooner; registered St Ives; 79.3ft × 19.7ft × 9.2ft; 72t net (*Schooner Port* gives no tonnage); official number 56589; signal hoist MQDK.

1868   Carp   flat   72t   T. Wilkinson
Vessel had a single mast and one deck, was flat-rigged, carvel-built on a wooden frame and had a round stern.

1868   Brill   flat   105t   T. Wilkinson
Vessel had a single mast and one deck, was flat-rigged, carvel-built on a wooden frame and had a round stern.

1868   Excelsior flat   28t   Wm. Cooper
1868?   Rival   lightship ?   ?
Overhaul and slight repairs completed at graving dock, Widnes, for the Upper Mersey Navigation Commissioners.*17

1869   Rudd   flat   78t   W. Wilkinson
Vessel had a single mast and one deck, was flat-rigged, carvel-built on a wooden frame and had a round stern.

1869   Perch   flat   81t   W. Wilkinson
Vessel had a single mast and one deck, was flat-rigged, carvel-built on a wooden frame and had a round stern.

1869   Maud   Schooner   71T   Samuel Stock
Presumably, the 1869-built "Barrow Flat" schooner, "Maude" mentioned in *Mersey Flats & Flatmen*.

Note: Schooner Sunset describes Maude thus: wood, auxiliary-engined ketch; registered Bideford; 47t net; official number 62010; no signal hoist.
    Presumably, a replacement for the schooner of the same name, noted on the Runcorn Register of Shipping (1847–1850) (or it may be a source quoting his

financial position in 1859) as owned by Samuel Stock. If she was owned by Samuel Stock, it can be assumed she was maintained at his yard. Converted to a houseboat in 1947.

1870   Dace   flat   141t   W. Wilkinson
Vessel had a single mast and one deck, was flat-rigged, carvel-built on a wooden frame and had a round stern.

1870   Try   schooner   75t   Samuel Stock
Presumably, a replacement for the schooner of the same name, noted on the Runcorn Register of Shipping (1847–1850) (or it may be a source quoting his financial position in 1859) as owned by Samuel Stock. If she was owned by Samuel Stock, it can be assumed she was maintained at his yard. Launched in September.

1871   Dab   flat   78t   T. Wilkinson
Vessel had a single mast and one deck, was flat-rigged, carvel-built on a wooden frame and had a round stern.

1871   Chub   flat   139t   W. Wilkinson
Vessel had a single mast and one deck, was flat-rigged, carvel-built on a wooden frame and had a round stern.

1872   Luce   flat   143t   W. Wilkinson
Vessel had a single mast and one deck, was flat-rigged, carvel-built on a wooden frame and had a round stern.

1875   Roach   flat   107t   T. Wilkinson
Vessel had a single mast and one deck, was flat-rigged, carvel-built on a wooden frame and had a round stern.

1875   Janie   schooner   172t   Samuel Stock
Presumably, a replacement for the schooner of the same name, noted on the Runcorn Register of Shipping (1847–1850) (or it may be a source quoting his financial position in 1859) as owned by Samuel Stock. If she was owned by Samuel Stock, it can be assumed she was maintained at his yard.

She was the largest vessel built in Widnes. Two-masted schooner. Wrecked off Rio Grande do Sul on 26th September 1884.

1877   Rose C   flat   82t   Hill and Grundy
1879   Edith Mary   flat   86t   Hill and Grundy
1879   Bret   flat   83t   W. Wilkinson

Vessel had a single mast and one deck, was flat-rigged, carvel-built on a wooden frame and had a round stern.

1879   Rav   flat   90t   T. Wilkinson

Vessel had a single mast and one deck, was flat-rigged, carvel-built on a wooden frame and had a round stern.

1879   Hettie   wood screw steamer   74t   Wm. Jamieson
Lasted until 1949.

1880   Ann and Martha   flat   70t   Hill and Grundy
1882   Grig   flat   78t   W. Wilkinson

Vessel had a single mast and one deck, was flat-rigged, carvel-built on a wooden frame and had a round stern.

1885   Sprat   flat   81t   T. Wilkinson

Vessel had a single mast and one deck, was flat-rigged, carvel-built on a wooden frame and had a round stern.

1890   Annie   flat   39t   Edward Gandy
1901   Bee   flat   ?   Wm. Cooper

Flat owned by M.S.C. Co. but hired by Coopers at the time and involved in a collision.*17

1902   Bee   flat   ?   Wm. Cooper

Flat owned by M.S.C. Co. but hired by Coopers at the time and involved in a collision.*17

1913   ?   ?   ?   Wm. Cooper*21
1913   ?   ?   ?   Wm. Cooper*21

Note: Mersey Flats and Flatmen states, according to the 1914 Mercantile Navy List, five flats were completed in Widnes in that year.
Therefore:

1914	?	flat	?	?
1914	?	flat	?	?
1914	?	flat	?	?
1914	?	flat	?	?
1914	?	flat	?	?

Note: *Mersey Flats and Flatmen* states, according to the 1914 Mercantile Navy List, seventeen flats were completed in Fiddler's Ferry in that year. Therefore:

1914	?	flat	?	?
1914	?	flat	?	?
1914	?	flat	?	?
1914	?	flat	?	?
1914	?	flat	?	?
1914	?	flat	?	?
1914	?	flat	?	?
1914	?	flat	?	?
1914	?	flat	?	?
1914	?	flat	?	?
1914	?	flat	?	?
1914	?	flat	?	?
1914	?	flat	?	?
1914	?	flat	?	?
1914	?	flat	?	?
1914	?	flat	?	?
1914	?	flat	?	?

1919 Elmarine   concrete barge   250t g   Concrete Seacraft

Information from David Long's research (*28).

Dumb barge but later fitted with an engine. Claimed to be the lightest sea-going barge in the world. Hull 1¾in thick.

Launched on 4th January 1919. Named by Mrs. Ritchie, the wife of the inventor of the system of prefabricated building used in the vessel's construction. Her husband, H. C. Ritchie, was part of the Ritchie and Black firm, engineers and patentees of the Royal Liver Building, Liverpool.

95ft × 21ft 4in × 8ft. Built for local grain carrying, registered on the Liverpool Shipping Register as No. 140629 on 27th May 1919.

Sank under tow in Morecambe Bay in 1919 and salvaged the following year. She was re-registered in 1920 as belonging to the Liverpool Grain

Storage and Transit Co. Ltd. and survived for many years. In the 1980s, she was towed from Birkenhead Docks (where she had been lying awaiting disposal) to Mostyn and scuttled along with a World War II concrete barge. This was part of the efforts to keep the DUKE OF LANCASTER upright in her role as a "fun ship" on the River Dee.

1919   Cretecamp   concrete coaster   c.710t?   Concrete Seacraft
Starkey gives her displacement as 753t. Alternatively, she may have been 1,000t and launched in 1918.*16

David Long (*28) describes her as being launched in December 1919. Apparently, her launch was something of an event as she hit the Cheshire shore and created a wash that beached a small yacht! The yacht was floated off at the next tide.

First registered in Liverpool in 1920/1 but left the register by 1925/6, having been bought by Norwegian owners.

According to *29: yard number 2; completed in October 1919; 753 grt, 726 nrt and later 717 nrt; 54.86m × 9.66m × 5.21m; official number 1443302;

Ordered in 1917 as PD45 and completed for the Shipping Controller, London; Transferred to the Board of Trade, London, in 1921; Sold to Crete Shipping Co. Ltd., London (managers Stelp and Leighton Ltd.) in 1922; sold to Norway in 1923; sold to Iceland in 1924.

1919   Cretecove   concrete coaster   c.710t?   Concrete Seacraft
Starkey gives her displacement as 747t. David Long (*28) describes her as having been launched in February 1920.

First Registered in Liverpool in 1920/1 but left the register by 1925/6, having been bought by Norwegian owners.

In 1942, the CRETECOVE was taken to the small harbour at Røssøyvågen on the island of Gossen. This was to bring materials for the building of a wooden landing strip by Russian prisoners of war under the control of the occupying forces. She is still there today as a part of the marina.

In 1995, the locals set up an exhibition to mark the 50th anniversary of their liberation and eventually it was turned into a permanent museum. It was set up in a house and includes a model of the vessel and the harbour with details of the work conducted there.

See www.mareud.com/Ferro-Concrete/f-c-list.htm or the SCARS website, www.scars.org.uk/cuttings/volume5/issue5-10/fiddlersf.html, for more details.

According to *29: yard number 1 or 3; completed in 1920; 747 grt, 712 nrt;

54.86m × 9.69m × 5.24m; official number 144300; ordered in 1917 as PD46 and completed for the Shipping Controller, London; transferred to the Board of Trade, London, in 1921; sold to Crete Shipping Co. Ltd., London (managers Stelp and Leighton Ltd.) in 1922; sold to Norway in 1924.

According to David Long (*28), ten 1,000t craft along similar lines to ELMARINE were planned for at the Fiddler's Ferry yard but only four more were begun after that barge was launched in January 1919. Of these four, only the two above were launched and that was the end of the yard's history.

I had believed that a further one (CRETEMANOR) was completed under the Ritchie and Black name but this ship was actually launched at Preston by Hughes and Stirling using the same patented construction system as those built in Fiddler's Ferry (invented by Ritchie and Black).

My error was from a couple of sources I believe (time has faded that, and many more memories), but including the book *Warrington at Work*. This is an excellent publication, from which I learned much, but one that made the connection between Ritchie and Black and the Fiddler's Ferry Yard and assumed they were one and the same. The book shows a photo of the recently-launched vessel and describes her as 180ft long and designed for a speed of nine or ten knots. She had three large cargo holds divided into five watertight compartments that were claimed to offer greater capacity than wooden or steel ships.

1920s?   Basuto   ?   ?   Wm. Cooper
Vessel built on the Clyde in 1902 and eventually sold by Mersey Docks and Harbour Co. (?) to Cooper's of Widnes in the 1920s. That firm converted her into a dumb barge.*23?

?   EUSTACE CAREY   steamer   ?   Wm. Cooper
Conversion only.
Converted to a barge (or "barged") by William Cooper when bought from the United Alkali Company.*31

?   DAVEY   steamer   ?   Wm. Cooper
Conversion only.
Converted to a barge (or "barged") by William Cooper when bought from the United Alkali Company.*31

Note: According to Starkey, all the vessels he discovered in his studies that were built by T. Wilkinson and W. Wilkinson were launched into the Mersey. All those he found that were built by Hill and Grundy were launched into the Sankey Canal.

The Concrete Seacraft vessels were launched into the Mersey.

Note: The Runcorn Register of Shipping (1847–1850) (or it may be a source quoting his financial position in 1859) noted Samuel Stock (Shipbuilder at Widnes) as owner of the following Schooners: TRY, EVA, MAUD, and JANIE. He is also listed as the owner of the following Flats: FLORA, LILLY, HIND, DORA, and RUSH. Possibly, some of these were built by Stock at his Widnes shipyard.

Note: William Cooper (and the firm's later guises) and Samuel Stock were ship owners as well as builders. It would be safe to say then, they maintained their own vessels at their yards.

Note: According to M.K. Stammers in his article, "Slipways and Steamchests" (as published in the *International Journal of Nautical Archaeology Vol. 28, Issue 3*), there were "19 [flats built at] Fiddler's Ferry between 1859 and 1880".

Ellesmere Port

1812   Bridgewater   brigantine   118t   Ellesmere Canal Co.?
Chester-registered; launched in July 1812 "if not earlier"; owner: Manley and Co.
65ft 1½in × 21ft ¾in × 10ft; 118t Burthen; small coaster; A1 at Lloyd's three or four years later.
*27

1812   Farmers Glory   Sloop   28t   Ellesmere Canal Co.?
Chester-registered; launched later in 1812; round-sterned sloop; owner: John Taylor, corn dealer of Liverpool, and two farmers of North Wales.
42ft 2 ½in × 12ft 10in; 28t Burthen.
Driven on shore at Leasowe Lighthouse in a storm in late December 1813, with one man drowning. She and her cargo were saved and she resumed her career.
*27

1813   Amelia and Hannah   schooner   108t   ?
Chester-registered; 108t Burthen.

Master and part-owner: John Garner. Other owners included: Samuel Yoxen (miller of Stanney), Thomas Whittle (brewer of Chester), and William Kirkham and Thomas Hazlehurst, merchants of Runcorn.
*27

1814   Katharine   brigantine   129t   Manley?
Chester-registered; 129t Burthen.

Owners: Ralph Manley and Co., and Runcorn merchants William Kirkham and Thomas Hazlehurst; A1 at Lloyd's in 1816.
*27

1814   Orford   flat   60t   Manley?
Chester-registered (in January 1817); 60t Burthen.

Owners: Ralph Manley and Co., under the wharfingers Joseph Manley (brother of Ralph) and John Sothern (related to the Sothern family of shipbuilders from Runcorn perhaps?) after the death of Ralph Manley in April 1815; square-sterned flat.
*27

1815   Catherine   schooner   94t   ?
Drogheda-registered; 94t Burthen.

Owner: Owens of Drogheda, Ireland; at some time in her career she was damaged and subsequently repaired and thus only stood E1 at Lloyd's.
*27

1816   Liverpool   brig/snow   127t   Charles Hickson
Liverpool-registered; 127t Burthen.

Owner: Manley and Co.; square-sterned brig or snow; sheathed with wood.

Classed A1 for 8 years at Lloyd's in 1818; sold to Belfast owners in 1824; belonged by 1835 to J. Ross of Maryport.
*27

1817   Mary Ann   schooner   108t   ?
Chester-registered initially and then Liverpool-registered in 1818; 108t Burthen.

Owners: John Threlfall (banker) and James Murrey (merchant) when registered at Liverpool.

A1 at Lloyd's for eight years. Registered in London in 1826 and then back Liverpool-registered in 1837.
*27

1819   Cheshire Lass   sloop   34t   George Dawson
Owner: George Dawson of Walton, near Liverpool: her builder; sold to owners in Kingstown, Jamaica in 1822.
*27

1820   Various – see below   Charles Hickson
Repair only.
When in this year he leased the Ellesmere Canal packets and the "Canal Tavern", Charles Hickson agreed to repair the boats after discovering they had dry rot.
*27

1826   City of Londonderry   paddle steamer   319t   Haselden
Launched 1st November; 201 net tons, 319 gross tons; 152.6ft × 22.6ft × 14.6ft; wooden paddle steamer; two-cylinder side-lever engines of 200hp;
   Owner: Liverpool and Londonderry Steam Navigation Company;
   Sold to Dublin Steam Packet Company in March 1837 and registered in London five years later; advertised for sale in April 1845 and later reported as broken up.
*27

1827   Rock Light   flat   61t   Haselden
Square-sterned flat; 61t Burthen, 40t new measurement.
*27

1827   ?   flat   ?   Haselden
When the company went bankrupt and the yard put up for sale, his stock of timber and other gear that went with it was advertised for sale alongside an unfinished flat.
*27

1864   Lorn   schooner   79t   Wm. Parkes
Lancaster-registered; small, wooden, two-masted topsail schooner; launched in August.
   Owner: Thomas Roper of Newland Furnace, Ulverston, Lancashire; later owned by: Aymer Ainslie of the Harrison, Ainslie Iron Ore Company; later part of the fleet of James Geldart, who was the shipping agent for the above company.
   On the night of 7th November, 1890, bound for Belfast from Connah's

Quay, she grounded in a storm to the north of Jurby Head off the Isle of Man. Overnight, she shifted position, fell on her side and broke her back. The crew of three were saved but the ship was a total wreck.
*27

1865   JCR   schooner   60t   Wm. Parkes
Chester-registered; small, wooden, two-masted topsail schooner; launched in early 1865.
Owner: James Reney of Connah's Quay, Flintshire; later owned by: Thomas Edwards of Railway Cottage, Saltney, Chester; by 1881 she was owned by Charles Clague of Castletown, Isle of Man; later still owned by: Captain Hugh Shaw, the famous "Schooner Captain". Vessel captained by the above's brother, William Shaw.
    Total wreck on Sprock Rock off Rosslare Harbour while sailing from Portmadoc to Waterford. Crew all saved. The ship was not insured.
*27

1865   Quickstep   schooner   103t   Wm. Parkes
Liverpool-registered; small, wooden, two-masted topsail schooner.
    Owners: Frederic Prince, firebrick manufacturer of Buckley, Flintshire (22/64), James Clarke of Buckley (21/64), and Thomas Bennett of Connah's Quay, her captain (21/64).
    Classed A1 at Lloyd's for twelve years; Wrecked on Puffin Island off the west coast of Ireland in April 1874.
*27

1865   Victor   narrowboat   ?   Wm. Parkes
For the Shropshire Union Canal Company.
*27

1866   Fanny Durant   schooner   60t   Wm. Parkes
Liverpool-registered in early 1866; small, wooden, two-masted topsail schooner.
    Laid down later in 1865 as a speculative venture and left unfinished until this date; advertised for sale (48/64 share was the offer, when the advert was placed during the building of this vessel in early November 1865).
    Owner: Edward Durant; later owned by: John Roberts of Rhyl; then sold to: James Grey of Berwick-on-Tweed in 1871.
    In January 1895, during a dense fog, the hull steamer JERANOS (1,288t)

struck FANNY DURANT amidships about twelve miles off Berwick-on-Tweed while she was bound for Sunderland from Invergordon. FANNY DURANT heeled over and sank in about one or two minutes but luckily the steamer saved all four crew. The schooner was left "stranded derelict at Whitley, near Blyth" according to the report sent to Lloyd's.
*27

1866   Stanney   narrowboat   ?   Wm. Parkes
For the Shropshire Union Canal Company.
*27

1866   Stanlow   narrowboat   ?   Wm. Parkes
For the Shropshire Union Canal Company.
*27

1866   ?   narrowboat   ?   Wm. Parkes
Advertised for sale in June 1866 as a part-finished vessel, along with various other vessels and gear when William Parkes went bankrupt in that year;

Details from the advertised sale in 1866: "Also, one canal boat, just launched, to carry about 40 tons, very strong, and admirably adapted to carry coal, lime, etc.".
*27

1866   ?   narrowboat   ?   Wm. Parkes
Partly-finished
Advertised for sale in June 1866 as a part-finished vessel, along with various other vessels and gear when William Parkes went bankrupt in that year;

Details from the advertised sale in 1866: "Also, a canal boat, part built, to carry about 25 tons, well adapted for canal purposes".
*27

1866   ?   flat   ?   Wm. Parkes
Frame only.
Advertised for sale in June 1866 as a part-finished vessel, along with various other vessels and gear when William Parkes went bankrupt in that year;

Details from the advertised sale in 1866: "The entire Frame, etc. of a Flat or River Lighter, to carry 50 tons, at 4 feet, or from 70 to 80 tons across the Mersey, and take the ground. Dimensions, 70ft by 14½ft by 6ft".
*27

1867 Triumph   schooner   73t   Wm. Parkes and ?
Liverpool-registered after her completion by an unknown builder in 1867; small, wooden, two-masted topsail schooner.

Laid down later in 1865 as a speculative venture and left unfinished until this date. Advertised for sale in June 1866 as a part-finished vessel, along with various other vessels and gear when William Parkes went bankrupt in that year;

Owners: James Reney, shipowner of Connah's Quay, and others; registered anew in Chester in 1874 under the same ownership;.

Totally wrecked on Langness Point in the Isle of Man on a voyage from Connah's Quay to Belfast in March 1880. Despite the very severe weather, the crew of three eventually reached safety.

Details from the advertised sale in 1866: "A Vessel, No.5, semi-clipper Schooner, of about 85 tons, NM, 135 tons, BM, and about 160 draw weight. Dimensions: Length, 76 feet; main breadth extreme, 20 feet; depth, 9½ to 10 feet hold; will class from 8 to 12 years [at Lloyd's]; keel laid, and stem and stern posts, etc., erected, and floors fixed in position; many of the frames are coupled ready for erection, and the other parts of the framing are upon the spot ready for connecting".

I have no idea who the builder was who finished this vessel.
*27

1873 Star   flat   ?   Wm. Skinner
Repair only.
According to the minutes of the Shropshire Union Canal Company meeting of May in this year, William Skinner had tendered to repair the above flat for £125. It is unclear whether or not he won the contract.
*27

1874 Charles   iron flat   ?   Wm. Newall
According to the minutes of the Shropshire Union Canal Company meeting of July 1874, the above was in need of repair to her "ceiling… and other" areas and was too large to get to the Chester yard. Therefore, a tender for the repair was received from William Newall for £82 10/-. This was approved, so I can only assume this work went ahead.
*27

1875   Garston?   dredger   ?   Wm. Newall
Minutes from a Shropshire Union Canal Company meeting of March 1875 give details of "Garston Old Dredger" being repaired at Newall's Yard.
*27

1875   Vanquish   flat   79t?   Wm. Newall
Launched April 1875; carrying capacity 180t; pronounced to be a model of her class and build by professed judges; christened by Miss. Newall; owners: William and George Alcock of Northwich and Winsford;
*27

1875   Probity   flat   79t   Wm. Newall
At the time of the launch of VANQUISH, there was another flat of the same dimensions on the stocks. It is unclear, but it may well have been this vessel, as this was one launched in the same year.

Liverpool-registered; owner: Sarah Ann Weedall of Seacombe, Cheshire; later sold to United Alkali Company (July 1912); register closed in December 1934 after she foundered and had to be broken up.
*27

1876   Thomas and Ann   flat   76t   Wm. Newall
Launched early in 1876; one-masted coasting flat.

Owners (16 shares each): Samuel Hickson of Barnton, Cheshire; her master; and three employees of Flint Chemical Works – Alfred Dyson (manager), Charles Edward Dyson (clerk, later managing owner of the vessel), and John Tweedie (foreman);

In February 1902, this vessel was altered in build and rig, becoming ketch-rigged and of 90t register; Broken up and registry closed in April 1932.
*27

1876   No Name   flat   ?   Wm. Newall
River flat; 200t carrying capacity.
*27

1878   Enterprise   flat   ?   Wm. Newall
River craft of similar dimensions to the NO NAME.
*27

1878   Louise   flat   ?   Wm. Newall
River craft of similar dimensions to the NO NAME.
*27

1878   Straight Tip   flat   93T   Wm. Newall
Sailing flat; Owner: William Beckett Hill of Liverpool; sold to Abel's of
Runcorn in 1926 and reconstructed, becoming BEDALE; registry closed on
her being broken up in 1959.
*27

1893   Beeswing   iron barque   1,392t   Manchester Dry Dock Ltd.
Repair only.
First vessel to use the pontoon dry dock (floating dock) at Ellesmere Port.
There for "repairs, painting, cleaning, etc.".
*27

1895   ?   steamer   ?   Manchester Dry Dock Ltd.
Repair only.
Large steamer. On the pontoon dock when it was struck by the steamer
NARAUJAH in July of that year.
*27

1895   ?   flat   ?   Manchester Dry Dock Ltd.
Repair only.
M.S.C. Co. mud-flat. On the pontoon dock when it was struck by the steamer
NARAUJAH in July of that year.
*27

1896   ?   barque   ?   Manchester Dry Dock Ltd.
Repair only.
As soon as the pontoon dock was moved to her new position, further inland of
the Ship Canal in a basin ("dock") purposely built for her, there were two large
barques on her for repairs.
See below.
*27

1896   ?   barque   ?   Manchester Dry Dock Ltd.
Repair only.

As soon as the pontoon dock was moved to her new position, further inland of the Ship Canal in a basin ("dock") purposely built for her, there were two large barques on her for repairs.
See above.
*27

1897   Queen Victoria   flat   92t   Shropshire Union
Launched early September; christened by J.R. Webb.

Length 75ft 6in; beam 17ft 11in; depth 9ft 4in; hold 54ft 2in; capable of carrying 220t.

Sold to M.S.C. Co. when the Shropshire Union Canal Company ceased carrying in 1921; sunk in the Mersey at Appley in 1943.
*27

1902   King Edward VII   flat   ?   Shropshire Union
Largest barge launched at Ellesmere Port up to that time; launched in September; christened by Mr. Brocklebank, chairman of the Shropshire Union Canal Company; designed by Mr. Hulse (the Chester Boatyard Superintendent); built entirely by Shropshire Union Canal Company staff.
*27

1904   Princess of Wales   barge   143t   Shropshire Union
Largest Flat ever built by the Shropshire union Canal Company at Ellesmere Port; launched in August; carrying capacity 300t; sold to M.S.C. Co. when the Shropshire Union Canal Company ceased carrying in 1921; broken up by 9th May 1944.

Information from visits to the Ellesmere Port Boat Museum and from *Waterways Journal, Vol. 15*, in an article by Terry Kavanagh named "Ship and Boat Building at Ellesmere Port: A History".

1904   Mullet   iron barge   160t   Manchester Dry Dock Ltd.
Iron coal barge but described later in the article as steel; 400t carrying capacity; built for R. and J. Rea of Liverpool; christened by Mrs. Shubrook, wife of the superintendent of Messrs. Rea; Nigel Bowker gives the information that she was broken up at Garston in the 1960s.
*27

1904   Shadiron   barge   160t   Manchester Dry Dock Ltd.
Iron coal barge but described later in the article as steel; 400t carrying capacity; built for R. and J. Rea of Liverpool; christened by Mrs. Grice, wife of the secretary of the Pontoon Company; sold to A.G. Diving Ltd. for breaking up in 1973 at Old Quay, Runcorn (on the shore of the Mersey adjacent to Old Quay Swing Bridge). Witnessed there by Nigel Bowker on 28th December 1973 whilst demolition was in progress, there was no trace of her left by 15th March 1974.
*27

1912   ?   ?   ?   Manchester Dry Dock Ltd.
Repair only.
One of two vessels on the pontoon dock when it was struck by the SS NYROCA in August of that year. See below.
*27

1912   ?   ?   ?   Manchester Dry Dock Ltd.
Repair only.
One of two vessels on the pontoon dock when it was struck by the SS NYROCA in August of that year. See above.
*27

1919   Ben Seyr   steel (?) coaster   c. 260t?   Manchester Dry Dock Ltd.
                      (steam)
Laid down as WAR DEVERON for shipping controller but cancelled in 1918; launched 11th October 1919 as Deveron; name changed to BEN SEYR in 1920, having been "launched" (?–*27) or completed as such in April; 120ft single hatch steam coaster; disappeared 2nd October 1938 after leaving Ramsey.
    Some notes for the above *27.
    Information on tonnage from *The Tow Line issue 33* (Feb 2014) in an article by John Huxley (who referred to the vessel as "Ben Sayr", and intimated her launch was 1920 in his later article for the Liverpool Nautical Research Society's *The Bulletin*). *30

1923   Ben Varrey/Mia   steel (?) coaster   c. 260t?   Manchester Dry
                            (steam)   Dock Ltd.
Laid down as WAR LOSSIE for shipping controller but cancelled in 1918; launched as LOSSIE; completed in 1923 as MIA; 120ft single hatch steam coaster; name changed to Beaconia and later to Ben Varrey; broken up at

Dublin 24th March 1957.

Information on tonnage from *The Tow Line issue 33* (Feb 2014) in an article by John Huxley (who referred to the vessel as being scrapped as "Ben Varry" in 1957, and, in *30, gave her launch date as 1932).

1924   Doris Head   steam coaster   c. 260t?   Manchester Dry Dock Ltd.
Name later changed to DENNIS HEAD; broken up at West Cork 5th June 1963. *27 gives the name of this vessel as the "Doris Thomas", with these details: 120ft single hatch steam coaster; launched April 1924.

Some notes for the above *27.

Information on tonnage from *The Tow Line issue 33* (Feb 2014) in an article by John Huxley (who referred to the vessel as "Doris Thomes", which was scrapped as BEN AIN in 1963). Mr. Huxley's later article (*30) gave the launch date as 1934.

1925   Penstone   steel (?) coaster   c. 260t?   Manchester Dry Dock Ltd.
        (steam)
Laid down 1919; launched 8th June 1925 (*27 and *30 give the date as December 1926); 120ft single hatch steam coaster; disappeared 2nd October 1938 after leaving Ramsey; sunk in collision with Norwegian motor vessel VILLANGER outside Liverpool Bay on 31st July 1948.

Some notes for the above *27.

Information on tonnage from *The Tow Line issue 33* (Feb 2014) in an article by John Huxley (who stated that the vessel was lost in 1963, but this may be a typo due to the same sentence also referring to the correctly reported scrapping of DORIS HEAD in that year).

1936   Ralph Brocklebank   tug/tender   ?   Manchester Dry Dock Ltd.
The RALPH BROCKLEBANK was docked on the pontoon dock twice in January of this year for survey and for repair of the hull and sea cocks., 17th January and 20th to 22nd January.

1953   Daniel Adamson   tug/tender   ?   Manchester Dry Dock Ltd.
Refit only.
New boiler installed (built by Kincaid of Scotland and installed using the crane at Eastham normally used for removal/refitting of ships' masts and funnels) as part of the job. Heaton Tabb and Co. refitted the accommodation areas again.

Information from *The Tow Line issue 33* (Feb 2014) in an article by John

Huxley. Refit begun following DANIEL ADAMSON's arrival in early 1953 and completed in 1955 after having been conducted as and when workers could be spared from other tasks (*30).

c. 1963   ?   barge   ?   Manchester Dry Dock Ltd.
Repair only.
Evidenced by a photo on the COBWEB site on Facebook from John Taylor.

1969?   Ben Ain   steel (?) coaster   ?   Manchester Dry Dock Ltd.
1976?   Worcester   tunnel tug   ?   North West Museum of (Preston Brook Tunnel?) Inland Navigation (now Ellesmere Port Boat Museum)
Rebuild/repair only.*19

1983   George   barge   ?   Ellesmere Port Boat Museum
Rebuild/repair.

1986   Mossdale   barge   ?   Ellesmere Port Boat Museum
Rebuild/repair.

1990   Mossdale   barge   ?   Ellesmere Port Boat Museum
Rebuild/repair.

And Also:
Early 1890s   Arrow   steam tug   ?   Shropshire Union
Repair only.
Steel, twin-screw steam tug; built 1889 in Dundee for the Shropshire Union Canal Company; official number 96276; beam 22ft 6in; length WL 103ft 8/10 in; draught fwd 5ft; draught aft 7ft 6in; triple expansion engines, stroke 14in; speed 10 knots.
*27

Before W.W. I   Clam   barge   160t   Manchester Dry Dock Ltd.
Steel coal barge; 400t carrying capacity; built for R. and J. Rea of Liverpool; badly damaged while in Huskisson Dock No. 3 Branch Dock during the night of 3rd/4th May 1941 as part of the May Blitz. Repaired and returned to service;
    Nigel Bowker discovered the fate of Clam: broken up by Pemberton and Carylon at Garston Beach, arriving there on 20th April 1970.
*27

Before W.W. I   Skate   barge   160t   Manchester Dry Dock Ltd.
Steel coal barge; 400t carrying capacity; built for R. and J. Rea of Liverpool.

Nigel Bowker gives this information on her fate: sold to Effluent Services Ltd. of Macclesfield (presumably for storage of waste); broken up by Pemberton and Carylon at Garston Beach in the 1960s.
*27

?   Stefano Razeto   sailing ship   ?   Manchester Dry Dock Ltd.
Repair only.
Three-masted.
*20/*27

?   Carbineer   steam ship   ?   Manchester Dry Dock Ltd.
Repair only.
At Ellesmere Port or Manchester?
*20

?   Huskinson   tug   ?   MSC Dry Dock Ltd.
Repair only.
A photograph from *The Tow Line issue 33* (Feb 2014) in an article by John Huxley gives this information, showing the tug entering the pontoon dock.

?   M.S.C. Ellesmere Port   tug   ?   MSC Dry Dock Ltd.
Repair only.
A photograph from *The Tow Line issue 33* (Feb 2014) in an article by John Huxley gives this information, showing the tug in the pontoon dock.

Early 1950s   Gowy   bucket dredger   ?   Manchester Dry Dock Ltd.
Major refurbishment only.
*30

Early   Irwell   bucket   ?   Manchester Dry Dock Ltd.
1950s   dredger
Major refurbishment only.
*30

?   Eric Cooper   barge   ?   Manchester Dry Dock Ltd.
Repair only.

Evidenced by a comment on the COBWEB site on Facebook from Tony Dowling.

? Tenacity cabin cruiser ? Reg Lindop (in his backyard?)
Note: Reg Lindop not only built his diesel-engined boat but later converted her to steam, with his own steam engine.

Note: *27 states that "four new single hatch steam coasters (120ft long)" were launched by the M.S.C. pontoon dock. The details are above but they are at odds with my earlier research as they give a ship I have as DORIS HEAD, as "Doris Thomas", they give different dates for launches and they do not mention BEN VAIN.

Note: Various companies sent their ships to the M.S.C. yard at Ellesmere Port for annual docking and other works, and this list included Coast Lines, Cooper's (of Widnes), Esso, Harker's, and Shell, as well as the M.S.C. Co. vessels, naturally.

Voyage repairs were conducted afloat for Esso, the Royal Fleet Auxiliary (RFA), and Shell, as well as several foreign oil tanker owners.

There was also work carried out for Liverpool-based tug operators.

The de-masting and de-funnelling work at Eastham was undertaken for various firms, such as American Lines, T and J Brocklebank Ltd., T and J Harrison Ltd., Lykes Lines, Strick Line, and Shell. According to John Huxley, "other contractors" did this work for City Line vessels but I do not know who these people were.

Manchester Liners famously had its ships designed so that they could pass clear of all obstacles on the Ship Canal without need for such modifications.
*30

Note: Other flats would probably have been built in Ellesmere Port in the early 1800s but because the inland navigation vessels were not required to be registered, it is difficult to prove.
*27

Note: Charles Hickson also lengthened the Ellesmere Canal Company's luggage boat sometime around 1820.
*27

Note: It has been said that William Parkes "built mainly flats, barges and canal boats". This implies that there is a greater list of his works still to be unearthed. *27

Note: When William Skinner left his occupancy of the Ellesmere Port Yard, there was an auction of various materials and such at the patent slip there. Advertised were the "remaining stock-in-trade of a shipwright, comprising the hulls of two North American-built schooners about 200 tons each, and pine mast 55ft long, three anchors, five chains 40 fathoms in length each, one steering wheel, two windlasses, one deckhouse 15ft. by 12ft., two boats, 400 cubic feet of English oak… and other effects". Any number of these vessels or component parts could have been built by, or repaired by, or otherwise worked upon by, William Skinner. *27

Sankey Bridges/Sankey/Sankey Brook

| 1807 | Hannah | flat | 79t | William Clare |

Owned by William Hazlehurst, coal merchant of Sutton, Frodsham.

1808	Mary	flat	64t	William Clare
1810	John	flat	59t	William Clare
1812	Royal Oak	flat	68t	William Clare
1822	John Clare	flat	56t	William Clare
1826	Wellington	flat	33t	William Clare
1826	Duke of York	flat	75t	William Clare
1828	Hugh	flat	47t	William Clare
1829	Clarence	schooner	82t	William Clare
1830	True Briton	flat	44t	William Clare
1832	Hero	flat	43t	John Clare
1834	Heart of Oak	flat	41t	John Clare
1836	Elizabeth	flat	51t	John Clare
1837	William	flat	44t	John Clare
1840	Bettys	flat	44t	John Clare
1841	Martha	flat	36t	John Clare
1842	Sarah	flat	?	John Clare
1843	Margaret	flat	43t	John Clare
1844	Alfred	flat	54t	John Clare
1846	Britannia	flat	60t	John Clare

Note: Mersey Flats and Flatmen states that, according to *Marwood's Register of Liverpool Shipping* (published in 1854), thirteen flats were completed in Sankey Bridges in 1854. Furthermore, the book states that "only two" flats "the Adelaide and the Jane – were built between 1847 and 1859" by "the Clares", so none of the following thirteen were built at that yard.

Therefore:

1854	?	flat	?	?
1854	?	flat	?	?
1854	?	flat	?	?
1854	?	flat	?	?
1854	?	flat	?	?
1854	?	flat	?	?
1854	?	flat	?	?
1854	?	flat	?	?
1854	?	flat	?	?
1854	?	flat	?	?
1854	?	flat	?	?
1854	?	flat	?	?
1854	?	flat	?	?
1855	Adelaide	flat	57t	John Clare
1857	Jane	flat	53t	John Clare

According to *Mersey Flats and Flatmen*, she was launched in 1858.

Note: Percy Dunbavand describes JANE thus: built 1858; mast flat with elliptic stern; registered Runcorn, No. 2/1875; registered Liverpool from 2nd June 1893; owner: Philip Speakman of Runcorn; 67.3ft × 16.7ft × 6.6ft; official number 67155.

1860	Gilbert Greenall	sloop	?	John Clare
1862	Hannah	flat	56t	Ex. Of John Clare
1863	Susanah Kurtz	flat	59t	Ex. Of John Clare?
1864	Bat	flat	62t	Ex. Of John Clare?
1868	Ellen	flat	38t	Clare and Ridgeway
1869	Mayfly	ketch	61t	Clare and Ridgeway
1871	Annie	flat	47t	Clare and Ridgeway
1872	Sankey	screw steamer	73t	Clare and Ridgeway

1875	Harold	screw steamer	78t	Clare and Ridgeway

Note: Percy Dunbavand describes HAROLD thus: wooden one-masted steamer, carvel-built with round stern; registered on 13th August 1887; registered Liverpool from 2nd June 1893.

Owner: Thomas Litton, gentleman of Grappenhall (64 shares); sold to Philip Speakman, merchant of Runcorn on 20th May 1889; sold to Samuel Higginbottom on 11th December 1891; sold to John Alfred Kelly on 30th May 1894; sold to Liverpool Lighterage Co. On 21st September 1896.

71.2ft × 18.3ft × 8ft; 53t; 30hp; official number 93738; registration closed on 16th November 1934; vessel brokenup and sunk.

1879	John	flat	74t	Clare and Ridgeway
1880	Edith	flat	82t	Clare and Ridgeway
1880	Harry	flat	67.5t	Clare and Ridgeway*
1887	Eccleston	flat	52t	Speakman of Runcorn

Built by Speakman in Runcorn in 1815; rebuilt by Clare and Ridgeway at Sankey Bridges in this year. This information comes from Percy Dunbavand, after researching the Liverpool registers.

1889	Harry	flat	67t	Clare and Ridgeway
1905	Eustace Carey	ketch	92t	Clare and Ridgeway

According to *Mersey Flats and Flatmen*, she was launched in 1906 and was 93t.

Warrington at Work gives these details: sister ship of the SANTA ROSA; built for the United Alkali Company.

Later sold to Cooper's, who turned her into a barge.*31

1906	Santa Rosa	ketch	94t	Clare and Ridgeway

According to *Mersey Flats and Flatmen*, she was a jigger flat. According to the same book (and that author's *Liverpool Sailing Ships*, which states she was 94 gross tons), she was the last sailing flat built.

Warrington at Work gives these details: launched in March 1906 and, at 200t, the maximum size possible to pass through the lock at Widnes and into the Mersey; sister ship of the EUSTACE CAREY; built for the United Alkali Company.

These two ships marked a revival of shipbuilding at Sankey Bridges.

1913   G.R. Jebb   lightship   69t   Clare and Ridgeway
According to Terry Kavanagh's article in *Waterways Journal Vol. 16* ("Richard Abel and Sons, of Runcorn and Liverpool"), this vessel was built by Richard G. Cross. The article states that the Upper Mersey Navigation Commissioners sold this vessel ten years later to Richard Abel and Sons of Runcorn.

In *Schooner Port*, Starkey says the yard at Sankey Bridges came under Clare and Ridgeway at an unknown date, so it may well be that he did not know when that firm wound up, and consequently, that the yard went to Mr. Cross.

The same volume of *Waterways* has an article by David Long that says the G. R. JEBB was built at Fiddler's Ferry. I believe he has got this wrong by a misreading of his source, *Schooner Port*.

Note: *Mersey Flats and Flatmen* states "a further eighteen" flats "were completed by the end of building in 1913" at the Clare's Yard.
   Therefore:

?	?	flat	?	Clare's Yard
?	?	flat	?	Clare's Yard

Note: *Mersey Flats and Flatmen* states, according to the 1914 Mercantile Navy List, thirteen flats were completed in Sankey Bridges in that year.
Therefore:

1914	?	flat	?	?
1914	?	flat	?	?
1914	?	flat	?	?
1914	?	flat	?	?
1914	?	flat	?	?
1914	?	flat	?	?
1914	?	flat	?	?
1914	?	flat	?	?
1914	?	flat	?	?
1914	?	flat	?	?
1914	?	flat	?	?
1914	?	flat	?	?
1914	?	flat	?	?

1929   Protection   jigger flat   ?   Clare and Ridgeway
Repair only.

Described in *Mersey Flats and Flatmen* as "the last flat to be dry docked" at Clare and Ridgeway.

1959   Widnes   dredger   ?   Winwick Yard
Dismantled in the dry dock but possibly after an attempted repair (?)*11.

Note: *Mersey Flats and Flatmen* states Crosfield of Warrington had its flats, AILEEN, AARON, FAIRY and INDUSTRY repaired at the Clare and Ridgeway Yard.

Note: According to M.K. Stammers in his article, "Slipways and Steamchests" (as published in the *International Journal of Nautical Archaeology Vol. 28, Issue 3*) "At Sankey Bridges thirty-seven [flats] were built between 1807 and 1913".

Warrington

1800   Mary   snow   111t   ?
Taken as a prize by the French but recaptured in 1804 and by 1807, registered at Whitehaven. Not on the list provided in *Iron Clipper 'Tayleur'*.

1840   Warrington   iron paddle   99t?   Bridge   Foundry
steamer
Described in *Schooner Port* in separate entries as either 99t or 100t, respectively. Not on the list provided in *Iron Clipper 'Tayleur'*.

1841   John Wilson Patten   iron brig   ?   Bridge Foundry
Not on the list provided in *Iron Clipper 'Tayleur'*.

1842   Libya   iron schooner   125t   Bridge Foundry
Not on the list provided in *Iron Clipper 'Tayleur'*.

1845   Die Schoen   iron paddle   108t   Bridge Foundry
Mainzen   steamer
Registered at Runcorn; the only steamer to be registered at the port. Not on the list provided in *Iron Clipper 'Tayleur'*.

1846   Enterprise   iron schooner   74t   Tayleur, Sanderson and Co.
Used on River Mersey, according to *Iron Clipper 'Tayleur'*.

1846   Neptune   iron sloop   42t   Tayleur, Sanderson and Co.
Described in *Schooner Port* in separate entries as either a schooner or a sloop, respectively.

Used on River Mersey, and described as a 70t schooner, according to *Iron Clipper 'Tayleur'*.

ENTERPRISE and NEPTUNE were, according to *Iron Clipper 'Tayleur'*, the first iron vessels built at the Bank Quay Yard and were launched on the same tide.

1849   Trout   iron schooner   58t   Tayleur, Sanderson and Co.
1852   Invincible   iron paddle   66t   Tayleur, Sanderson and Co.
                      steamer
1853   La Perlita   iron screw   84t   Tayleur and Co.?
                      steamer
Owned by the Pacific Steam Navigation Co., according to *Iron Clipper 'Tayleur'*.

1853   Startled Fawn   iron ship   1,165t   Tayleur and Co.?
Described in *Schooner Port* in separate entries as either built in 1853 or 1855, respectively.
1853   Tayleur   iron ship/   1,750t?   Tayleur and Co.?
                   clipper
1,979t according to **Schooner Port**. 230ft × 40ft; carrying capacity said to be nearly 4,000t.

Owned by C. Moore and Co., Liverpool, according to **Iron Clipper 'Tayleur'**. See that book for an excellent full history of the ship.

Warrington at Work says TAYLEUR was:the largest iron ship yet launched on the Mersey, with accommodation for 680 passengers; chartered by the White Star Line. See also the website at http://tayleurarms.co.uk/history.net

1854   Lady Octavia   iron ship   1,272t   Tayleur and Co.
Described in *Schooner Port* in separate entries as either 1,132t or 1,272t, respectively.

Owned by Adams and Co., Greenock, and described as 1,272t, according to *Iron Clipper 'Tayleur'*.

1854   Medora   iron barque   392t   Tayleur and Co.
Described in *Schooner Port* in separate entries as either 357t or 392t,

respectively.

Owned by G.W. Turner, Liverpool, and described as 392t, according to *Iron Clipper 'Tayleur'*.

1854   Deerslayer   iron barque   500t   Tayleur and Co.
Described in *Schooner Port* in separate entries as either 390t or 500t, respectively.

Owned or sailed out of Blythe, and described as 500t, according to *Iron Clipper 'Tayleur'*.

1854   Liverpooliana   iron ship/   800t   Tayleur and Co.
                    clipper
Owned by C. Moore and Co., Liverpool, and name changed to MEDORA when sold to Shallcross and Company, according to *Iron Clipper 'Tayleur'*.

1854   Golden Vale?   iron ship   1,440t   Tayleur and Co.
Note: According to the *Warrington Guardian* newspaper, in 1854 (29th April according to *Iron Clipper 'Tayleur'*) the Bank Quay Yard of Tayleur and Co. had the vessel "Golden Vale" nearing completion, two other vessels of 500t on the stocks and a further two vessels of greater tonnage to be started that year. By 1855, the same newspaper reported that, after the launch of the SARAH PALMER, no other keels were at the yard. The GOLDEN VALE was either renamed before launching (most likely to SARAH PALMER) or maybe not completed for some reason; the other four vessels mentioned could easily be some of the ones listed here as launched in 1854/5.

1855   Retriever   iron screw   500t   Tayleur and Co.
                    steamer
Described as 410t, according to *Iron Clipper 'Tayleur'*.

1855   Conference   iron ship   531t   Tayleur and Co.
Owned by H. Moore, Liverpool, according to *Iron Clipper 'Tayleur'*.

1855   Sarah Palmer   iron ship   1,301t   Tayleur and Co.
Described in **Schooner Port** in separate entries as either 1,325t or 1,301t, respectively. Owned by Palmer and Co., according to **Iron Clipper 'Tayleur'**. 1, 325t, and the largest of all Warrington vessels, according to *Warrington at Work*.

1855   Mystery   iron barque   424t   Tayleur and Co.
Not on the list provided in *Iron Clipper 'Tayleur'*.

1855   Startled Fawn   iron ship   1,165t   Tayleur and Company
Owned by G.H. Fletcher, Liverpool, according to ***Iron Clipper 'Tayleur'***. Not
on the list provided in *Schooner Port*.

1857   Sarah Sands   iron ship   ?   Bank Quay Foundry Co.

And Also:
1840s   ?   iron paddle steamer   ?   Bridge Foundry
1840s   ?   iron paddle steamer   ?   Bridge Foundry
Warrington at Work states the Bridge Foundry built four iron paddle steamers
in the 1840s but I only have records for two such vessels, above. Hence, there
are two more unknown ships listed here.

Note: As early as 1830, iron barges had been built locally.

Note: The existence of the ferry at Thelwall suggests some sort of boat building
experience was known in the area since the medieval times when the service
started but was this at Runcorn (within which Parish Thelwall traditionally
resided) or within what is now the boundary of Warrington (where Thelwall
is now a part)?

Note: The discovery of the Howley Canoe, an ancient dug-out canoe at Arpley
(?) near Warrington, suggests there may have been ancient boat builders
nearby (or perhaps just visiting).

LOCAL SHIP TYPES

The North-west's unique style of vessel was the (Mersey) flat. It was known and built on the Mersey, Weaver and Dee Rivers, as well as other tributaries and canals (such as the Mersey and Irwell Canal, River Ribble, Rochdale Canal, St Helens Canal and Weaver Navigation) and built as far away as North Wales and Cumbria. Various sub-types existed, broadly divided between "cut" flats (for the canals), "inside"/"river" flats (for the rivers) and "outside" flats (used as coasters) and further sub-classified as follows:

Barrow flat: A flat-bottomed, flat-like topsail schooner.
Bridgewater/Duker flat: The type of barge used on the Bridgewater Canal; the type of vessels for which the canal was built. Originally of no known set dimensions, but eventually built in three sizes:
Birkenhead flats – which were too large for Runcorn Docks,
Preston flats – which could be used as far as the transhipment port of Preston Brook, and Manchester flats – which could travel all the way to Manchester and were horse-drawn.
Market flat: A type of flat that was horse-drawn and intended for use around Chester.
Douglas flat: Flats built for the dimensions of the Douglas Canal.
Dumb flat: A flat-like barge, as in wide boat – barges are either wide or narrow boats.
Float: A subgroup of flat, with no hold, cargo being carried on deck; otherwise, the name for high-sterned cabin tanker-barges.
Galliot flat: A galliot-rigged flat.
Jigger flat: A flat-bottomed ketch-rigged flat or flat-like ketch.
Leeds and Liverpool short boat: The type of barge used on the Leeds and Liverpool Canal (similar vessels existing on the Lancaster Canal and River Ribble); known as a "boat" but really a barge due to its width.
Leeds and Liverpool steamer: The engined version of the above.
Naked flat: Those flats with no rail, as most river flats were designed (except for a small iron "horse" at the extreme stern).
Powder hoy: An explosives-carrying flat.

Rochdale (Canal) flat: The type of barge used on the Rochdale Canal, with narrow side-decking and mainly used for cotton bales.

Rochdale Canal steamer: The engined version of the above.

Sand hooker: The name given to flats used for collecting sand in the Mersey.

Weaver flat: A shorter flat, with a square stern, contested by many as a different sub-type.

Weaver or Bridgewater (little) packet/(steam) packet: The engined versions of the above; one larger than the other (operated by the Bridgewater Department of the M.S.C. Co.) (sometimes called Weaver steam flat).

Weaver motor or diesel packet/Brunner flat/Brunners: The ultimate flat; the most modern type built before the style died out; sometimes known as Brunners after the Brunner Mond company, which owned the majority of them.

Some vessels known as schooners, ketches, galliots or barges, etc. were actually flats rigged or used as such.

Varieties of schooner seem to have made up the bulk of the coasters and ocean-going vessels built locally, with variations of rig giving rise to different names in some cases, such as snow.

The flat probably derived from the medieval ships of the Irish Sea. Therefore, there may have been many more vessels built locally going back to that era and perhaps beyond.

Note that among the sea-going vessels of the 1800s, Liverpool builders became famous for creating an accommodation block amidships, which kept crews sheltered and safe where previously they would have laid exposed to the elements on the open decks of ships. This Liverpool House also helped make ships more sturdy and this was adopted across the globe. This may or may not have been something adopted early on by Runcorn shipwrights.

Note that the Humber keel and North Sea herring bus were similar to the flat and that the West Country keel was similar to a Rochdale (Canal) flat.

Further to the above, what we now know as Humber keels were more properly called Yorkshire keels, Humber keels being a deeper (by a foot) draught version of them. The Yorkshire keels were built in localised types, according to the maximum width of vessel which could be accommodated in the specific canal locks of each area. Hence there were Sheffield, Lincoln, Beverley, Barnsley and West Country keels (or "-size keels"). There were also billy boys, coal slackers and Mallion boats; all built on similar lines to keels.

Other local vessels were:

Barge: Both wide and narrow boats; the former being those most usually known as barges (properly, a canal or river craft of not less than 11ft width, anything narrower being a boat) and the latter being those more usually known as narrowboats; the barges were often built along the same lines as flats.

Narrowboat: Boats designed specifically for canals, with various sub-types as follows:

*Butty: In the days of motorised vessels, these were the engineless ones, designed basically like the original horse-drawn narrowboats.

*Day boat: A narrowboat without any overnight accommodation.

Dukers or Dukes: The name given to all craft operated (mainly wooden, but later steel ones also) by the Bridgewater Canal proprietors, although most usually the term applied to the flats used on that canal. (See entry for Bridgewater/Duker flat, above.)

*Fly boat: A narrowboat with finer lines for increased speed.

*Joey boat: A narrowboat with accommodation space.

*Knobsticks: narrowboats of the Alexander Reid and Co./Anderton Co. were called knobsticks, although no real difference between them and other narrowboats has been discerned (Edward Paget-Tomlinson suggests they were known as such possibly because they belonged to the Anderton Company that operated on the Trent and Mersey. The latter company employed baton-carrying patrolmen, those weapons giving their names to the company's vessels).

Little packet/Jack Sharps: The name given to Duker tugs; the tugs of the Bridgewater Canal.

*Packet boats/market boats: An early version of the narrowboat, with fine lines and a reduced beam.

*Runcorn boat/Runcorn six-planker/wooden header/northern boat: The deeper-hulled type of narrowboat developed in Runcorn for the Bridgewater Canal that were like scaled down barges/wide boats, mainly built by Simpson, Davies and Co.; the "wooden header" name came from the wooden bollards at the bows.

*Trench boat: A very narrow narrowboat for use on the Shropshire Union Canal.

And there were also:

Cock boat: The carvel-built tender to most local vessels, known by this name on the River Weaver (and also in Runcorn); the same boat being known as a punt, on the Mersey. The cock boat's name came from medieval times.

Liverpool boat: The Liverpool-style boat was developed by Liverpool boat builder Thomas Coastain and was adopted by the RNLI as it was light and seaworthy and could be easily launched from beaches. May or not have been built in the Runcorn area.

Nobby: A fishing vessel designed along the lines of contemporary yachts of the day (late 1800s and early 1900s), built from North Wales to Cumbria. May or may not have been built in the Runcorn area, but certainly there were many registered in Runcorn.

Various types of yacht were also designed and built locally, some being developments of the former working boats (such as the nobby, which is raced in the region to this day).

Note that the cog or coggy boats of Humber keels probably derived from the same root name from medieval times as the cock boats of Weaver flats.

Furthermore, local yards produced these vessels:

Ship	=	Full-rigged sailing vessels or ocean-going steamers.
Barque	=	Usually three-masted vessel, square-rigged on both fwd masts (fore and main) and fore-and-aft-rigged on the mizzen.
Brig	=	Square-rigged two-masters.
Snow	=	Brigs wherein the main try-sail is set on a separate try-sail mast or pole, rather than on the lower mainmast as in standard brigs.
Brigantine	=	Two-master, square-rigged on the foremast and fore-and-aft-rigged on the main, but with square sails on the topmast.
Schooner	=	Two-or-more-masted vessel that is fore-and-aft-rigged.
(Square) topsail schooner	=	Fore-and-aft-rigged throughout but with square sails on the fore topmast.
Ketch	=	Two-masted vessel wherein the forward of the two masts is the mainmast, and the after mast is a small mast known as the mizzen (normally a term applied to the after of three masts in most ships).
Sloop	=	One-masted fore-and-aft-rigged vessel.

Note: The following local vessels are, or may be, still in existence:

DENNIS BRUNDRIT – The 462t ship built by Brundrit and Whiteway in 1856.

Remains can be seen in the waters off Centre Island, near Salvadore Settlement, Falkland Islands. Her figurehead is preserved at the Stanley Museum (in a barn nearby, with half the face on show in the museum itself).

HARVEST KING – The schooner built by Brundrit and Co. in 1879.

The figurehead was saved and is the Arklow Maritime Museum in Ireland.

FOX – The 100t schooner built by Brundrit and Co, in 1883.

The figurehead was saved and erected at the entrance to a bungalow named Fox Cottage in a small village called Stop and Call, Pembrokeshire.

SNOWFLAKE – The 96t schooner built by Brundrit and Co. in 1880.

Withdrawn from service when her master, Captain Pinch died, she was eventually bought by a Yugoslavian owner in 1934 for trading in the Mediterranean and fitted with an auxiliary motor. She was renamed HRVAT and was still in use in 1975. There are rumours she was being used for tourist trips in the 1980s, and she may yet still be in existence.

MAUD(E) – The 71t schooner built by Samuel Stock in 1869.

She lasted in the coastal trade until 1947 and her hulk remains on Appledore Beach, Devon.

MOSSDALE – The barge built as RUBY by ? in c.1860, and bought by Richard Abel and Sons in 1921.

She was renamed MOSSDALE, and later rebuilt by the company. She is preserved at The Boat Museum, Ellesmere Port.

OAKDALE – The barge built by Richard Abel and Sons in 1950/1.

Owned by Dave Keenan, she has for some time been preserved at the Merseyside Maritime Museum, Liverpool. She began leaking in 2002 and was taken to Barrow-in-Furness for repairs. On the way she was beached at Lytham St Annes, near Blackpool. Sometime in 2007(?) she slipped her moorings in a storm but was recovered and is now moored at Askam-in-Furness, Cumbria.

Listed on the National Historic Ships Register., this vessel is critically in need of help to maintain her. Her owner David Keenan has intimated that if he cannot keep up with the costs of maintaining her, OAKDALE will have to be sold for scrap. As she is one of the last two surviving Mersey flats, the second-to-last built and sister-ship to the last one built (which has now already been scrapped), this is a potential travesty. In much the same way that we can consider the Weaver packet as the most modern development of a Mersey flat, the design being taken to its natural conclusion in those motor vessels, OAKDALE represents the very same level of development along the traditional sailing line and is therefore a vessel of great historical importance.

Any help in preserving this vessel would be an aid to keeping alive a very important facet of our national shipping heritage. One man's struggle to keep this vessel going is a very compelling story and the efforts deserve much more attention and as much support from the public as possible. Mr. Keenan is a very friendly man with lots of experience and knowledge of local maritime affairs (having worked in the coastal trade for many years) and clearly loves the OAKDALE, realising her almost unique status.

Therefore, I intend to donate money to this cause and implore anyone who can volunteer to help with maintenance work (particularly in the summer months) to get along to Askam-in-Furness to help. Alternatively, I can act as a go-between for anyone wishing to assist, via the e-mail address at the end of the foreword of this book.

Thank you in advance for your help.

MULL – The narrowboat built by Simpson, Davies and Co. in 1914.
Launched as the MULL, she later became the HAZEL, a pleasure cruiser. The HAZEL is now owned by the Wooden Canal Boat Society, was being restored in Runcorn, and now lies in Portland Basin Museum awaiting further work. Listed on the National Historic Ships Register.

TENACITY – The ?t pleasure cruiser built by the late Mr. Reg Lindop in Ellesmere Port.
Still in use and berthed at Preston Brook Marina (but there are plans to move her to the Lake District for use by surviving members of Reg Lindop's family).
Many pleasure cruisers built by the local builders must still be around.

The Steam Engine built in 1900 by E. Timmins and Sons Ltd. For the paddle launch FIREFLY.
Preserved at the Ben Shaw Gallery, Merseyside Maritime Museum, Liverpool.

Note:

SARA – The 68t vessel built by Wm Hazlehurst, Frodsham, in 1838.
A model of this vessel is in storage at the Merseyside Maritime Museum, Liverpool.

ISAAC – The pilot vessel built at Frodsham Bridge in 1805.
A model or picture of this vessel is in the Science Museum, London.

EUSTACE CAREY – The ketch built by Clare and Ridgeway at Sankey in 1905.
A model of this vessel is on display at the Merseyside Maritime Museum.

ELIZABETH BENNET – The schooner built by Brundrit at Runcorn.
A painting of this vessel still exists and was auctioned in 2013 by Bonham's for more than £16,000. Abel's former barge STAINTONDALE was recently broken up after years serving as the clubhouse for the sailing club on the Weaver at Frodsham.

It is worth noting here that the DANIEL ADAMSON is also listed on the National Historic Ships Register. Although this remarkable vessel was not built on the Upper Mersey, she was based there, at Runcorn, for many years and maintained not only in that town but also at Ellesmere Port. She was built only a few miles away, by the Tranmere Bay Development Company (a branch of the Lairds empire), and was an oft seen and popular addition to the colourful maritime scene of this part of the world.

Any and every effort should be made to try to keep what is left of this group of vessels preserved. This should also be the case for any from the other former shipbuilding towns of Cheshire. Some years ago I emailed both the Merseyside Maritime Museum and the Ellesmere Port Boat Museum to try to encourage the saving of a Northwich-built barge then in use (and about to be replaced) as the Seamanship Training Barge AJAX, moored near HMS RALEIGH in Cornwall.

She was a former World War II Admiralty dumb barge (C626 – aviation fuel lighter). I never heard anything more about it and the barge went for scrap. Even though she was of no special interest for being a "first" or a largest, or any sort of innovative design, she was one of the last of a breed and I felt sad at her loss. I would hope future opportunities such as this are not missed.

Some other evidence of our now-lost industries exists if you just cast a casual eye over local maps or have a little stroll around our towns. The importance in the local way of life of local rivers, particularly the Mersey and Irwell, is evident in place names in Runcorn, Widnes, Ellesmere Port, and Warrington. The Big Pool in Runcorn and its associated waters are remembered in Poolside Lane, Pool Lane, and Water Street. Canal Street in Runcorn, Dock Street in both Widnes and Ellesmere Port, Ship Street and The Quay in Frodsham, and Wharf Street in Warrington all reflect the port histories of those towns. A plethora of names connected to the Bridgewater family show the importance of the canal network locally, and Runcorn alone has Dukesfield, Duke Close, and Bridgewater Street, with a Bridgewater Avenue appearing in Warrington. Speakman Street in Runcorn probably relates to the shipbuilder of that name and Dockyard Road in Ellesmere Port is in clear reference to the facility that once stood beside the docks where the boat museum now stands.

There are many more such naming conventions in existence and it is worth considering the contribution made to the local economy by these industries and industrialists as you amble along those old roads, perhaps heading towards one of the many nautically-named alehouses to be enjoyed in that part of the world.

NOTES FROM THE MAIN TEXT OF THIS WORK

* = Information from *Mersey Flats and Flatmen* by Michael Stammers.

*1 = Information from Uphill Village, Somerset's website, at www.uphillvillage.org.uk/History.htm.

*2 = Information from *Waterways Journal, May 1999.*

*3 = Information from Kirkcudbright website, at www.old-kirkcudbright.net.books/sailing.htm.

*4 = Information from Canal website, at www.canaljunction.com/news/info9.htm

*5 = Information from the Frodsham and District Local History Group's *The Port of Frodsham* booklet by Wm. R. Hawkin.

*6 = Information solely from a photo in *Mersey Flats and Flatmen* by Michael Stammers.

*7 = Information from Wooden Canal Boat Society website, at www.wcbs.org.uk/autoindex.htm?/society/soc_southam_elton.htm

*8 = Information *from Colours of the Cut: The Company Colours of the Inland Waterway Working Boats of Britain* by Edward Paget-Tomlinson.

*9 = Information from Mary Gordon website, at www.marygordon.org.uk/marygordon.htm

*10 = Information from *Images of England: Runcorn, a Century of Change* by Bert Starkey.

*11 = Information from the Sankey Valley Park website, at www.warrington.gov.uk/images/sankey_winwick_history_trail_tcm15-5312.pdf

*12 = Information from *Port and People: A Newsletter for the Port of Manchester, April 1975*

*13 = Information from photograph taken during author's trip with his father Ian and Reg Lindop in Reg's boat Tenacity.

*14 = Information from a photograph by K.M. Holt in *Port of Manchester Review*. (May also be another vessel on the smaller slipway further east in the yard, if it was indeed there in 1960).

*15 = Information from a famous photograph of the packet dry dock.

*16 = Information from the Sankey Canal Restoration Society (SCARS)

website, at www.scars.org.uk/cuttings/volume5/issue5-10/fiddlersf.html

*17 = Information from photographs and documents in the collection of/ conversations with, Mr. Percy Dunbavand.

*18 = Information from **Schooner Sunset: The Last British Sailing Coasters** by Douglas Bennet.

*19 = Information from *Port of Manchester Review.*

*20 = Information from **Sutton's Photographic History of Transport: Manchester** *Ship Canal* by Edward Gray

*21 = Information from a photograph in **Britain in Old Photographs: Widnes** by Cliff Hayes

*22 = Information from a photograph in **A Pictorial History of the Mersey and Irwell Navigation** by John Corbridge, stating "flats at the Castle Rock Shipbuilding yard", although it only appears to show one vessel.

*23 = Information from **Mersey Docks Fleet List 1850–1980** compiled by Gordon F. Wright

*24 = Information from *A Pictorial History of Canal Craft* by Peter L. Smith

*25 = Information from a photograph deposited in the Runcorn Shopping City/Halton Lea Library Local History Archives

*26 = Article by William E. "Bill" Leathwood for **Sea Breezes** in June 1974, entitled "Days of Sail on the Upper Mersey".

*27 = Information from Terry Kavanagh's article, "Richard Abel and Sons, of Runcorn and Liverpool" (*Waterways Journal Vol. 16*).

*28 = Information from David Long's article, "Concrete Boats and Barges – Solutions for Wartime Steel Shortages" (*Waterways Journal Vol. 16*). Mr. Long is a former chairman of the Sankey Canal Restoration Society (SCARS) and is editor of its magazine.

*29 = Information from www.mareud.com/Ferro-Concrete/concrete_seacraft_co.html

*30 = Further information from John Huxley, this time from his article on "The Manchester Dry Docks at Ellesmere Port", from the Liverpool Nautical Research Society magazine *The Bulletin*.

*31 = Information from *Sea Breezes* magazine of December 1971, in the article "Mainly About Flats" by Frank L. Ogle.

Appendix B

The Port of Runcorn

Runcorn is likely to have been some form of port since it was founded more than 1,000 years ago. In an earlier guise it may have been a port during the Roman period of English history, as evidenced by archaeological finds in the River Mersey (either products lost overboard on their way to the Roman settlement at Wilderspool, near Warrington or goods destined for the town known today as Runcorn).

Later, Runcorn was a definite landing place, which developed into a minor port within the customs port (authority) Liverpool.

Runcorn is at the termini of several waterways: The Bridgewater Canal, the Mersey and Irwell Canal (Runcorn to Latchford or Blackbear Canal), the Weaver Navigation (alternatively known as the Weaver Canal or Weston Canal), the River Weaver, and the Runcorn and Weston Canal. Runcorn is also sited on the River Mersey and the Manchester Ship Canal.

At Widnes is the terminus of the St Helens, or Sankey, Canal and Ditton Brook.

The head office of the Bridgewater Company and later the Bridgewater Department of the M.S.C. Co. were sited at Runcorn, or Bridgewater, Docks. Later, the head office of the M.S.C. Co. itself was also sited there. The offices of the Upper Mersey Navigation Commission were also at Runcorn Docks.

Coastal and International Port

The town was in a great position to overtake Chester as the leading port of the county of Cheshire but legislation was enacted on that city's behalf to prevent any foreign trade passing through any other county port. Runcorn suffered a major decline and lost its trade with Dublin. This also meant the much younger town of Liverpool soon became the dominant port of the area; a position Runcorn may well have filled.

Runcorn became a port within the customs port of Liverpool but won independence as a customs port in its own right in 1847.

Runcorn later once again became part of the port of Liverpool in 1850, when expected levels of foreign trade to Old Quay Docks failed to materialise, but was granted independence again in 1862.

Finally, Runcorn and Weston Point became deep water ports after centuries of being subject to the ever changing tidal streams of the River Mersey when the Manchester Ship Canal was constructed. Furthermore, a temporary port, Saltport, was created at Frodsham Marshes (at the mouth of the River Weaver) in 1892. It was in use until 1894, with the jetties getting little use after that date until they were dismantled in 1905.

With the passing of the act to create the Manchester Ship Canal, Runcorn and all the other ports along the canal's route were to become part of the new customs port of Manchester (a port 36 miles long), with effect from 1st January, 1894. The remaining ports returned to Liverpool's jurisdiction.

The port of Manchester became the fourth largest port of the United Kingdom.

The M.S.C. Co. owned the largest private railway network in the British Isles: At its peak, the network was 230 miles long and saw not only engines and coaches of the company's railway department but also some belonging to various of the companies based at the estates in Manchester that bordered the M.S.C. The company had its own police force and fire brigade: It was the largest (and one of the oldest) private polices force in the U.K.

The head office of the M.S.C. Co. port operations (port division HQ) were, until recently, located at Runcorn Docks (now the enterprise is run from Liverpool, whose docks the owner of the M.S.C., Peel Holdings, also own).

Canal Port

Runcorn was also a canal port in the sense it was an inland waterway port (for canals smaller than a ship canal). The town became the country's premier canal port, with more than 1,000 narrowboats registered there.

Many firms were situated on the banks of the canals in order to bring in their raw materials and ship out their finished products. These firms included the many tanneries of Runcorn (which at one time was the largest leather producer in the country), the various chemical works of the town, which was the joint birthplace of the chemical industry (with Widnes and Northwich) and the other factories and mills situated there.

This status as a canal port is considered to have ended in the 1960s, with the infilling of the lines of locks from the Bridgewater Canal to Runcorn (formerly, Bridgewater) Docks and the Ship Canal beyond (the new line of locks closed after a Ship Canal Act of 1966).

Preston Brook was a trans-shipment port from where loads could be transferred between the small boats of the Trent and Mersey Canal and the bigger vessels of the Bridgewater Canal.

Fishing Port

Runcorn was also a fishing port, having many fishing vessels registered there. *Note:* Runcorn-registered vessels carried the letters RN to signify such.

Ship Owners

Runcorn had many ship owners. These were not just those who held shares in certain vessels that they worked on or captained but powerful and rich individuals who owned fleets of vessels.

These included The Abel family, the Brundrit family, the Johnson brothers and William Rowland.

The Port of Frodsham

In years gone by, Frodsham may have been a more important port than Runcorn due to the trade in Cheshire cheese and salt; she was an important port from early medieval times.

Late in the Thirteenth century, Frodsham was named in connection with the summoning of vessels for the king's fleet. There must therefore have been enough substantial vessels working out of that port to be of service to national defence.

Frodsham developed into a trans-shipment port for cargoes to Northwich and other towns on the River Weaver due to the limitations put on vessels travelling down the River Weaver by Frodsham Bridge and the subsequent need to lighten the vessels' cargoes at the port.

Before the reclamation of land leading to the creation of Frodsham Marshes, the River Mersey came up to a line along today's Ship Street and on behind the Bear's Paw Pub. Up until recent times (1980s/90s?), bollards could still be seen near the playing fields behind that pub, meaning that the port of Frodsham stretched beyond Frodsham Bridge.

Most trade later bypassed Frodsham via the Weaver Navigation Canal but a small trade to the industrial estate at Frodsham Bridge's East shore still exists today, with regular voyages of the barge PANARY back and forth to Liverpool.

Frodsham was once also a fishing port.

Port Facilities of Runcorn

These included some examples of private facilities along the Bridgewater

Canal, although by no means all, due to the great number there have been over the years.

Runcorn was once a major leather-producing town, purportedly providing the boots for the Duke of Wellington's army in Spain and later becoming the premier British town in the trade, and as a result there were many waterside tannery facilities.

Furthermore, as Runcorn and Widnes were two the chemical industry's birthplaces, there were many such works along the waterways. Many of Runcorn's other diverse firms will also have had river or canalside locations for importing raw materials and exporting finished goods.

Key
All details in red text show currently existing facilities.

Location	Facility	Owner/Operator	Status Today
Bridgewater or Duke's/Runcorn Docks (River Mersey/Manchester Ship Canal and Bridgewater Canal)	Fenton Dock	Duke of Bridgewater/ Bridgewater Trustees/M.S.C. Co.	In use
	Basin/Tidal Dock/Francis Dock		In use
	Alfred Dock		In use
	Old Dock		Closed & filled in
	Francis Dock (separate from the above)		Closed & filled in
	Coal basin		Closed & filled in
	Middle basin		Closed & filled in
	Old basin/Harriet Dock (originally the basin or lower basin that was the sole such facility at Bridgewater Docks, with only an upper basin at Top Locks to accompany it)		Closed & filled in
	Iron ore arm		Closed & filled in
	Arnold Dock(s)		Built from the end of the Runcorn and Weston Canal, which was expanded to make the facility.
			Closed & filled in

Name / Location	Feature	Owner	Status
Bridgewater Lay-By / Runcorn Lay-By (River Mersey/Manchester Ship Canal)	Basin/Sevastopol arm		Later used as a boatyard, then Closed & filled in
	Lay-By	M.S.C. Co.	In use
Salt Union Berth (Manchester Ship Canal)	Wharf	Salt Union Ltd.	In use
Old Quay (River Mersey/Runcorn and Latchford Canal – part of the Mersey and Irwell Navigation/M.S.C.)	Lower dock	Mersey and Irwell Navigation Co./ Bridgewater Trustees/M.S.C. Co.	Closed & filled in
	Old dock		Closed & filled in
	Tidal basin		Closed & filled in
Boat House Pool (River Mersey)	Stone loading wharf and coal yard	Bridgewater Trustees	Not in use & facility removed
Boat House Pool (River Mersey)	Public landing place	Free	Not in use & facility removed
Ferry Hut (River Mersey)	Ferry landing place	Ferry	Not in use & facility removed
Saltport (M.S.C.) (Temporary port that existed during the period that Runcorn and Weston Point were cut off from the water as the M.S.C. was under construction)	Wharfs		Closed & facilities removed (Saltport is remembered today in the name "Saltport Bend", a curve in the Ship Canal just after Frodsham Strait on the approach to Weston Point and Runcorn).

Location	Feature	Owner/Operator	Notes
Wigg Island (Runcorn and Latchford Canal – part of the Mersey and Irwell Navigation/M.S.C.)	Wigg wharf	Charles Wigg and Co./Guinness/various	In use
Astmoor (M.S.C.)	Sludge berth	Sewage works	?
Astmoor (M.S.C.)	Stonedelph dock and turning basin	Various	?
Weaver Docks/Weston Point Docks/Port Weston (River Mersey/Manchester Ship Canal/Weaver Navigation)	Church Cut/Tollemache Dock	Weaver Trustees/British Waterways Board/Port Weston	Part of an extended Delamere Dock
	Delamere Dock		Delamere Dock is now one long facility taking in what was Tollemache Dock, which was widened and the lock between the two removed.
	Old basin		Currently, there are proposals to fill-in this dock, for wharfage space and create a lay-by outboard of the area.
	New basin/new dock		
Basin (Runcorn and Weston Canal)	Basin	Unknown	Closed & filled in
Wright's Dock (Weaver Navigation)	Wright's dock	Local quarry owners	Closed & filled in
I.C.I. Castner Kellner Berth (Weaver Navigation)	Wharf	I.C.I.	

Clifton (Now Ashville Point) (Weaver Navigation)	Wharf	Parkes? Steel Works (built tanks during W.W.I)	Not in use
	Sutton Dock	Abel's Repair Yard (now closed)	Used for a sailing club mooring and repair yard
Frodsham Bridge (River Weaver)	Wharfs	?	Liverpool Lighterage?
Top Locks (Bridgewater Canal)	Wharfs (This area was originally the upper basin, as opposed to the sole basin, or lower basin, at Bridgewater Docks)	Various	Not in use Commercially, but now used for pleasure craft moorings
Stone Loading Wharf, Big Pool (Bridgewater Canal)	Wharf	Duke of Bridgewater/ Bridgewater Trustees/M.S.C. Co.	Not in use & facility removed
Hazlehurst's Soap Works/ Camden Tannery (Bridgewater Canal)	Wharf	Hazlehurst's Soap Works Camden Tannery	Not in use
Highfield Tannery (Bridgewater Canal)	Wharf	Highfield Tannery	Not in use
Royal Oak Tannery (Bridgewater Canal)	Wharf	Royal Oak Tannery	Not in use

Puritan Tannery (Bridgewater Canal)	Wharf	Puritan Tannery	Not in use
Ockleston's Tannery (Bridgewater Canal)	Wharf	Ockleston's Tannery	Not in use
Runcorn Soap and Alkali Works (Bridgewater Canal)	Wharf	Runcorn Soap and Alkali Works	Not in use
Borax Works (Bridgewater Canal)	Wharf	Borax Works	Not in use
E. Timmins (Bridgewater Canal)	Wharf	E. Timmins Foundry	Not in use
Australian Alum Works (Bridgewater Canal)	Wharf	Australian Alum Works	Not in use
Wigan Coal and Iron Company Coalyard (Bridgewater Canal)	Wharf	Wigan Coal and Iron Company	Not in use
Horsefields Coalyard (Bridgewater Canal)	Wharf	Horsefields	Not in use
Runcorn Co-op Coalyard (Bridgewater Canal)	Wharf	Runcorn Co-op	Not in use
Rayner's Coalyard (Bridgewater Canal)	Wharf	Rayner's	Not in use

Limits of the Port of Runcorn, as Drawn up for 5th April 1847

River Mersey

Both shores from Warrington Bridge to Chapel Farm House in Lancashire and Eastham Church in Cheshire. Alternate sources cite the western end to be at the site of the Ince Ferry (through a line to Dungeon Point on the north shore) but this I believe to have been the limits of the later independent port before the opening of the Manchester Ship Canal. I say this because the current port of Manchester's limits are down the River Mersey to that same point as well as, of course, the entire length of the Ship Canal to Eastham.

River Weaver
To Frodsham Bridge.

The port ceased to be independent on 16th April 1850.

Hopefully, this illustrates the extent of the network of Runcorn's port, which was by far the most developed of those in the area.

Widnes had the two-armed West Bank Dock, Widnes Dock, and some wharfage on the Mersey and the St Helens Canal. Warrington and its suburbs had the Warrington Dock or Walton Basin at the entrance to the Ship Canal from the Mersey (Walton Lock), the DuPont Wharf at Acton Grange (Acton Grange Wharf), the Moore Lane Lay-by, and some wharfage on the Mersey at Bank Quay and Warrington Bridge.

Ellesmere Port had the, very *complex*, docks complex and a number of wharves on the Ship Canal. Other local towns only received port facilities with the coming of the M.S.C. and they were limited to a handful of wharves (such as the container and barge berths at Ince Bay near the village of Ince, or Manisty Wharf, opposite the north bank's Mount Manisty) or the small oil docks on the north bank at Stanlow (Stanlow oil docks 1 and 2 and turning basin).

None of these settlements came close to Runcorn in terms of complexity and diversity of port activity.

APPENDIX C

New Word for all Pertaining to Waterborne Craft and Trades

The idea of this chapter is to come up with an all-encompassing term to describe all items and persons who work in an environment pertaining to ocean, sea, river, canal or any other body of water, whether to do with the building, repair or operation of ships, boats or other craft, or with any other associated and ancillary trade.

I come from a family with a strong tradition of work as sailors or as bargemen/lightermen (working on the rivers and canals between the shore and the ships), or as watermen (working the sailing flats) and boatmen (on the narrowboats). So they were either at sea (in the "deep sea" trades on the oceans and seas that link the continents), or on the rivers and canals/cuts in various craft. They also counted among their number shipwrights in various yards engaged in building and repair of such vessels.

In my genealogy there were fishermen; beatsters (who made and repaired fishing nets); sailmakers; dockers; members of the customs service; at least one Royal Marine and a number of Royal Navy personnel; and ostlers who handled the horses used to tow canal craft, families who lived on canal craft and navigated the canals and rivers either by engine or by towing these boats (by hand or horse).

In so many other families in this country, there were more of the same, and there were also shipbuilders; ship riveters; shipwrights and engineers (who built or repaired ships, boats, whatever craft and their engines); boilermakers; chain and anchor smiths; mast and spar makers; divers; longshoremen; personnel from roperies/rope works/walks or who repaired ropes and rigging; lighthouse keepers; chandlers; etc. As you can imagine, for an island nation, the list is extensive.

I therefore wanted to come up with a term that would encompass all these persons, rather than using a combination of terms that were designed to be analogous with specific areas of the aforementioned, such as "nautical", which pertains to the sea. I looked at the definitions of "marine", "maritime", "shippage", "shipping", and "water-borne", among others, and found nothing to fully conform to the ideal I was after.

Nothing could quite grasp the idea of corralling all in this extended field, so that we could equally speak of a sailing master mariner the same as we could someone who worked in a shipyard in an administrative role, or as a millwright, an electrician, or first-aider. Not one word satisfactorily allowed a Manchester Ship Canal constable to be included alongside a tug or barge skipper. Neither could I find a way to group a beach lifeguard and a marine biologist. Yet all in one way or another belonged in certain circumstances to the same area of business: water.

I desired to use a word from Old English, rather than the more usual Greek or Latin, as I am an Englishman.

My first port of call (sorry for that obvious pun), therefore, was the website www.oldenglishtranslator.co.uk

There I found the term I thought most appropriate:

fléot Strong Masculine Noun

1. water sea estuary river 2. raft ship

fléot	Singular	Plural
Nominative	(the/that se) fléot	(the/those þá) fléotas
Accusative	(the/that þone) fléot	(the/those þá) fléotas
Genitive	(the/that þæs) fléotes	(the/those þára) fléota
Dative	(the/that þæm) fléote	(the/those þæm) fléotum

From this, I tried some manipulation of the word and I suggest the following for my proposed word: fleotical.

AFTERWORD

These are letters I sent to the *Runcorn Weekly News* and various other publications a few years ago. The *Weekly News* printed a condensed version of the letter concerning the Royal Naval Association.

Perhaps one day, some people in my town will have the appetite for such ventures.

18th December 2006

Subject: Maritime Runcorn and the Royal Naval Association.

Dear Mr. Miller,

You may remember me from nearly five years ago, when we met to discuss the DENNIS BRUNDRIT and my pictures of her from the Falkland Islands. I keep meaning to speak to you about the latest updates to my research into local ship and boat building, so I hope you find the enclosed of interest (it is very much a work in progress, I must mention though!). If you wish to see the whole file, with photographs and PowerPoint briefs via memory stick, drop me a line and I'll sort it out.

I read in a recent article of yours (my mother always sends the paper on to me) about the ailing fortunes of Runcorn RNA and although I can understand why times have changed, with fewer serving or veteran matelots around and younger people not so inclined towards working clubs as they used to be, I am still upset about this development.

What is the answer? Lottery money probably won't be the solution per se, but what about a scheme to make a local Maritime Centre? The Borough Council seem pleased to market our heritage with new canal-side projects, such as The Deck and the proposed building beside the Brindley Arts Centre, so what about a small Maritime Museum at the RNA?

There is supposedly a Marine Engine built by Timmins and a builder's model of a Frodsham-built ship, both at the Maritime Museum in Liverpool, yet neither were on display when I last visited (four years ago, when I got my phone call to pack for sunny climes and ended up in the escort force for the Gulf; deep joy). Perhaps the museum could be persuaded to loan these and any other pertinent items to a small gallery in Runcorn, with maybe some maps and books from Halton Lea Library? Lottery money would be more likely if the plan was for an amenity open to the general public and I suspect that volunteers from the RNA would be forthcoming.

Perhaps I am over-optimistic but we need to start thinking laterally if we are to stave-off the loss of another part of our rich nautical history. We have already lost Old Quay Yard, the last of our commercial ship and boat yards, but with a little flair and imagination we may yet save our Naval club and perhaps keep an interest alive in our handful of surviving boat builders and repairers, who may wish to contribute some information and photographs of their pleasure boating activities to a Halton Maritime Museum.

The Borough of Halton had many nautical links, with the world's first dock-terminating railway at Widnes and many local shipping firms and families. We still have a world-class marine engine-builder in Runcorn and we have Europe's leading kayak canoe building company also. In years gone by, many of the local world-beating industries, such as the chemical and tannery firms used the canals and rivers of the district to transport their raw materials and finished products. What better way to celebrate this than by opening a museum, especially if it helps keep the great institution of the RNA alive?

Thanks for your time; take care.

21st August 2010

Subject: Open Letter to Curiosity Bookshop, Robert Greig Industrial Textile Products, Halton Borough Council, Ineos Chlor, Peel Group/Holdings and Peel Ports (Manchester Ship Canal Company), Riverside College, Runcorn and District Historical Society, Runcorn Linnets F.C., Runcorn Locks Restoration Society, Runcorn Town F.C., Salt Union Ltd., Sankey Canal Restoration Society, Stobart Group (Port of Weston), James Troop and Co. Ltd., and Widnes Vikings R.L.F.C., as well as all concerned parties within Halton Borough and surrounds.

To Whom it May Concern,

Many readers may remember me from earlier letters and articles on our nautical heritage and I would now like to offer a suggestion which may boost the local economy and reputation as well as provide entertainment and a reminder to our populace of our earlier triumphs.

Having recently visited my in-laws in Hartlepool and seen the excellent Tall Ships weekend held there, it occurred to me, a former Runcornian and current sailor, that such an extravaganza could do wonders for the town of Runcorn and the borough of Halton in general.

I have thought about it all and wonder if any of the above named companies and institutions feel as I do that hosting a Tall Ships event would do wonders for local prestige and economics. If I set my stall, perhaps men and women more intelligent than I and more current on local information could put a plan in motion for my suggestion.

I would propose that berths for the Tall Ships could be made from the Salt Union berth and Runcorn Lay-by to Runcorn Docks and 'round to the new Maritime Quarter surrounding Bridgewater House. Berths could then be provided beyond that point, to the Runcorn Promenade along Mersey Road and onto the Deck. Across the Old Quay Swing Bridge, the Wigg Wharf formerly used by Guinness, back to the Old Quay Lock and beyond to the former Lay-bys at what was Runcorn Island (opposite the Maritime Quarter), could be further berths for ships and boats. Admittedly, a lot of refurbishment would be required to bollards and quaysides across these areas if they have been damaged or removed at the Deck and elsewhere; and also work would need to be done to repair railings along the Gantry Wall and fit mooring posts and pontoons along Mersey Road. Notwithstanding this, I think it would be doable and also very worthwhile, in terms of prestige, tourism and a regeneration of maritime infrastructure which could well be key to further development in trade and tourism.

Further plans I will break down as follows:

1. Centre the display on Runcorn Docks, using a Park-and-Ride system from points in outer Runcorn, Frodsham and Widnes and only allowing motor vehicle access to Old Town Runcorn for the event to public service vehicles and disabled badge holders. Parking for this could be afforded at Astmoor, Ashville Point and various green field sites, such as at Frodsham Bridge (where they used to hold car boot sales), for example. Obviously, business traffic must be allowed to continue, but a minimising of vehicular access will be imperative to keep the event flowing.

2. Allow a walking public to transit a cordoned-off Runcorn Docks and surrounding areas as listed above, visiting all the Class A Ships and also the smaller vessels, which will be able to pass under the bridges to berth at those areas listed to the East.

3. Parking for the Park-and-Ride organisation could be augmented by land from the various big businesses of the borough, including the Ineos Chlor and Port of Weston concerns and the existence of the various Busways must be a bonus to setting-up a successful car-free access to a Tall Ships event.

4. Opportunities could be taken in preparation for any such event, for the development of the local canal infrastructure, from reopening the Locks to the Ship Canal from Top Locks, to the promotion of the Sankey Canal and facilities at Widnes. Yachts and canal craft should be encouraged to visit the twin towns and berth in both at the various facilities available locally. Perhaps hosting a canal regatta in the borough could be a good precursor or a future event on completion of the Tall Ships visit. Our remaining boatyards may be interested in supporting this facet of any Tall Ships event and especially, any such canal-based festival in its own right. The borough is, after all the birthplace of the canal network of the UK.

5. Local companies and institutions should be encouraged to support and sponsor the event, especially those with a maritime bent, such as Greig's, James Troop and also Port of Weston, who may also be able to offer overspill berths for some of the ships and boats. Others who may wish to become involved include Riverside College, whose Runcorn Campus is in the Maritime Quarter and also our local sports teams, who could offer facilities for recreation to the Tall Ships crews and may even wish to challenge them to friendly matches to raise money and awareness.

6. Egerton Street Library could be granted an Annex at the former Runcorn Technical Institute/Runcorn Grammar School around the corner in Waterloo Road, which could be transformed into a "Halton Borough Museum". This museum could be divided into areas such as a Maritime Wing, with Shipbuilding and Repairing, Docks and Shipping and other sections; as well as a Chemical Industries section and Leather Industries section, amongst others. Reference would of course have to be made to

other local museums, such as Catalyst and the War Museum at Halton Royal British Legion (which seems to have embraced a similar idea I once muted for the old Royal Naval Club at Halton Road to have a Maritime Museum) and also such businesses as the Curiosity Bookshop, who have long aided local awareness of our rich history. Furthermore, a formal request may be put to Warrington to recover items held in their local museum that came from Runcorn.

7. A Maritime Heritage Walk could be established along existing pathways, as I suggested to Peel Holdings a few years ago. My proposal is that a plaque be erected at the Deck to detail some of the shipbuilders and yards that once occupied the site and that a plan for a circular walk from there also be established. This walk would take the pedestrian along Mersey Road to the Maritime Quarter, up to Top Locks and along the Bridgewater Canal past the Bridgewater Motor Boat Club to the former Timmins works and then back to the Deck. Along the way, small notice boards would inform people of what used to be at each point in terms of ship and boat builders/repairers, sailmakers, rope walks, etc.

I may be out of touch and wildly offside with any feel for local desire to host such an event and bring yards of canvas back to our maritime borough, but I hope that I have hit a chord of harmony with enough of my fellow Runcornians and neighbouring Widnesians and that the idea I have briefly outlined above is a workable concept that finds favour with the council.

I am willing to assist in any way I can, starting by detailing the ideas I mention in para 7 above with regard to a plaque at the Deck and a heritage walk if anyone is interested in taking the notion up. I also have a great deal of information on our former shipyards which I am willing to share in any museum the council wishes to establish.

Thanks as ever for your time.

Yours faithfully,

Bob Ratcliffe.

Bibliography and Recommended Reading

A Hundred Years of the Manchester Ship Canal Ted Gray
A Towpath Walkers Guide to the History of the River Weaver Colin Edmondson
Navigation, Vol 2
Birkenhead Docks Ian Collard
The Bridgewater Canal Bi-Centenary Handbook ?
Britain's Lost Commercial Waterways Michael E. Ware
Chemical Manufacture in Runcorn and Weston 1800–1930 Gordon Rintoul

via the Internet
Cheshire Historic Towns Survey: Runcorn and Halton Cheshire County
    Archaeological Assessment Council
Cheshire Shipyards Antony J Barratt
(A book for which I, for personal interest, wrote an addendum that also covered
    the Wirral and then the rest of Merseyside. It is a pure list rather than a
    book in its own right and remains unpublished)
*Colours of the Cut: The Company Colours of the Inland Waterway Working
    Boats of Britain* Edward Paget-Tomlinson
Crossing the Runcorn Gap Vol I: Runcorn Ferry and Hale Ford C.A. Cowan
Discovering Old Frodsham: A Trail to Follow devised by the Frodsham and
    District Local History Group
The Duke's Cut: The Bridgewater Canal Cyril J. Wood
Edwardian A–Z and Directory of Liverpool and Bootle Paul Bolger
Frodsham: The History of a Cheshire Town Frank A. Latham (Research
    Organiser and Editor)
History of Runcorn Nickson
The Horse on the Cut Donald J. Smith
Images of England: Runcorn Bert Starkey
Note: Same book as "The Old Photographs Series: Runcorn"
Images of England: Liverpool Docks Michael Stammers
Images of England: Runcorn, a Century of Change Bert Starkey
Images of England: Runcorn, the Second Series Bert Starkey

Iron Clipper 'Tayleur' – the White Star Line's "First Titanic" H.F. Starkey

Kelly's Directory of Cheshire, 1906, 1910, 1923, 1934 and 1939 ?

Liverpool and the Battle of the Atlantic, 1939–1945 Paul Kemp

Liverpool's Historic Waterfront: The World's First Mercantile Dock System Nancy Ritchie-Noakes

Liverpool Sailing Ships Michael Stammers

Liverpool Ships of the Eighteenth Century R. Stewart-Brown, M.A., F.S.A.

McTay: A Wirral Shipbuilder Antony J. Barratt

Mersey Docks and Harbour Board Fleet List, 1850–1980 Gordon F. Wright

Mersey Flats and Flatmen Michael Stammers

No Tides to Stem: A History of the Manchester Pilot Service Derek A. Clulow (in three volumes)

The Old Photographs Series: Runcorn Bert Starkey

Note: Same book as Images of England: Runcorn

Old Runcorn H.F. Starkey (Bert Starkey)

Runcorn Through Time Roy Gough

The Sankey Canal: A Towpath Guide to England's First Industrial Waterway Colin Greenall and Peter G. Keen

The Schooner: Its Design and Development from 1600 to the Present David R. MacGregor

Schooner Port: Two Centuries of Upper Mersey Sail H.F. Starkey

Schooners in Four Centuries David R. MacGregor

Schooner Sunset: The Last British Sailing Coasters Douglas Bennet

The Ship Models Collection, Merseyside Maritime Museum Alan J. Scarth

Smith's Almanack Directory 1888 ?

Tales from the Old Inland Waterways Euan Corrie

Tugs of the Manchester Ship Canal W. B. Hallam

Warrington at Work Jamie Hayes and Alan Crosby

The Way We Were; Runcorn Remembered: A Social History Liz Howard

White's Directory, 1860 ?

Worsley to Top Locks: Life on the Bridgewater Canal Edited by Tracy Aston

Various magazines and newspapers, such as:

Sea Breezes, December 1971. Mainly About Flats by Frank L. Ogle.

Shipping, Today and Yesterday No. 239 (January 2010). 'The Wanderer of *Liverpool* by John Richardson

Warship World, Issue 11 Number 5. 'The Royal Navy's First Manned Aircraft Project' by David Hobbs

Waterways World, September 2005. 'Changing Places: Preston Brook' by Harry Arnold

All editions of Waterways Journal (particularly those containing the articles by):
Alan Faulkner (who wrote about "Chester and Liverpool Lighterage and Wharehousing Co. Ltd.")
The late Alf Hayman, a former employee of the M.S.C. Co. at Sprinch Yard and later manager of the Bridgewater Department
The late Michael Stammers
Terry Kavanagh
Rev David Long (who wrote about "Concrete Boats and Barges – Solutions for Wartime Steel Shortages")

Various editions of the Port of Manchester Review.

Various editions of the Runcorn Weekly News (particularly, but not exclusively, the Ray Miller column)
These include articles written by Ray Miller after I sent in some historical details (such as my visit to the wreck of the DENNIS BRUNDRIT and my subsequent report on it).

Various maps, booklets, pamphlets and packs (including from visits to local libraries, especially using the local history packs at Halton Lea Library, in the former Shopping City facility in Runcorn).

Peeps into the Past: Runcorn (DVD).

Various websites and pages, chatrooms and groups, as mentioned throughout this work. Have a search of the internet using, as key words, various phrases and names from within this study and you will find lots to immerse yourself in. This includes:
Conversation threads on Facebook pages "Runcorn Photos", "Runcorn past and present", "You know your (sic) from Runcorn when…", and "COBWEB"; Ship's Nostalgia site; The TugTalk site.
These sites gave me the opportunity to learn from, talk to and befriend various people.

The website www.oldenglishtranslator.co.uk, from where I took inspiration for the new word, fleotical.

Visits to the following museums:
Ellesmere Port Boat Museum and Gloucester Waterways Museum (now branches of the Inland Waterways Museum).

Merseyside Maritime Museum, Hull Maritime Museum.

In fact, there can't be many books, booklets, leaflets, DVDs or other material I have not bought and thoroughly consulted in the making of this work. This includes general history publications as well as river and canal ones, and also those on railways.

Conversations with various local people, discussing their reminiscences:
Father of the author, Mr. Ian Ratcliffe.

Great uncle of the author, the late Mr. Frank LeCouteur.

My cousin-once-removed, Frank LeCouteur, son of the above.

Friend of the family of the author, Mr. Percy Dunbavand, a man from a long maritime lineage of Runcorn men and himself a tug skipper with the M.S.C. Co. (from where he was a friend of the author's grandfather, George).

His son followed him into the tug world and was the tug skipper who transported the fore end of the first Type 45 Destroyer HMS *Daring* from Portsmouth to the Clyde for completion (thanks to Percy also for a number of photographs).

Mr. Roy Gough (thanks also to him for a number of photographs).

Mr. Ken Stubbs (great grandson of Samuel Stubbs and grandson of Jack Stubbs, shipwrights of Runcorn).

Mr. Ron Turner (local boat builder, who learned various skills of his trade from the late Mr. Jimmy LeCouteur, brother of my great uncle Frank).

Mr. Dave Keenan (owner and master of OAKDALE).

Finally, a big thank you to all others who have helped by providing pictures, etc. I have seen so many and received so many over the years it is hard to know where they all originated from. Apart from those named sources above, I have also received pictures from my friends Brian Janion and Chris Oakley, and there are some CDs locally doing the rounds. No one at the Runcorn and District Historical Society, or those contacted by my aforementioned friends, seems to know the origin of them.

Every reasonable step has been taken to name and credit all sources of information and material. After twenty and more years of researching this project part-time, and as an amateur who had originally intended it only for his own use, I hope not to have caused offence should there be any person or organisation I have failed to mention. Any omission is not intentional and no plagiarism or rudeness was meant.

As an aside, the BBC TV series *Mersey Beat* (set in Runcorn and Frodsham) has long been on my list to buy should the corporation ever decide to make it available on DVD. As I recall, every scene involving chasing villains ended up being down the docks or at Old Quay, and I would really love to see it again to see what was going on in the background!

Illustration 64

Illustration 65

ABOUT THE AUTHOR

Bob Ratcliffe is a Warrant Officer First Class Seamanship Specialist in the Royal Navy, having joined the service in the 1990s following a couple of years in the Royal Naval Reserve whilst initially training for a career in the Merchant Navy. He is a member of the Liverpool Nautical Research Society and the DANIEL ADAMSON Preservation Society. He has been a supporter of the Runcorn and District Historical Society, Runcorn Locks Restoration Society, and the River Weaver Navigation Society for many years, supporting these causes and submitting work to the former for their archives.

His wife, Julie, joined the Women's Royal Naval Service (WRNS) as a member of the Fleet Air Arm (FAA) in 1989, before transferring from the Wrens to the RN and leaving as a Petty Officer Air Engineering Mechanic in mid-2013 after twenty-four years.

Some of Bob's relatives have been mentioned in this work, such as his great uncle Frank LeCouteur, who served in Abel's vessels as chief engineer and also worked at Castle Rock Yard. His son Frank also served in Abel's vessels before going deep-sea in Blue Funnel Line ships. The LeCouteurs are a nautical family originally from Jersey and great uncle Frank's daughter Yvonne was a Wren (a member of the Women's Royal Naval Service) who married a Royal Marine and had a son Carl (son of Yvonne) who joined the Fleet Air Arm.

Uncle Frank's grandfather was the partner of Anderton at Castle Rock Yard and his father was partner of Withington in a concern based at Top Locks.

The author comes from a nautical family, which he has traced back to around 1700 so far, with possible connections back still further.

His father, Ian, is a retired chief engineer in the Merchant Navy who has worked for various shipping groups both at sea and as machinery inspector or project manager in shipyards across the globe.

Bob's mother Rita herself worked in the maritime field, as a secretary in shipyards and marine engineering firms, and her side of the family are also firmly established in the same field, with merchant and naval sailors, fishermen and shipyard workers back through at least four generations.

The Ratcliffes were sailors for generations also, with Ian Ratcliffe's father

George being a prime example. He worked for the Upper Mersey Navigation Commissioners as a seaman, before joining the M.S.C. Co. dredging department. He later went to sea in coasters, joined the Royal Naval Reserve at Liverpool (where his grandson would many years later follow suit), and served in the Navy throughout World War II.

He then went to work for Cooper's at Widnes, serving as a barge skipper until he broke his leg and as a result lost his job (they could not hold it for him any longer). He then re-trained as a fireman on M.S.C. tugs and rose to become chief engineer, retiring in 1979. Bob's grandmother Maud worked at BICC in Helsby for a long while.

George Ratcliffe's father and grandfather were also mariners , and so too were all three of his sons: The author's father having been discussed above, there are also Bob's uncles, Harry and David, both of whom served at sea in the Merchant Navy.

No matter where he has looked in his family tree, Bob has found uncles, cousins, brothers, wives and husbands that have been connected to the sea, from sailors to beatsters, engineers to dockers. His fascination with the sea and his love for his home town have inspired him to conduct this research and produce this publication.

BRIEF FAMILY TREE

As well as a lot of time devoted to this study (and to its wider field covering the rest of Cheshire and the Mersey), I have spent a considerable amount of effort on researching my family history. This has meant unearthing a lot of interesting links to this study and to other things, and I have taken immense pride in discovering just how many of my (both paternal and maternal), and wife's family members have been connected to seafaring and shipbuilding.

Below is a small snippet of the Ratcliffe family tree with some local maritime (or is that fleotical?) connections:

William Henry Ratcliffe
1828–1890
Waterman and dock labourer
Served as mate in EGERTON and Able Rate (AB) in ALICE
My second great grandfather
His sons included:

John Ratcliffe	William Henry Ratcliffe
1859–?	1865–1896
Waterman	Sailmaker and waterman
Possibly served in BLANCHE	Possibly served in schooner SARAH JANE

(John Ratcliffe's son Frederick was a labourer who built ship and boat models, of which my father has three).

George Albert Ratcliffe
1873–1945
Waterman, later coal dealer
Recipient of Liverpool Shipwreck and Humane Society Silver Marine Medal for rescue of a boy from the Bridgewater Canal; his fourth such rescue.
His youngest daughter married into the Grounds family of Runcorn, perhaps the once famous local ship owners, although research is ongoing.

Arthur Ratcliffe   Walter Ratcliffe
1881–1902   1879–1898
waterman   waterman

Frederick Ratcliffe
1869–1917
Mariner, waterman and lighterman
Served as cook in FOUR BROTHERS and AB in CAERNARVONSHIRE
Possibly served as mate in SARAH McDONALD
My great grandfather
His sons included:

George Ratcliffe (my grandfather)
1914–1984
Mariner, waterman and naval seaman
Served as boy/ordinary rate (OD) in Upper Mersey Navigation Commission's
     JESSE WALLWORK and LADY WINDSOR.
Served as OD in coaster BROADGREEN.
Served as AB in MSC Co. dredging craft, incl. PRINCESS JULIANA.
Served throughout World War II as a Royal Naval Reserve (RNR) gunner in a
     variety of HM ships.
Served as AB in vessels owned by Cooper's of Widnes, eventually rising to
     skipper of barge EMILY II.
Re-trained as a fireman with the MSC Co. after breaking his leg and thus
     losing his job.
Served as fireman in tugs ARCHER and FIREFLY, second engineer in
     NEPTUNE, ONSET and PANTHER, and chief engineer in ROVER,
     RANGER, QUARRY, QUEST, PANTHER, and SABRE.
Possibly served as chief engineer in SCIMITAR.
As a younger man, with my grandmother and father, he rented rooms from,
and lived with, the mother of Harold Whitby; one of Stubbs's shipwrights.

All three of my grandfather's sons served at sea in a variety of merchant ships.
     My father, George Ian (known as Ian), later went on to serve in shipyards,
and then for a while ran the Drammen Maritime business discussed in this
booklet.
     My uncles, Harry and David both served in merchant ships (David also
having just joined the Royal Fleet Auxiliary), and Uncle Harry worked as a

lock boy at Old Quay before he went to sea.

My grandfather's sister, Aunt Alice, married Frank LeCouteur, whose maritime lineage is also discussed in this book

Their children were also involved in the sea. Their son, also Frank, served in several of Abel's vessels (BRETHERDALE, MONSDALE, SAXONDALE, and ROSSENDALE among them). He later joined the Blue Funnel Line. Their daughter Yvonne served in the WRNS and married a Royal Marine, David Eaton. Their son, Carl, served in the Fleet Air Arm.

A number of other Ratcliffes served on the Manchester Ship and Bridgewater canals; some of them were related to us. Keith, who worked on the tugs out of Old Quay, for example, was a cousin of my grandfather. I am still investigating the links to others including the family of siblings Brian Ratcliffe and Elaine Slevin, my friends and, as I call them, "cousins".

As for me, I still serve in the Royal Navy as a searider and section head for Flag Officer Sea Training, working our ships up ready for operations. My wife, Julie, having left the Navy, decided on a complete break from her former career and now works for the NHS.

My son Billy is too young yet to decide if he wants to keep up the family tradition but he seems to love ships and the sea and is a big fan of *Octonauts* on the television, so you never know…

This was a snapshot of life in five British urban areas: four industrial towns and a market town, and only of course, focusing on one industry area. Whole books could be written on the tanneries, chemical works, and breweries. So, here's hoping…

I am not entirely sure how much interest my work will garner (or how much I will be able to offset the costs), but wanting to help local nautical organisations, I have decided for every book sold, I will make a donation to the Liverpool Shipwreck and Humane Society, the DANIEL ADAMSON Preservation Society (DAPS) and Mr. David Keenan for the upkeep of the OAKDALE.

If I have achieved the wrong thing and managed to depress some readers as to just how much we have lost over the years of "progress", I leave you with this thought…

Whenever I saw, on the television or in the papers, the latest bit of bad news about closing yards and factories, paid off ships and regiments, and other indicators of the decline of this once mighty nation, my grandmother used to console me with a simple phrase: "It'll all come full circle".

I believe this to be true, and one day we will build again.

282

END WORD: A COCKTAIL RECIPE TO ENJOY WHILE READING THIS WORK

Top Locks

This drink was invented by my wife Julie to celebrate my fortieth birthday in 2014. It was two months after the date but was made the night we went to see Lisa Stansfield on her Northern Soul Tour in Gateshead as part of my birthday treats.

The recipe is as follows:

Take one long drink glass
Fill it a quarter full with Archer's peach schnapps
Add a splash of brandy
Fill near to top with lime soda water
Squeeze half a lime into the glass
Add a slice of lime

I named the drink Top Locks because Napoleon (brandy) gets drowned just as at Waterloo, Waterloo Bridge is atop the arches (Archer's) over Top Locks, Top Locks was a transhipment port where limes might have been brought in and soda ash fell over the whole thing from the chemical works.

Enjoy!

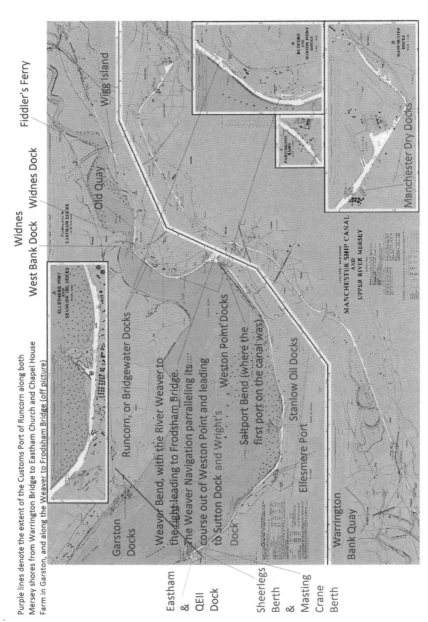

Fiddler's Ferry

Wigg Island

Widnes

Widnes Dock

West Bank Dock

Old Quay

Runcorn, or Bridgewater Docks

Weaver Bend, with the River Weaver to the right leading to Frodsham Bridge.

The Weaver Navigation parralleling its course out of Weston Point and leading to Sutton Dock and Wright's Dock

Weston Point Docks

Saltport Bend (where the first port on the canal was)

Stanlow Oil Docks

Ellesmere Port

Warrington Bank Quay

Eastham & QEII Dock

Sheerlegs Berth & Masting Crane Berth

Manchester Dry Docks

Garston Docks

Purple lines denote the extent of the Customs Port of Runcorn along both Mersey shores from Warrington Bridge to Eastham Church and Chapel House Farm in Garston, and along the Weaver to Frodsham Bridge (off picture)

Chart shows berth numbers in circles beside each wharf for docks and basins that hold several ships

Illustration 66

284

Mersey flat OAKDALE Refit Society

To garner support and volunteer workers to help preserve this unique craft.

Please visit:
http@//bobratcliffeupperm.wix.com/
mersey-flat-oakdale
or
Our Facebook page

ADDENDUM

This insert slip details information discovered subsequent to the original acceptance of my book for publication. It is laid out here for the purposes of completeness.

Shipbuilders at Runcorn
Richard Abel & Sons

Dave Keenan has revealed some titbits about this family, starting with the fact that when they first appeared in Runcorn (having moved there in the 1850s) they went straight into shipbuilding. The usual route is some sort of repair business, wherein one would build experience and then move on to building a vessel of one's own. However, it seems that the Abel family did not need this and that leads to speculation that they had a background in the trade before moving to Runcorn. He also said that they bought many vessels from Bristol, which is true (a number of former Severn Trows, etc. having been bought by Abel's over the years), and speculated that there may be a family connection there. There is a shipyard still operating in Bristol that is owned by a similar-named family, but they are the Abels family, and their business only begun in 1980 (taking over the former Charles Hill yard). There may be another blood link in the area though, or perhaps the Abels and Abel families have a more distant connection in times past when they perhaps spelled their names the same.

Dave actually met Jack Abel many years ago, as his father was an ex-Royal and Merchant Navy engineer who worked as an inspector on the Mersey, including surveying Abel's vessels.

Bridgewater

I had taken the best guess for the start of the Duke's Yard at Bridgewater Docks to be 1785, when Bert Starkey states (in *Schooner Port*) that by that year "the line of canal locks ended in a tidal basin... and, two locks up from the tideway, a small dry dock". However, the Bridgewater Canal opened "locally at Runcorn" in 1773 and was in its full glory in 1776, also according to that seminal work. There is a map of 1782, furthermore, that shows the graving dock beside Bridgewater House, so a date of establishment must in reality be some point between 1773 and 1782. The graving dock was latterly known as "Big House Dry Dock", due to it being near to Bridgewater House (always known as the "Big House" locally). Mr. Geoff Dutton kindly reminded me of this fact with his reminiscences on Facebook (please see below for more on that subject).

Brundrits & Whiteways

This is how the name of the famous Runcorn firm was rendered by D.G. Bennet in *Mariner's Mirror* Vol. 58, No. 3 and 4. He states that the yard was taken over by the MSC Co. in 1891 and used by that firm for the repair of wooden vessels into the 1930s. Clearly, what he is talking about here is the letting of that area of what had become Old Quay Yard to Messrs. Stubbs, who used what had once been the Brundrit Slip, into the 1950s.

Joseph Parks and Son(s)

Joseph Parks set up a yard at Northwich in 1861 for the building and repair of boats for the salt trade. He later branched into iron vessels and, eventually, steel ones. He went on to open a steelworks at Sutton Weaver, which I am still investigating (for example, my father believes they may have made tanks for the British Army at one time, but as yet I have found no proof of this). They built radar towers for the Air Ministry during the early stages of W.W. II. This steelworks was beside Sutton Dock and slipway. Did the Parks' concern also conduct maritime business at this site prior to the slipway being owned by Richard Abel & Sons?

Alex Cowan of the Runcorn Historical Society provided information for the above in an article for Ray Miller's column in the *Runcorn Weekly News*, and if you search online for information on the firm (known either as "and Son" or "and Sons"), you can see that the Northwich works was the contractor for the steelwork on the Sutton Weaver Swing Bridge.

Philip Speakman & Sons

See comments under entry for *MOSSDALE* in section on vessels built or repaired at Runcorn.

Megan Posnett's information from an article in the *Runcorn Weekly News* of 25th December 2014 (Ray Miller's column) states that the Speakman residence was known as The Mount and was sold to the Posnett family (Robert H. Posnett, specifically, who was the great grandafather of Megan Posnett) of tanners when the shipbuilder sold the property in 1896. Philip Speakman had moved to Fox Hill in Frodsham in December 1895, where he lived until his death in 1899. The

Mount previously belonged to Charles Wigg, the industrial chemist. Apparently, Mr. Speakman "channelled his energies into coal, lime and salt" after ending his shipbuilding enterprises, so these were probably what his own fleet of vessels (for which he had the building and repair facilities in the first place, I believe) carried. Megan Posnett says that Philip Speakman was an "Alderman, he served on Cheshire County Council, and was also Chairman of the Board of Commissioners and President of Runcorn Football Club" (which I had believed to be founded in 1918 by the tanneries, so I think this may have been confused with the information on Mr. Posnett). The article states that the building of the Manchester Ship Canal forced Philip Speakman to close, but I detail more about the effects of the MSC on Runcorn in the main text of the book.

Also, note that there was a Samuel Speakman in business as a shipbuilder at Preston, Lancashire. Perhaps (and this is purely speculation) another family connection?

Stubbs family
Note that there was a Stubbs family at Northwich that was engaged in the boat building trade. Was there a connection between these two clans?

Vessels Built or Repaired at Runcorn
MOSSDALE
The Mersey (Bridgewater) Flat I had previously thought was built in Northwich, seems to have been built in Chester in 1860 by William Speakman. This information is care of the National Historic Ships Register (NHSR). This has further led me to speculate that the Speakman family of Chester may be related to that of Runcorn, but this is pure conjecture. See Dave Keenan's comments at the end of this section on vessels built or repaired at Runcorn, marked by an asterisk.

The NHSR also states that as part of the rebuild, Abel's lengthened her.

RUTH BATE
This vessel, built by Richard Abel & Sons in 1953, was 62 tons according to Dave Keenan.

PROTECTION
Dis-masted (and other sailing equipment removed) at Old Quay Yard when it was decided to keep her under motor.
Unknown date.

JESSE WALLWORK II

Repaired at Old Quay Yard, having to be slipped due to a hole being found in the forward plates during an operation to concrete the banks near the Crane Berth at Eastham.

Unknown date.

Mr. Geoff Dutton provides some more information on repair work conducted in Runcorn via various contributions to local history pages on Facebook (supplied with copies of photographs from the 1950s that he took himself). He speaks of how the Graving Dock at Runcorn Docks was "extremely busy" in those days. It was also from him that I got the information that the area otherwise known as Runcorn Wall (north of Bridgewater House on the Manchester Ship Canal) was called "Cocky's Hut" by the local Dukesfield residents (or "Dukesfielders"). This was due to the watchmen employed by Harker's to look after their boats tied up there, that were called "Cocky Watchmen" by the locals (for reasons unknown but perhaps, one could surmise, because they were "cock of the walk" so to speak?). The name then conjugated to the watchmen's hut and took on significance for the locale. Here is the information Mr. Dutton has shared on Facebook:

MSC DOLPHIN

Repaired in the Big House Dry Dock. Various repairs conducted, including repair of the propeller.

MSC EVA

Painted at Big House Dry Dock. I had her listed in the book, but this confirms the work I had seen in a photograph of this event was painting and not repairs.
Unknown Barge
Caulked at Big House Dry Dock.

A list of vessels built by "Brundrits & Whiteways" at Runcorn is supplied with D.G. Bennet's article on flats in *Mariner's Mirror* Vol. 58, No. 3 and 4. The following are the discrepancies I have found with my own list (asterisked items concur with the information given me by Ken Stubbs):

Name as given by D.G. Bennet	Date of Launch	Issue
DENIS BRUNDRIT	1857	Second "n" missing from "DENNIS".

Date should be 1856.

| *ANNIE CHESHIRE** | 1859* | Spelling of name different. |

Date should be 1853.
Described as a Barque, rather than a Ship*.
Note that, from 1878 onwards, I have the firm as Brundrit & Co.

| *MARTYN* | 1878 | Described as a Flat, rather than a Ketch. |

| *A.M. BRUNDRIT* | 1879 | Date should be 1878. |

| *SNOWFLAKE* | 1881 | Date should be 1880. |

| *SUNBEAM* | 1883 | Corroborates statement from Ken Stubbs that she was 3-Masted. |

| *ELIZABETH BENNET* | 1884 | Corroborates statement from Ken Stubbs that she was 3-Masted. |

| *LILY HEAPS* | 1885 | Second "l" missing from "LILLY". |

Date should be 1882.

| *EDWARD WHITTLEY* | 1886 | No second "t" required in "WHITLEY". |

Date should be 1880.
Described as a Flat, rather than a Barge*.

| *DISPATCH* | 1886 | Spelling of name with "i" rather than "E". |

Corroborates statement from Ken Stubbs that she was 3-Masted.

The article also gives this information:

| *HANNAH* | 1807 | Built at "Sanky Bridge". |

78 Tons, rather than 79; Draught 8'. Liverpool to Dublin, classed E1.
"Hough master... W. Clare Master", which I take to be a typo giving the information that a Mr. Hough was Master, and W. Clare was the Owner (given that the Flat was built at the Clare Yard).

TRAFFIC	1892	Built by Speakman.

Described thus –
155 Tons; 101.8' Length; 23.6' Beam; 9.6' Hold Depth; Wood Flat.

Vessels Built or Repaired at Frodsham

ANN	1799	As described in the main body of the book, but more information found to complement this.

This Flat, described as being launched in 1795 on at least website (but I believe that to be erroneously), is described in some detail at:
http://www.rhiw.com/y_mor/hanes_llongau_llyn/flat_ann/flat_ann.htm

ANN was registered at Liverpool until 1848, when she was sold to owners in Caernarfon (4th August of that year). She was 60 tons, 61.8' long, 15' 1" wide, with a draft of 6' 6" and a crew of three. She had a square stern and a lifting bowsprit and was carvel-built as other Mersey Flats. Her master, once in Welsh ownership and for some years before this, was a Hugh Pugh, who owned 20 shares in her.

She ran aground during a gale of the 18th October 1858 in St. Tudwell's Roads and was destroyed.

The story of her wreck is recalled in the Welsh sea shanty, *Fflat Huw Puw* and was the inspiration for *The Songs of Huw Puw* by J. Glynne Davies.

Note: The fact that one person describes a vessel as a Flat and another as a Ketch or Barge is not mutually exclusive: A Flat could easily be used as a Barge or Ketch-rigged, Schooner-rigged, etc.

* = Dave Keenan recalls, from his research and his interaction over the years with so many of the characters from the maritime history of Merseyside, that Runcorn in the 1850s – 80s had a good reputation for building strong ships (mainly of Welsh Oak). He states that there were eight yards, and that many of the shipwrights moved to Runcorn from Chester when the River Dee silted up and ended the industry there. Runcorn, he told me, was the largest centre for the building of wooden two-masted ketches and schooners, etc.

Mr. Keenan was a friend of an Albert Slack, whom he recalls was born in the 1860s or 70s. Mr. Slack told Dave much about the history of shipbuilding in Runcorn as he himself had learned from his grandfather. One anecdote was that there were always men walking the forests picking the right branches and trunks for specific parts of boats and ships. He also spoke of an area of Runcorn known as the "Cast Iron Forest" due to the weights hung off trees in order to bend and shape the branches into the forms required by the shipwrights.

The mystery of the local method of disposal of vessels seems to have been answered by Dave as well. He told me that often, barges and flats would be sunk up to deck level in order to preserve them in salt water when work was scarce. Stoves and canvas, etc. were all removed prior to such action and then the vessel could be left for prolonged periods when not needed. The wood would tighten and help seal the boats so that when pumped-out and raised, they were soon good to go straight back to work. Hence, all the old vessels left in locks and other bodies of water when they were filled-in for "improvements" (such as Runcorn's two flights of locks down to the docks and Big Pool, also in Runcorn) were probably there awaiting future work that never came.

Another little piece of local maritime custom was the use of wooden dowels (known as "treenails" – pronounced "trenels" and sometimes spelled this way, but can be seen as "trenails" or "trunnels"), rather than iron or steel nails, in the building of boats. These were hexagonal pieces inserted into the round holes in hulls for better purchase and were used in lieu of metal fixtures due to the latter's susceptibility to corrosion in the chemically-contaminated canals of the area. Working in the Sankey Canal, for example, such nails would last the life of a boat whereas the metal ones would probably dissolve within three weeks! Even wholly-metal barges suffered, with paint falling straight off and then the iron or steel disappearing over time once exposed to the heavily polluted waters. The Weaver was one local waterway that was relatively clean and hence the proliferation of iron and, later, steel vessels on her waters and being built in her shipyards.

Bibliography

Sailing Barges by Frank G. G. Carr.
Sea Breezes Vol. 6, 1948: Article on the Flat, PROTECTION, by John Sutton
Sea Breezes Vol. 8, 1949: Article on the Flats by ?
The Mariner's Mirror Vol. 58, No.s 3 and 4 (1972): Article on Flats by D.G. Bennet
Dave Keenan's opinion is that the finest writer of books on the river and canal craft of this country was Edward Paget-Tomlinson. His work certainly was of high quality and based on first-hand knowledge of these vessels built-up over many years, so it seems a fair assessment.